FROM ADOBE OF INDIA

TO THE KILLER WHALE OF THE US NAVY

BY BRAMVEL CHRISTIAN

TRILOGY

Trilogy Christian Publishers

A Wholly Owned Subsidiary of Trinity Broadcasting Network

2442 Michelle Drive

Tustin, CA 92780

For information, address Trilogy Christian Publishing

Rights Department, 2442 Michelle Drive, Tustin, Ca 92780.

Trilogy Christian Publishing/ TBN and colophon are trademarks of Trinity Broadcasting Network.

For information about special discounts for bulk purchases, please contact Trilogy Christian Publishing.

Trilogy Disclaimer: The views and content expressed in this book are those of the author and may not necessarily reflect the views and doctrine of Trilogy Christian Publishing or the Trinity Broadcasting Network.

10 9 8 7 6 5 4 3 2 1

Library of Congress Cataloging-in-Publication Data is available.

ISBN 979-8-89333-410-4

ISBN 979-8-89333-411-1 (ebook)

This book is dedicated to my wife, Janet, my daughters, Marilyn and Joan, and my sister, Pushpa, for their love, help, compassion, and lots of patience while I was sweating on this book over the period of three years and three months.

ENDORSEMENT

From Adobe of India to the Killer Whale of the US Navy *is the story of my brother in Christ, Bram Christian.*

I remember meeting Bram when I was the Executive Officer (EO) for the Program Management Office in Pittsfield, Massachusetts. I needed an experienced engineer to lead one of our many efforts in our Anaheim, California, office. I had several interviews scheduled for that week, and there were several qualified applicants. I completed two interviews before meeting Bram, and in walked this unassuming man, very polite with a pleasant accent, who looked me in the eye when we shook hands. He introduced himself as Bramvel Christian, but he preferred to be called Bram. I asked my planned questions, which he answered without pause and expertly, and I sensed in my spirit something different about this man.

I remember wondering why a person retiring from such a prestigious company as Boeing wanted to come to work for the US government versus enjoying his retirement and spending time with his grandchildren, so I asked him. I remember him stating, "I am ready for a new challenge, and I still have so much more to give." At that point in the interview, I decided that this was the man for the job. He had a passion for our nation's strategic deterrence mission, and he was more than qualified for the position.

Fast forward several months until my next visit, when I was able to learn more about Bram, and my suspicion was correct; Bram was a brother in Christ, and we had a bond that can only be described as Spirit recognizing Spirit. What a joy for me to know that there was an engineer on my team in California who knows and loves the same Jesus that I do. However, I did not know the depth of his life story until reading his draft transcript. Seeing the challenges that he has overcome in his life to become the brother in Christ that he is today gives me even more respect for this man.

This book should cause each of us to examine ourselves and make sure that we are not holding any personal bias against another person. We may not show it like the people that Bram encountered, but it is a sin and one that we should repent from and ask the Lord to forgive us. One of my favorite passages of Scripture is found in Proverbs 3:5–6 (KJV), "Trust in the Lord with all thine heart; and lean not unto thine own understanding. In all thy ways acknowledge him, and he shall direct thy paths."

Bram's life has seen many paths, but along each of his journeys, Bram has trusted His Lord, the same one that I trust, and if you are reading this, you either know and trust, or by the end of this book, you will have a deep desire to ask Christ into your heart. Please do not wait a moment longer because we do not know what tomorrow holds, but we know who holds tomorrow.

Read on, friend, and see how God led a man and his wife from a class-drive regime to a nation where dreams are possible and where Jesus is still on His throne and still answering prayer.

May the Lord of lords and King of kings bless you as you read Bram's journey.

—Dennis R. Mohr LCDR, USN (Ret)

God bless against every odd,
From Adobe of India to the Killer Whale of the US Navy.

To: _____

From: Your Friend in Christ, Bramvel D. Christian.

TABLE OF CONTENTS

INVITATION

Hello, my international friends,

I don't call it introduction but an invitation to a book-reading party. My memoir is not in chronological order but rather in emotional order. Why? It is because, after I retired in December 2020, when I got up early one morning, the past episodes floated in front of my eyes, and I simply penned them down.

I invite every person from every nation, tribe, and trade to hold a book-reading party of this book. I hope this book will change your life forever, you will think differently than ever before, and you will have a dream that will chart your path in an unchartered territory you never dreamed of. The dream you see while you are sleeping is not a dream but an illusion only. The dream you see while you are awake is the real dream that will shape your destiny.

This is a true story woven with the true stories of millions like me in India. The story is of pieces of memories, recollections, and episodes of how I navigated the tough times being the son of a Christian pastor in a country with a majority of Hindu friends. Then, the story moves to unveil how I came to America with hardly any money in my pocket and how I became successful in Fortune 100 American iconic companies. The story ends with the climax of my life when I got an opportunity to be the chief engineer of the nuclear missiles submarine navigation system Navy Program Office in Huntington Beach, California, and solved the most difficult technical problems nobody else was able to resolve. The power that turbined all these triumphs and protected me from the double-edged sword of the evil descended on me from the Father, Son, and Holy Spirit, not because of me but because He lives and because of His love, mercy, and forgiveness.

Because He lives, yes, there is a tomorrow. Because there is a tomorrow, plant the seeds today; it might rain tomorrow. You may wait for tomorrow (opportunity), but perhaps tomorrow (opportunity) will not wait for you; tomorrow begins today because we believe in the risen Lord.

Isaiah 60:1 (KJV), "Arise, shine; for thy light is come, and the glory of the LORD is risen upon thee."

Matthew 28:6 (KJV), "He is not here: for he is risen."

I want you to receive the same power; it's free. I have tried to unfold the secret of winning the war most of the time and not worry when I lose it. I hope you will throw this book-reading party. You will be blessed, and in turn, you will be a blessing to others. Read on.

If you are encouraged by reading this book, give it as a gift to someone you love, one who stands with you, encourages you, shakes your hands, and wipes your tears. You will ignite a nuclear fusion that will generate enough power of love, peace, joy, happiness, and wealth to illuminate your friends' circles and community.

As I was penning this book, more bad news came from the Manipur State of India, where the Christians are persecuted, tortured, and burned alive. I dedicate this book to all Manipur Christians who have lost their lives and those who continue to lose their lives every day due to the oppressive apartheid behavior of extremist groups around the world. Jesus said, "But I say to you, love your enemies, bless those who curse you, do good to those who hate you, and pray for those who spitefully use you and persecute you" (Matthew 5:44, NKJV).

Luke 6:27 (NKJV), "But I say to you who hear: Love your enemies, do good to those who hate you."

Luke 6:35 (NKJV), "But love your enemies, do good, and lend, hoping for nothing in return; and your reward will be great, and you will be sons of the Most High. For He is kind to the unthankful and evil."

God bless America, my adopted home; God bless you, your family, your friends, and your enemies. To spice up your book-reading party, I have sprinkled bold text you will see as you read, and also provided dessert called "Takeaway" at the end of each episode.

> **Takeaway:** I repeat, I invite every person from every nation, tribe, race, and trade to hold a book-reading party of this book. I hope this book will change your life forever and that you will think differently than ever before. And that you will have a dream that will charter your path in an unchartered territory you never dreamed.

Note: These episodes are not in chronological order, but as they appeared in front of my eyes at night time, I penned them down in the early morning before they evaporated like morning dews.

1. SON OF A PASTOR IN INDIA

It was a cold winter morning, and I was sitting on the bench at Anand railway station, Gujarat state, India, waiting for the train. My parents, the Salvation Army officers, sent me off to another town, Napad, to my grandpa's home to attend school because my parents were appointed in a far, remote, small village, and in that town, there was no high school. I didn't want to go. I was crying, but I didn't have a choice. Finally, the train arrived. They pushed me onto the train; it was like a tug-of-war game.

First day of the school. The bell rang. Mr. Patel, my teacher, said, "Boys, we will learn math first. Whoever writes down the answer, sit down."

I was the first to sit down every time. I was correct every time. He liked me. All the boys liked me. I was the only Christian student. I taught my classmates how to do math faster. They shared mango chutney and purees with me at lunch. Some teachers and parents did not like that. They hated me. Why? I did not know at that time. But at the end of the day, Mr. Patel put his hand on my shoulder and shouted, "Attaboy, hang in there; you are my favorite boy."

> Takeaway: If you are the son of a pastor, the blood of the Bible runs in your veins. Use it, donate it, sacrifice it; it will replenish seventy times seven.

2. CHRISTMAS EVE, DORM ALONE

It was December 24, 1967. I was a physics student for a master's degree at UCLA.

The final exams were over. All the students, except me, went home.

I was home alone, far, far away from home in India. I hear an angel far away, singing and scaring me,
"Silent night, lonely night, Baily calm.
BP mounts, tears run down, sick for home alone.
Where to go, whom to talk to, all are gone, no one calls.
Oh, Lord, where are You? Help me get this over with."

The devil pushed me into a corner and whispered in my ears, "There is only one route out. Go home, go home, go home. Oh, homesick boy, go home now. Pack up your sack and run to LAX."

It felt like high 200, low 50, and I was in between. What do I do? Where do I go?

My roommate laughed, and he was happy to let me go. "Go, you are not made for Yankee's home." He laughed again, louder and louder, then took off.

I was alone, homesick, and crying. I could not sleep for three nights. In India, Christians go house to house on Christmas Eve to sing Christmas carols to bring joy to their neighbors. In America, shopping malls sing Christmas carols to bring money in. It made me more homesick and depressed.

Takeaway: Depression is a disease, and only two doctors and one vaccine can cure it. Make Jesus Christ your physician friend and find a friend you can trust; the Bible is your only vaccine.

New Year's Eve. I headed to LAX, and I can't describe how I felt. Now I realized depression is a disease, and only love, a real friend, and a comforting hand on the back from heaven above could calm it.

The train arrived at Anand station. I looked around, but nobody was there. I was shaking. I suffered from depression for a long time. Thanks to my VP Science College, Vidyanagar, India, the physics department's faculty staff, and the head of the physics department, with their love and friendship, I overcame the disorder that can kill if not controlled.

3. THREE-THOUSAND-YEAR-OLD CASTEISM IS STILL ALIVE IN INDIA, EVEN IN HIGHER LEARNING CENTERS. UNBELIEVABLE!

Casteism is a deadly disease India has suffered for two thousand years and is not willing to immunize. India is the only country on the surface of the universe that poisoned its own people with stingy casteism. What is surprising is that even after high education and observing other civilized nations, people are not ashamed of it for their personal socio-economic gain. If you are a human being, you need to understand that class is not your birthright; you have to earn it. Why don't people understand this even after going to school? It is because they learn how to read and write but don't acquire the knowledge and wisdom that comes from above. This explains why a PhD-earned man acts like an animal in a civilized community. Learning is not the source of knowledge and wisdom; it is only a tool to obtain them. If you use your tools to suppress other mankind, you are a universal criminal. If you label others as lower than you, you are insulting the creator who created you, and you have committed a crime by civilized world standards.

It was the summer of 1970. College was closed. Vacation time. The campus was quiet. A visiting Peace Corps American professor from the University of Arkansas was conducting physics seminars for the undergraduate faculty members of S. P. University, Vidyanagar, Gujarat state, India. Dr. A. R. Patel, head of physics and dean of PhD students, appointed me as an assistant for the American visiting professor. He taught physics fundamental theory class. Each lesson was followed by an experiment and demonstration to support the theory. Dr. A. R. Patel appointed me his teaching assistant because no other faculty member was willing to accept that responsibility since they could not understand American English. I designed and demonstrated experiments to illustrate the theory he taught in the morning class. I don't know how I did it, but it was a great success in every class he taught.

One day, the American professor asked, "Which is the latest element discovered and listed in the periodic table?"

I answered, "Dubnium."

His eyes turned as wide as I had ever seen, his face turned pink, and he smiled with both of his hands stretched and hugged me. We broke for lunch. I was going down the stairs. Several faculty members were walking behind me also. They were talking, discussing, and commenting on that day's class.

One of Mr. Patel's faculty members shouted behind me, "What is the name of the latest discovered element?" Then, he himself shouted, "Low Casteium."

I immediately realized he was making a mockery of me because I was Christian. He was jealous of my success. Everybody in his group bent forward and laughed louder and louder. As I ran down the staircase steps of the university building at forty miles per hour, tears ran down my eyes, but I did not say a word.

A few minutes earlier, the whole class and the same group were clapping to see my demo, but now nobody was on my side. It was a behavior typically of self-emblemed upper-class Indians, friendly as an individual but posing the lowest of the lowest as a group mentality. The roots are so deep that Gandhi and the Nehru family failed to root it out. The pH of the casteism acidic poison is at the highest level in India, the highest the world has ever seen in any modern society in the world.

India is the only country in the world that classifies its own human beings into high and low classes even before the baby is born. Unbelievable, but true even in the twenty-first century. Can you believe a man with a PhD degree in physics still lives in the Stone Age cocoon of casteism?

I can't stop the nightmare of what I had heard in India while I was teaching at the science college. My jealous Hindu colleague got a habit of using racially motivated language to insult me in front of college staff, and everybody got a kick out of it. In any civilized community, racist slurs, epithets, and insensitive, hateful phrases toward any minority group are a lack of high-class culture in the modern world. I was empathetic to this highly educated but ignorant, stupid Hindu guy who lacked knowledge and wisdom because my guru, Jesus Christ, taught me to forgive those who trespass against me.

I didn't say a word, but my heart was broken into a million pieces. A man with a PhD degree behaves like a monkey! Is it a mark of human values? It stinks. It's a trademark of low culture, low thinking, and a shame for India. Surprisingly, it still continues in civilized world.

Thanks to missionaries who left the highest living standard with all the modern amenities of their homelands, responded to the call of humanity, and pulled the innocent victims of socio-economics manmade social structure of darkness into a new life when their own countrymen were pressing them down. The blind eyes are opening but very slowly, at the turtle's pace. Will it take centuries to cure this disease, or will it ever be cured? Even today, living in America, these self-proclaimed so-called upper-class Indians are suffering from this disease. Oh Lord, when will this end? In the meantime, give us more strength to love them and witness them.

Casteism is torture. India is slowly changing at a snail's pace. The majority of those self-proclaimed upper-class clowns draw the invisible lines in everyday religious, social, and educational life. Hardly will you see intercast marriages. A victim of casteism can't even dare to enter the temple. How would you feel if those who practice casteism had to stay on the outskirts of the American towns? That is how some of these victims live in villages in India.

Takeaway: The strength of God's given talents, skills, knowledge, and wisdom to His blessed ones is always threatened by the terror of the beasts called casteism and racism.

Jeremiah 1:8 (NIV), "'Do not be afraid of them, for I am with you and will rescue you,' declares the LORD."

(7/1/2022)

4. THE DREAM OF AMERICA

It had always been my dream since I was in high school to go to California. I read about the orchards of California in geography textbooks, and since then, I always wanted to go to California. In Gujarat state, India, as soon as a Gujarati student graduates from college, the next move is to go to America, no matter what it takes. I was no different, except I didn't have the money or a sponsor to do so. Most of these dreamers, 95 percent of them, are Patels. Although their ancestors were farmers, they are rich; they have money and lands. Why do they have 80 percent of the farming land and others don't? Why are they rich and others are not? The socioeconomic structure of India is wrapped in a caste system, layer after layer. It will take a century to peel them off.

Ninety-five percent of the advertisements in Gujarati newspapers right after college graduation day that say, "Going America for further study" are from rich Hindu families.

I would read this and cry, "Oh, Lord, when will be my day?"

My Lord said, "Trust and obey. Tomorrow is just behind today; wait upon the Lord."

In 1966, I graduated with a master of science in solid-state physics. I read the morning newspaper. Every day was full of advertisements of my classmates and hundreds of others, "My son, Patel Hari is going to America for further study." Their credentials were lower than mine, so why couldn't I go to America? I didn't have money. I waited two more years.

The newspaper was full of advertisements—Patel Hamant and hundreds of others, "My son Amish Patel is visiting India for a short time after working in a highly reputed company in America. Matrimonials are invited for a bright, beautiful girl to go to America." The parents of dozens of girls would line up to see the boy.

I asked myself, "Can this happen to me?" Never, but I kept praying and dreaming.

I was desperate for a job after a master's degree in physics. The science college needed a physics teacher. More than twenty candidates lined up. All were Hindus except for me, mostly Patels. "Do you know anybody who can influence the selection committee chairman, Mr. Patel?" The answer was no for me. All others had some connection. All I could do was pray and wait upon the Lord.

The interview went very well. I was sitting outside in the hallway when the VP Science College's, Vidyanagar, Gujarat state, India, principal, Mr. R. P. Patel, came out of the committee conference room.

He placed his hand on my shoulder and said, "Bramvel, come and see me tomorrow at 10 a.m."

There was some hope. I could not sleep the whole night. The next day morning, well before 10 a.m., I was waiting outside of the VP Science College's, Vidyanagar, Gujarat state, principal's office.

Mr. R. P. Patel walked out of the office and said, "Come on in, sit down."

My heartbeat was 280. He pulled open the desk drawer and handed me a letter. "Sign this; you got the job. Welcome to the faculty. You will teach first-, second-, third-, and final-year physics classes. Congratulations."

I signed it; I could not say a word. Tears ran down my cheeks. I shook his hands and ran out of the office. Mr. R. P. Patel, a man of integrity and honor, would have my respect for my whole life. How did that happen? I don't know. There is a science that maneuvers the universe, but there is something called "beyond the science" that maneuvers the science. His name is "Creator of the universe," "I am who I am," my living God.

I paddled my bicycle back home as fast as I could. I couldn't wait to break the news to Janet, the most beautiful girl in the town, sculptured from the icy white Italian marble, the same as used to flourish the Taj Mahal. I called her Mona Lisa, the lily of the valley, Babee's Barbee.

"I got the job. Now, I can go to America in two years. I will find a second job, private tutoring, and make money. I will take you to America. Now, my dream will come true."

It was not easy. I had to commute to science college, a ten-mile round trip by bike, come home at around 5 p.m., have a cup of tea, and run to for private tutoring class. I saved every penny I could. I borrowed money from friends and took loans from education charity organizations. I also sold everything I had.

January 11, 1972, was a big day. All faculty members, all Hindus except one of my closest Muslim friends, Yosef, attended my wedding.

As a wedding vow, I whispered in her ear privately, "And God willing, I will take you to the promised land."

She chuckled.

Takeaway: My Lord said, "Trust and obey. Tomorrow is just behind today; wait upon the Lord."

Isaiah 40:31 (KJV), "But they that wait upon the LORD shall renew their strength; they shall mount up with wings as eagles; they shall run, and not be weary; and they shall walk, and not faint."

(7/3/2022)

5. THE SECRET OF SUCCESS

Is there a magic wand to be successful and win? Yes, there is. Listen carefully. Here is lesson 101 of the technique that will lead you to hit the high goal.

1. Believe in yourself because the one in you is greater than anybody else outside of you.

   "You are of God, little children, and have overcome them, because He who is in you is greater than he who is in the world" (1 John 4:4, NKJV).

2. Don't let anybody tell you that you can't do it.

So, Jesus said to them, 'Because of your unbelief; for assuredly, I say to you, if you have faith as a mustard seed, you will say to this mountain, "Move from here to there," and it will move; and nothing will be impossible for you.'

Matthew 17:20 (NKJV)

3. Before the sun sets, review what tangible credits you earned today, then draw a plan for tomorrow.
4. Get up before the sun rises, add the vitamins of inspiring devotion to your breakfast, be ignited with prayer, and be delighted with His words.
5. Come out of the cocoon of fear and start your day with a smile on your face because a smile on your face will bring grace for your day ahead.

   "The LORD make His face shine upon you, And be gracious to you" (Numbers 6:25, NKJV).

6. **Take time out with your family always and recharge your battery.**

7. Be like a child. When you accomplish something, shout as loud as a goalie does in a football game, "Goooaaal." The game is over. You are the winner. Move on to the next goal.

Takeaway: Everyone is given a staff called talent; learn a new skill and keep striving until the goalie roars, "Gooaaal." Remember, even Moses had to strike twice.

Numbers 20:11 (NLT), "Then Moses raised his hand and struck the rock twice with the staff, and water gushed out. So the entire community and their livestock drank their fill."

(7/11/2022)

6. WHY ONLY IN AMERICA
AND NOT IN ANY OTHER NATION?

Why does America exceed, excel, acclaim, and achieve the highest technical breakthroughs? The answer is that it is injected into her DNA. Look how many Nobel Prize American winners are and how many Gold, Silver, and Bronze medals are awarded to Americans each time in the Olympic games. As of today, only American footprints are sculptured on the sand of the moon, and a fifty-star banner is flying on the peak of the moon. I envision that the moon will be declared as the fifty-first, and Mars will be the fifty-second state of the USA soon. Now, you know.

When the evil covered the globe with COVID-19, American scientists had already figured out how to kill the monster. In 1966, at a university in India called Sardar Patel University in the state of Gujarat, American textbooks on physics, chemistry, mathematics, and biology became the officially approved textbooks for the first time in India's history. Thousands of these books were donated by American universities. Many American professors spent their summer vacation teaching and preparing college staff to teach these textbooks that emphasize how to solve scientific and technical problems rather than learning the theory behind them. How do I know? I was there as an assistant to a visiting professor from the University of Kansas at S. P. University, Vidyanagar, Gujarat state, India.

Today, all major Indian universities use versions of American textbooks. How generous is America? Can India learn a lesson from this? People all over the world ask the same question, "Why is America so technologically and educationally advanced and economically wealthy and yet such a generous nation?" The answer is that America is a Judeo-Christian nation with the DNA of Jacob's twelve sons. The Americans are descendants of Jacob's thirteenth son, unknown. Now, you know.

Americans are born engineers. My students, when I was teaching at Cantwell High School, Montebello, California, would change my car oil in a swift during lunchtime and offer me to rebuild the old engine of my old 1965 Dodge Plymouth over the weekend. Can students in any other country do this? Breathtaking, marvelous, amazing, wonderful, and beyond-the-imagination! New inventions are born in the incubator called "garage" in America. Apple computers are one example. There is a Home Depot and electronics store within ten miles of every American town. In America, name after name, top-notch universities are encyclopedias of science, math, and technology that students from all over the world want to get into. Can any other nation boast like this? That's why America remains number one in cutting-edge technology. Now, you know.

The world said, "Impossible." But Neal Armstrong said, "A small step for man, a giant step for mankind." America, you will be the first to step on Mars and beyond. The moon and Mars will be American Puerto Rico in space soon. We, Americans, move mountains from Earth to space because of our faith because He went from the cross to the grave and from grave to heaven. Now, you know.

> "You don't have enough faith," Jesus told them. "I tell you the truth, if you had faith even as small as a mustard seed, you could say to this mountain, 'Move from here to there,' and it would move. Nothing would be impossible."
>
> Matthew 17:20 (NLT)

Why do American men's and women's teams dominate World Cups and Olympic games?

Here is the clue: Because Moses' Olympians survived forty years in the wilderness, the toughest mankind made of 60/40 steel, blessed by the living God. Americans are Judeo-Christian descendants in the line of Moses and the thirteenth sons of Jacob, that's why. Now, you know.

America has sent more missionaries to other countries than any other nation in the world. If the missionaries had not brought hope, dreams, joy, education, and new life to the millions of victims of socio-economic-religious persecution in India, they still would be at the bottom of the community. This is a historical fact, and no one can deny it. My dear missionaries and your families, job well done, and billions of thanks from the bottom of our hearts. America, carry on the gospel's baton because it is your mandate. Go ye into the world and preach the gospel. Now, you know.

Mark 16:15 (NASB), "And He said to them, 'Go into all the world and preach the gospel to all creation.'"

America has shared with others more food, medicine, clothes, American cheese, and apple pie than any other nation. There is no other nation in the world that has so many varieties and options and an ample supply of lavish food, state-of-the-art appliances, automobiles built with cutting-edge technology, and comfort houses with all the amenities the world can offer. Go and see the American supermarkets and department stores to believe it. America, trust me, you are a new Canaan; you are blessed abundantly, exceedingly. Don't forget your giver, the living God, the Jehovah (Psalm 13:6).

The day the American president raises a book other than the Bible on the front of Capitol Hill in January will be the first day of forty years in the wilderness. America, you are warned, "Thou shalt have no any other Gods before me" (Exodus 20:3) (read Exodus 20:2–17). How can you forget after all these showers of blessings from heaven above that no other nation in the world has received? Now, you know.

(7/29/2023, Saturday)

To be successful, you don't have to be perfect or an expert or have a degree from a renowned institution; all you need is willingness to take a calculated risk, endurance to go through the expected fire, and courage to start the journey no matter where it leads. If you wait to plant the olive tree in the desert until the perfect weather arrives, your olive oil jar will always remain empty. Just get started and wait upon the Lord; the showers of blessings will ascend even though you don't see clouds, and come harvest, your jar will be full of the most delicious olives you have ever tested.

> Farmers who wait for perfect weather never plant. If they watch every cloud, they never harvest. Just as you cannot understand the path of the wind or the mystery of a tiny baby growing in its mother's womb, so you cannot understand the activity of God, who does all things. Plant your seed in the morning and keep busy all afternoon,

for you don't know if profit will come from one activity or another—
or maybe both.

Ecclesiastes 11:4–6 (NLT)

Now, you know.

(7/27/2023, Thursday)

America, your basket will be full of bread, vine, figs, pomegranates, and olive oil as long as the American president takes oath with the family Bible in his right hand on Capitol Hill.

Haggai 2:19 (KJV), "Is the seed yet in the barn? yea, as yet the vine, and the fig tree, and the pomegranate, and the olive tree, hath not brought forth: from this day will I bless you."

(8/8/2022)

7. WHAT HAPPENS IN AMERICAN GIANT CORPORATION WAR ROOMS?

Do you know what happens behind the mahogany lane and on the cement floor in American corporations?

CEOs in the mahogany lane, do you really know what's happening on the cement floor?

White- and blue-collar men and women on the cement floor, do you know what's happening behind the mahogany lane?

This is an American corporate world called free enterprise, a child of democracy, a savior of a booming economy that the other side of the world is envious of.

Do you know how this game behind the mahogany lane and on the cement floor is played out every day to keep the numbers of Dow, Nasdaq, and S&P 500 flying higher and higher than the day before?

How do American corporations thrive in technical excellence and achieve the world's largest gold pot year after year? Why are the richest on Wall Street, the most famous on the screen, and the brightest of the Nobel Prize winners born in the land called the USA?

This is the answer:

It's a contest for the money. It's a win-or-die Olympic. It's a position. It's a promotion. It's the stock price that keeps up at any cost. It's power lunch. It's a bloody war game. It's a game of winning the hearts, minds, souls, and brains of Navy, Air Force, and Army colonels. It's a war game that ends at Wall Street but starts in a corporate cherry-furnished war room. The soldiers are die-hard engineers, computer scientists, chemists, mathematicians, biologists, and doctors. The cream of the crop harvested from around the world is attracted to the center of the American dream.

From Boston to Silicon Valley and from Seattle to San Diego, every corporate CEO proclaims the same slogan, **"We are here to make it** possible that others say is not possible. Never say it will not happen. Don't even think it does not exist; it is in the making. I want to solve this problem. Let me know what tools you need, but I want to win this contract at any cost. You are the best and brightest brains in the industry, and we are so fortunate to have you on the board. Go figure it out. You have my back."

And war begins. There is something in the American air that inspires, promotes, and pushes engineers to the edge to achieve excellence and to go where nobody else has gone. However, there are many enemies in the corporate world. They look like friends, but they aim to distract you. They are jealous. They put you down. They always search for your weaknesses and spread rumors. They munch on gossiping at lunchtime in the cafeteria.

Uncle Sam whispers in the ear of the selected few to drive beyond the speed of light. It's that drive that becomes life for the innovator. All of a sudden, this individual sees a carbon-tungsten sharp arrow in his hand and seven concentric circles. He has to shoot the arrow at the center of seven circles.

The crowd behind me shouts, "You are so weak. You hardly weigh 100 pounds. This is not your game; you can't do it. Sit down. Go home."

But the inner voice tells me, "Close your eyes and ears. What do you see?"

I answer, "A tiny dot in the middle of the innermost circle."

And I hear, "My son, that's it. Don't move, don't even blink. Go for it. It's all over. Pull the trigger."

That is where I get the strength and expertise to solve the most challenging technical problems. In 1974, in a town called Torrance, located in Southern California, on 228 Street, the outside billboard read, "Doctor's Office," but the world did not know what was going on inside. A subsidiary of Universal Studios, MCA Records Company invested in a research initiative, later named MCA Disco Vision. The story I heard was that Universal Studios made tons of money on the *Ten Commandments* movie, thanks to those Universal visionaries for granting this windfall in research of laser recording medium. Guess what? The first CD/DVD in the world was born in this tiny building in Torrance, California. I was part of a pretty smart team of a dedicated bunch of visionaries.

One day, the chief scientist Mr. Gary Slaten, a very talented physicist and the owner of hundreds of breakthrough patents, announced, "We are going public, and Bram Christian will be the production manager of the pilot production line of the DVD laser discs first ever produced in the world."

I knelt down on my knees, and tears ran down my cheeks. "O Lord, who am I? I am the poorest of the poor, the son of the Salvation Army officer from India! Oh, God, give me the knowledge and wisdom to win the hearts of those with whom I work and the intelligence and creativity to make this product a grand success."

I visited the Museum of Science and Technology in Washington, DC. There, the original DVD disks and player are on the display platform. The tag reads, "Invented by Pioneer Corporation of Japan." Not true. The original laser-recorded DVD and player were invented by MCA Disco Vision in Torrance, California, a subsidiary of Universal Studios, California. Later on, the rights were sold to Pioneer to mass produce and distribute. It is true that Pioneer turned this bulky new invention into a compact, consumer-friendly, marketable product at an affordable price. But the inventor was MCA Disco Vision; I was there and watched its birth in the lab to the winner at market. Today's CD and CD ROM are the byproduct of the original CD that was twelve inches in diameter, I still have it.

> Takeaway: Every American has Columbus' blood; no turning back, invent, invent, and invent, and then give away free to the thirsty and hungry world and move on in search of the next golden pot.

(8/20/2022)

8. THE SAILORS FIRST: IS THERE A GHOST ON THE SUBMARINE?

Boeing Company, the world's largest aerospace giant, is an American icon and pioneer of the aviation, aerospace, and satellite breakthrough industry. It was early morning when the program manager called all the managers and engineers.

"I got the call last night. Lt. Commander Wesley is catching the Red Eyes flight and will be here at 10 a.m. I want everybody with secret clearance in conference room 1177."

"What is the issue? Why so sudden? Why is it an emergency?"

The program manager said, "I don't know." He knew but didn't want to tell us; we could tell by looking at his face.

Lt. Commander arrived at exactly 10 a.m. It was a closed-door meeting. This building had no windows. The walls were secured. Radio frequencies couldn't penetrate the communication.

"What you hear here stays here," the commander addressed a small, invited group of top-notch engineers. "Listen carefully, can you imagine navigation mode 302, power supply module 6XXX OPRT, down mode 607, power loss 303. Urgent message 1404. At 2 a.m. Atlantic 55 degrees north. Switch to NVGTN 2. Okay. One hour in NAV. SYS 1 secured. No command. Now, in NAV. What is going on here? I want the answer by 10 a.m. tomorrow. Sailors first. That's it. Go figure it out. I have to catch my next flight. I flew in to deliver this message in person."

Could there be a ghost in the submarine? Commander Christianson was very angry and wanted Boeing to fix it right away. How in the world could that happen?

"Hey Bram, you are on the hook. You three go to the lab and do whatever you need to do. Let me know what support, tool, or funding you need, and report back to me by 6 p.m. That's all. Go figure it out; don't take it lightly."

Commander left. Pin drop silence. Mr. Eggnora, the manager, pointed at me. "Bram, you are in charge. Go to the lab. Report to me by 4 p.m. The race is on. Pressure mounts. No lunch today."

I got the module and went to the top-secret lab. The module behaved unpredictable functionally. I designed an experiment to back up the gold module. It was secured control. A few hours later, it moved to OP. The sailor operator would go crazy. Is it a ghost? Oh my God! What do I do now?

I spent hour after hour and day after day. Chasing the host was not an easy assignment. Finally, I figured it out. The solution was implemented. As far as I know, many Halloweens have gone but the sailors have not seen the electronic ghost since then again.

The Navy commander of the submarine sent me a message with only three words, "Bram, Bravo Julu." He took me to lunch when he visited the Boeing gigantic facility in Huntington Beach, California, at the superclass cafeteria. The tears ran down my eyes. These American military men and women are made with 60/40 stainless steel outside and strawberry Jell-O hearts inside. God bless America. God bless our troops. God bless our sailors and commanders who put their lives on the line day in and day out every day.

I had the privilege to walk on the submarine floor to provide technical support. The words are not enough to thank these young heroes for what they do to protect our liberty and justice for all. As an immigrant from India, I ask myself, what have I done for this amazing nation that gave me a new life that the country I left behind couldn't give me?

I want to bow down and express my gratitude every day to these unsung heroes, and I pray that God bless them and their families and God bless America, a hope, a beacon of freedom, a lighthouse for justice, and an emblem of equal opportunities for all.

Takeaway: The words of thanks are not enough to thank those ordinary young boys and girls performing extraordinary tasks above the ocean and under the ocean to keep us safe twenty-four seven. Every one of you is an American hero; every American salutes you. Your name is engraved on the fifty stars that will shine on every Fourth of July.

(8/22/2022)

9. THE GAME OF CARDBOARD BOXES

America and Wall Street are synonyms. Look at some of the dramatic headlines that unfold when Wall Street goes on a roller coaster ride. The impact on the workforce and the aftermath of the layoff is devastating.

NASDAQ is down, again and again, week after week. Stockholders' eyes are glued to the big board. Board of directors urgent meeting today. Executive conference room in Cherry Lane, closed-door brouhaha. We lost ten million. Enough is enough. CEO must resign. The CFO should quit. We want our money back. Do whatever it takes. Cut to the chest to reduce payroll. Some good news: a new baby has arrived. Vacation to Hawaii will be canceled. Forget to marry this spring. He just got married, planning to buy a new house, forget it. The American dream, where is it? The cubicles are filled with card boxes. The tears run down in her eyes. Adios!

I hear the inner voice. There is an angel. And he says this is not the end of my life. There is a tomorrow. Beautiful sunshine is waiting; just get it over with this dark night. Morning will be brighter and even more beautiful. There is always a tomorrow. Yes, there is an angel. Yes, there is an Almighty who knows your needs. He counts your hair. A company may let you go, but He will not.

The cubicles are filled with the card boxes. Engineers pack up the stuff. The party is over; turn off the light.

But a miracle happened in my case.

My director, a brilliant scholar, an amazing man, Moses' heir, Mr. Roseberry, called me. "Your pink slip is canceled. Go to Anaheim."

It's a Navy nuclear missile submarine program. A major unit was failing, and all engineering efforts were exhausted. It is a high reliability government program; national security depends on this program that draws high visibility at the Admiral level. It would cost thousands of dollars and two years to redesign, qualify, build a prototype, perform engineering evaluation, test at the system level, get the customer approval, and finally build a new unit.

The program manager couldn't sleep at night and was looking for a magnetic expert.

I was transferred from Boeing Satellite Division, El Segundo, California, to Boeing Nuclear Submarine Navigation System, Anaheim, California, to take charge of this technical problem. The challenge was to solve the problem or go home. I committed to solving the problem. I spent hours and hours without enough sleep, and the war room was full of experimental test data.

Finally, one beautiful morning, the test engineer, Paul, came to my office running and shouted, "Bram, it works. It works! You did it." Boeing awarded me a hundred dollars.

(8/23/2022)

Again, a few months later, we gathered in the war room. The engineers with secret clearance were listening to a panicked phone call from the Navy nuclear submarine senior commander. The thermal electronic heater was burning.

"You can smell everywhere. If not controlled, it can burn the whole system unit."

I was Technical Director (TD) in the Navy Program Office in Huntington Beach, California.

At the end of the meeting, the Navy commander announced, "Bram, you lead the team. I want symptom, cause, and impact charts by tomorrow and a Fault Tree analysis by Friday 5 a.m. to present to the Admiral's staff meeting. Coordinate with SP24, Boeing, General Dynamics, and Lockheed-Martin technical teams. Let me know what tools you need. I will support you with whatever you need, but I want an answer. I'll give you two weeks. The meeting is adjourned. Go to work; thanks for attending."

This was my first protocol after being the Technical Director (TD) of the Navy Program Office, and I had to learn the military work ethic, no guesswork, straight talk, straight answer, timeline, deadline, and life on the line.

Another Navy call. I was a senior engineer at Boeing, Huntington Beach, California.

The Navy nuclear submarine commander was on the line. "It's an electronic box. I can't get the signal out. The technician inspection reports a strange white powder residue around the box terminals. I need an answer really quick."

Mr. Segram, a very intelligent manager, looked at me and said, "Here we go again. Bram, take charge."

So, we teamed up again. Within two weeks, I determined the problem and proposed a technical solution. The Navy was very happy. Boeing gave me an appreciation award with the wording, "Congratulations. Job well done." I played a small role in the country that had done so much for me and millions of immigrants from South Asia like me.

Mattel in Hawthorn, California, is the largest toy company in the world. Believe it or not, it takes a team of brilliant mechanical engineers, electrical engineers, and chemists to innovate, prototype, and mass-produce toys that meet very stringent health and safety standards of USA regulatory agencies. In 1980, Mattel opened a new enterprise called Mattel Electronics to invent and market state-of-the-art electronic musical players. Today's electronic drum was first invented by this company. The heart of the instrument, the electrical signal generator, is a piezo crystal.

I was a new quality assurance engineer just hired. My assignment was to establish quality control standards for the new product. Although I didn't have any talent for playing any musical instrument, I designed a test fixture to characterize the sound quality of the new product electronic drum that can be used on the assembly line. I gave a demonstration to the director of the company. The conference room was full of newly hired director's staff members. There were two sets of electronic drums, one that met the quality parameters and the other that did not, but you couldn't tell just by looking at it. I placed the electronic drum under the tester and dropped the ball from the top of the tester. The light comes on if it meets the quality standard. The tester identified each instrument correctly.

The director shouted, "Amazing! It works. It works. Thank you, Bram."

That year, my amazing director, the descendant of Moses Mr. Singer, sent me to Japan to work with Toshiba to establish a quality control lab and get the Japanese government's approval to produce electronic drums and other electronic toys in Japan. I went to the Japanese government office with Toshiba's two engineers. I saw piles and piles of documents on the tables lined up in the Japanese government licensing office, the red tape and bureaucracy similar to what I have seen in India. Thank God, the license was granted.

Takeaway: In your lifetime, you will go through the game of card boxes, but remember, the darker the cloud, the more rain is on the way. A beautiful morning will arrive right after the stormy night. He has counted the hairs on your head; He can pull you out of the cardboard boxes.

Luke 12:7 (KJV), "But even the very hairs of your head are all numbered. Fear not therefore: ye are of more value than many sparrows."

10. I CAN ENTER A SATELLITE IN AMERICA BUT NOT A HINDU TEMPLE IN INDIA

I was a senior magnetic engineer at Boeing Satellite, El Segundo, California, the world's largest state-of-the-art, cutting-edge technology satellite research, design, and manufacturing company. One day, bad news came. The sub-contractor in Portland, Oregon, refused to build our designed transformers because the magnetic cores were cracking during prototyping, evident in radiographs. These devices were very critical to building several satellites for the Air Force contract. The very smart, intelligent director and my mentor, Mr. Roseberry, assigned me to spearhead the challenge.

Amazingly, a miracle happened. By the grace of God, I was able to formulate a special process to encapsulate the magnetic devices in such a way that the magnetic core would not split down the further processing and thermal shock. Bingo, we were able to build the transformers successfully. Boeing awarded me a Technical Karate Kid Award and an Amy Award trophy on Christmas party day, I still have it on my desk.

Darkness through the Pin Hole: Hindu Temple in
Vadtal for Excursion Picnic

I was in ninth-grade class a long, long time ago, about seventy years ago. One day, the teacher announced, "We are going on a school excursion to Vadtal."

The location was a very popular Hindu temple. All the students were Hindu except me, but they all were my friends. We arrived at the temple.

My teacher, a very nice Hindu gentleman, took me to a corner and whispered in my ears, "Look, Christian. No offense. I don't want to get into trouble. Do you mind just not going inside the temple, please? We will be back in a few minutes."

I said, "No, I don't mind." What choice did I have? What god would hide inside the temple? Why can't I see their god? Why would their god meet only to certain group? What qualifications do you need to meet and greet their god? What does their god look like?

So, I went behind the temple and looked inside through a small opening between two gigantic doors. It was dark inside, except for a small earthen lamp filled with ghee (Indian butter) that was burning. You could also smell the burning incents. Tons of flowers were on the floor.

Every minute, someone entered the temple, rang the bell, and offered mouthwatering, colorful pastries to the monk, and the monk dedicated them to their god; the aroma made me hungry. I could hear the chanting but couldn't understand what they were saying. It might have been in Sanskrit.

My classmates came back. I didn't utter a single word; it was a calm, pin-drop silence, but I could read their lips saying, "Sorry." Even today, I ask the same question, but there is no answer: If god doesn't want to see me, why do I want to see him?

Takeaway: I want to see Your face, touch the wounds in Your chest, the nails on Your hands, and the thorns on Your head. I want to see You.

Psalm 100:4 (KJV), "Enter into his gates with thanksgiving, and into his courts with praise: be thankful unto him, and bless his name."

(9/1/2022)

11. THE RED BLOOD OF THE AMERICAN HEROES TURNS BLACK UPON ARRIVAL AT HOME

Arrived at LAX. The Salvation Army captain was waiting for me.

"Hello, I am Captain Williams. Welcome to California. How was the flight? We are going to Harmony Hall in Los Angeles."

This was a halfway house for rehabilitated alcoholics, fine young men. They came from all walks of life. Many returned from the Vietnam, Korean, Gulf, and other wars.

Listen to their stories:

"Hey, young man. How in the world you ended up here?"

"I have a master's degree in physics. I am a Christian. We are a minority in India. There are no opportunities for me in India."

"Opportunities in this country?" He spread out his hands and laughed and laughed. "Look, I was a salesperson in Sears. They drafted me for the Vietnam War. I left my family. It was pretty hard on me. My son was four years old, and my daughter was two years old. We were very happy. We went to church every Sunday there in Orange Grove. We picked up Kentucky fried chicken boxes free from the church and sat down on the bench in the grove, and it was so refreshing. When the war was over, I came home. I don't know where my family is. There was no place to go. Thanks to the Salvation Army, I got a roof over my head and a cup of soup on my plate. I became an alcoholic to forget all the old memories and pain."

It was the same story after story after story from all of these heroes.

"I gave my blood for my country; the country put alcohol in my blood." I could see the tears running down in his eyes.

"Go to Little Saigon, only ten miles from here. All Vietnamese are driving Mercedes, Volvo, and Cadillacs. What did I do wrong?"

"Brother, hang in there. I got this shirt for you. I sell shirts at the Veteran Hospital in Los Angeles. Good luck to you, and God bless you."

Go to Artesia, Pioneer Street, California, Edison, Green Street, New Jersey, Clearwater, Florida, or Chicago, Illinois. These Indians, Pakistanis, and Bangla Deshi immigrants did not shed a single drop of blood in any war Americans fought. I don't understand the politics of our nation. Why do we Americans send our young sons and daughters to the battlefield every time there is a crisis and open the door for immigrants when the crisis is over?

Why did we invent the electric bulb, the electricity, the gramophone record, the cinema, the phone, the X-rays, the stethoscopes, the automobile, the vaccines, the plane, the rocket, the TV, the diode, the transistor, the computer, the laser, and millions of other inventions and then gave away to the world free?

Why did we send tons of food cans and medicines worldwide when our veterans camp on the sidewalks of all major cities of America?

The answer is:

This is a second promised land, a land of honey and milk. From Anchorage to San Diego and from Boston to Honolulu, the sons and daughters of fifty stars are so generous as their Almighty living God is. Believe it or not, love, kindness, generosity, and wealth are inherited assets for Americans from Jacob's twelves.

God said, "I will bless you because you have blessed others around the world."

Americans asked, "When did we do all this?"

And God said,

And he shall set the sheep on his right hand, but the goats on the left. Then shall the King say unto them on his right hand, Come, ye blessed of my Father, inherit the kingdom prepared for you from the foundation of the world: For I was a hungered, and ye gave me meat: I was thirsty, and ye gave me drink: I was a stranger, and ye took me in: Naked, and ye clothed me: I was sick, and ye visited me: I was in prison, and ye came unto me. Then shall the righteous answer him, saying, Lord, when saw we thee an hungred, and fed thee? or thirsty, and gave thee drink? When saw we thee a stranger, and took thee in? or naked, and clothed thee? Or when saw we thee sick, or in prison, and came unto thee? And the King shall answer and say unto them,

Verily I say unto you, inasmuch as ye have done it unto one of the least of these my brethren, ye have done it unto me.

Matthew 25:33–40 (KJV)

And He said, "Because you did all these for all who were in need, you did to Me."

Now you know why Americans sing, "Awesome is our God."

The fifty stars and stripes will fly on the earth, moon, Mars, and beyond shortly, as long as Americans keep singing this song.

The immigrants claim, "We are the minority wealthiest population in the top 10 percent of Americans." True, but ask yourself, "Why could I not become so wealthy in my own homeland?"

The fact is that the majority of us came from poor or middle-class Asia and South Asia and immigrated to America because our homeland did not offer the opportunities to match our education, talents, and skills.

The correct answer is: It is a magic of 30/70 miracle. Thirty percent is your hard work and intelligence, and 70 percent is the opportunities offered by Judeo-Christian America, the living God's promised land, the second Canaan, the land of milk and honey. Read the Bible.

Message for the immigrants: Watch American history TV channels and see how many young American lives have been sacrificed in World War I, World War II, the Korean War, the Vietnam War, the Gulf War, and many others. What we enjoy today is the gift of their sacrifice and the blessings from our living God, not because of our hard work and smartness.

And one more reminder: Always remember the hard work and brilliance of our Judeo-Christian founding fathers and pioneers who built America from scratch. God bless America, the beacon of real freedom and justice for all, an example to follow for the world.

Takeaway: What is true for Israel is also true for America because America is a new Canaan.

Genesis 12:2 (KJV), "And I will make of thee a great nation, and I will bless thee, and make thy name great; and thou shalt be a blessing."

(9/5/2022)

12. HOW SHOULD IMMIGRANTS LOOK LIKE? THEY SHOULD LOOK LIKE THE PARSIS IN INDIA

This is a well-known real story everybody knows in Gujarat state, India. The father of India's independent movement, the great man Mr. Gandhi, was from this state. The Parsis were persecuted in Iran because of their religion. They migrated to India between the eighth and the tenth century, but no exact record is found. They arrived first by sea at the harbor of north Gujarat state, India, and asked for permission from the king ruler of that area to enter into country. The king sent a glass of milk filled to the rim as a gesture of symbolizing that his kingdom was overpopulated and couldn't accommodate the newly arrived foreigners. The intelligent Parsis leader of the immigrants added sugar to the glass of milk and sent it back, signifying that they were desperate and would melt in his community just like sugar melts in milk and makes it sweeter. The king smiled and welcomed the Parsis in India. That is a Parsis history, but how true it is. Parsis have melted into the Indian community and made it much sweeter.

Have a look at some of the prominent Parsis figures:

The father of nuclear energy in India, Homi J. Bhabha; nuclear scientist, Homi N. Sethna; the fathers of the steel industry in India, J. R. D. Tata and Jamsetji Tata; and the father of the construction industry, Pallonji Mistry.

The other notables are Godrej, Mistry, Tata, Petit, Cowasjee, Poonawalla, and Wadia. They are highly distinguished industrial Parsi families.

Other great Parsi well-known businessmen are Ratan Tata, Cyrus Mistry, Ratanji Dadabhoy Tata, Dinshaw Maneckji Petit, Ness Wadia, Neville Wadia, Jehangir Wadia, and Nusli Wadia Feroze Gandhi married Indira Gandhi, the daughter of first Indian prime minister, Jawaharlal

Nehru. The brave military officer Field Marshal Sam Hormusji Framji Jamshedji Manekshaw was Parsis. And the list goes on.

Here is an example of how the immigrants should melt into "the glass of honey and milk called America" from the heaven above, the Judeo-Christian land, the greatest nation on Earth. Let us be like Parsis and melt into the American glass of milk and honey to make it sweeter. My immigrant friends, leave your old rugged luggage behind you and embrace the rugged cross. Listen, the church bells are ringing in your honor:

"On a hill (of America) far away stood an old, rugged cross

"The emblem of (immigrants) suffering and shame

"And I love (freedom and justice for all) that old cross where the dearest and best

"For a world of lost sinners was slain (so I left my old luggage behind, far away in India)."

"No man can serve two masters, for either he will hate the one, and love the other; or else he will hold to the one, and despise the other. Ye cannot serve God and mammon" (Matthew 6:24, KJV).

Should an immigrant in the Big Apple say, "I am a New Yorker and proud to be an American"?

Should an immigrant in Los Angeles say, "I am an Angeleno and proud to be an American"?

If the answer is yes, welcome to America.

If the answer is no, you are an alien. Did you see ET?—Home! Home! You forgot to leave your old luggage behind.

Takeaway: China and India are boasting as the largest economies in the world after America. But the highest number of immigrants coming to America are from these two countries in 2023. Why? It is because Washington, DC, is a new Jerusalem. His name is written on Pennsylvania Avenue.

Him that overcometh will I make a pillar in the temple of my God, and he shall go no more out: and I will write upon him the name of my God, and the name of the city of my God, which is new Jerusalem, which cometh down out of heaven from my God: and I will write upon him my new name.

Revelation 3:12 (KJV)

(9/14/2022)

13. THERE IS A SCIENCE, AND THEN THERE IS BEYOND THE SCIENCE

There are two disciplines that govern and control the universe. One is called science; we partly understand it, and man constantly keeps trying to understand it more and more. However, only the knowledge, wisdom, and power that come from above can reveal it. America is a champion of science and technology in this discipline. Look how many Nobel Prizes in all fields America has won. Who has landed on the moon? Do you watch the Olympics? Gold after gold, silver after silver, bronze after bronze, American athletes stand high on the Olympia stage and sing, "America, home, my sweet home." And every American places their right hand on their heart when they sing (except those who forgot to leave their old luggage at home).

The common Joe of the world, all he wants is to live in peace and let others live in peace. But then there is always a Hitler rising in some dark corner of the world. Guess who shuts him down? America. Don't believe it? Go back and look at the history. First World War, Second World War, Korean War, Vietnam War, Gulf War, 9/11, and now Ukraine.

Where in the world does every ninth-grade student drive a car at school? Only in America. The high school kid of Cantwell High School in Montebello, California, opened up my car hood during lunchtime and changed the spark plugs and oil of my 1970 Dodge in the school parking lot while I was their science and math teacher. I was impressed to see these "born American mechanics" at the age of eighteen. No wonder they aim to join NASA, and next thing you know, they will step on Mars.

The second discipline is called "beyond the science." It can't be understood by the principles of the science. To receive it, you have to humble yourself. The only way you can understand it is by trust, faith, and obedience. It does not require earthy knowledge of math, physics, chemistry, or biology. It comes from above. It is a free gift, and still, people deny receiving it. It's granted by the Holy Spirit. That is a mystery. It is a free gift. The Bible says, "It will be given to those who humble themselves and seek me."

Proverbs 11:2 (NKJV), "When pride comes, then comes shame; But with the humble is wisdom."

Proverbs 11:2 (LSB), "When arrogance comes, then comes disgrace, But with the meek is wisdom."

Matthew 10:33 (BBE), "But if anyone says before men that he has no knowledge of me, I will say that I have no knowledge of him before my Father in heaven."

> Then he said to me, "Don't be afraid, Daniel, for from the very first day you applied your mind to understand and to humble yourself before your God, your words were heard. I have come in response to your words."
>
> Daniel 10:12 (NET)

Takeaway: The presence of God cannot be understood by earthly science and technology. But make yourself humble, open your eyes and ears and surrender to Him; the knowledge and wisdom of the Trinity will be revealed to you.

Matthew 13:11 (NIV), "He replied, 'Because the knowledge of the secrets of the kingdom of heaven has been given to you, but not to them.'"

14. WHAT IS IN YOUR BACKPACK?

A sling and five stones from the bank of the Hudson River.

Then he took his staff in his hand and chose for himself five smooth stones from the brook, and put them in the shepherd's bag which he had, that is, in his shepherd's pouch, and his sling was in his hand; and he approached the Philistine.

1 Samuel 17:40 (NASB)

America, the God of Abraham, Isaac, Jacob, and Moses is on your side as long as the American president will raise the Bible in his right hand when he proclaims presidency on Capitol Hill and takes the oath, "And so Almighty God, help me to protect and preserve this second promise land of yours [the New Canaan]."

Why? It is because our Declaration of Independence says so. Abolitionist leaders Benjamin Lundy and William Lloyd Garrison adopted the "twin rocks" of "the Bible and the Declaration of Independence" as the basis for their philosophies. He wrote, "As long as there remains a single copy of the Declaration of Independence, or of the Bible, in our land, we will not despair."

The war can't be won on the battlefield of Ukraine, Afghanistan, Vietnam, Iraq, or Korea, but go and see the war we have won, the towering prosperity on the bank of the Hudson River. The fire from the devil's jealous eyes generated 2500 degrees Fahrenheit, the melting point of the steel. But the next day at dawn, when the sun has risen, behold, at the sound of the trumpet, out of the ashes, a magnificent victorious monument has emerged again. It is so shiny. Next time, if the devil looks at it, he will be knocked out blind. This is where the eagle dares, and the wind of the towering economy starts flowing again from the bank of the Hudson River of the Empire State to the Silicon Valley of the Golden State.

Exodus 14:14 (NASB), "The LORD will fight for you, while you keep silent."

Deuteronomy 1:30 (NASB), "The LORD your God, who goes before you, will Himself fight for you, just as He did for you in Egypt before your eyes."

Deuteronomy 20:4 (NASB), "For the LORD your God is the One who is going with you, to fight for you against your enemies, to save you."

Joshua 10:25 (NASB), "Joshua then said to them, 'Do not fear or be dismayed! Be strong and courageous, for the LORD will do this to all your enemies with whom you fight.'"

Nehemiah 4:14 (NASB),

When I saw their fear, I stood and said to the nobles, the officials, and the rest of the people: "Do not be afraid of them; remember the Lord who is great and awesome, and fight for your brothers, your sons, your daughters, your wives, and your houses."

Nehemiah 4:20 (NASB), "At whatever place you hear the sound of the trumpet, assemble to us there. Our God will fight for us."

Psalm 35:1 (NASB), "A Psalm of David. Contend, LORD, with those who contend with me; Fight against those who fight against me."

Exodus 15:6 (NASB), "Your right hand, LORD, is majestic in power; Your right hand, LORD, destroys the enemy."

First Chronicles 29:12 (NASB), "Both riches and honor come from You, and You rule over all, and in Your hand is power and might; and it lies in Your hand to make great and to strengthen everyone."

Job 9:19 (NASB), "If it is a matter of power, behold, He is the strong one! And if it is a matter of justice, who can summon Him?"

Psalm 78:26 (NASB), "He made the east wind blow in the sky And by His power He directed the south wind."

Proverbs 24:5 (NASB), "A wise man is strong, And a person of knowledge increases power."

Isaiah 40:29 (NASB), "He gives strength to the weary, And to the one who lacks might He increases power."

Jeremiah 16:21 (NASB), "Therefore behold, I am going to make them know—This time I will make them know My power and My might; And they will know that My name is the LORD."

Matthew 22:29 (NASB), "But Jesus answered and said to them, 'You are mistaken, since you do not understand the Scriptures nor the power of God.'"

Luke 10:19 (NASB), "Behold, I have given you authority to walk on snakes and scorpions, and authority over all the power of the enemy, and nothing will injure you."

Takeaway: To fight with Goliath, you need five stones in your backpack. Guaranteed, you will win.

Colossians 3:12 (NIV), "Therefore, as God's chosen people, holy and dearly loved, clothe yourselves with compassion, kindness, humility, gentleness and patience."

Colossians 3:13–14 (NIV), Bear with each other and forgive one another if any of you has a grievance against someone. Forgive as the Lord forgave you. And over all these virtues put on love, which binds them all together in perfect unity.

15. OH, MY BELOVED INDIA, UNLOCK THE TWO-THOUSAND-YEAR-OLD SHACKLES OF CASTEISM

Casteism is a 2000-year-old cancer that has poisoned India. India was largely isolated from the modern world's social structure, Western education, and advanced science and technology up until the British arrived. Mr. K. Gandhi, Mr. Jawaharlal Nehru, Mr. Vallabhbhai Patel, and other Indian independent pioneers studied in England and carried the modern world ideas home.

Mr. Gandhi, living in England, realized what a shameful ideology the caste system was. The honest mistake he made was that he named those who were socially and economically suppressed and exploited as God's people. Although he had good intentions, the term he used turned out to be an abusive mockery, a sarcastic name of the millions of socially and economically crushed people. The appropriate term would have been the victims of socio-economic and cultural injustice (VSECI).

By international civilized world standards, this casteism is deemed as a violation of human rights and dignity. If this happens in the Western world, it would be considered a crime, and punishment would be very severe. India is still struggling with this disease on a large scale behind the curtain. It will take another hundred years to wipe out this COVID of casteism pandemic from their hearts and minds. Believe it or not, the Five Eyes are also infected by the traces of this COVID-Casteism spread by the infected few blind-minded religious extremists who sneaked into the Five Eyes. India, it's about time now. The Son rose on Easter Sunday; He came out of the grave. You need to come out of the cocoon of casteism and racism. He loves every caste, race, and culture equally. Let the Philadelphia Bells of socio-economic equality, religious freedom, and justice for all ring on the Red Fort of New Delhi.

Uma Shankar Joshi, a renounce poet of Gujarat state, India, and the vice chancellor of the Gujarat University, India 19060–64, visited America. He was amazed to see the beauty, the culture, the wealth, the community, the unity, the New York, the grocery stores, the malls, the schools, the hospitals, the department stores, the world-class universities, and the houses of worship across America. When he returned to India, he penned a poem. What impressed him most was that there was no casteism in the melting pot, even though there were people from all over the world. One nation under the living God, no matter where you come from. That message he took home.

I still remember one of his poems that was in my Gujarati textbook during my high school year in 1957. "Pasteem na vira via, Uth ne ukarda joto nathee." (Gujarati luggage.)

Abstract English translation, "The revolutionary wind is blowing from the west. Get up, oh, pile of dung. Are you blind? Can't you see?"

Mahatma Gandhi tried to break this chain, but he could not overcome the ugly old evil. Young India, now is the time, now is your turn. Wake up, don't let anybody tell you you can't. Break the chain. Answer Mr. Uma Joshi's call.

You hosted G20, and now G20 will expect you to break the chains because you are the only nation in G20 that suffers from this infectious disease: the chain of casteism. Chain of religious intolerance, chain of supremacy. Free the victims you have held up for 2000 years. Let their light shine to make India even more beautiful.

> Takeaway: If you label someone backward class or lower class, your brain must be wired backward, and your tongue is hanging lower. I recommend checking it out with an American neurologist.
>
> Matthew 23:8 (NLT), "Don't let anyone call you 'Rabbi,' for you have only one teacher, and all of you are equal as brothers and sisters."

16. SILENT NIGHT, HOLY NIGHT, IS IT?

I was in the Gaily Street apartment, very close to UCLA, with all the students. The first-semester exam was over just before Christmas. All students packed up their stuff and went home. It was like a ghost town. No friends, no relatives. Home alone. Loneliness was killing me. The blanket of homesickness covered me. You don't know how it feels unless you experience it yourself. I wanted to go home. America was not for me.

Silent Night, Holy Night. All Is Calm, All Is Dark

It is LA. It's UC. As far as I can see, it's gloomy, it's scary.
Searching Christ, in gaily light, no Bethel star in smog full sky,
Angel lost in Los Angeles, only palm trees, no Christmas tree.
It's blowing sand on Santa Monica beach. It's the darkest night; all I can see, the doors are closed.
Where is a hope? Where is a dream? Where is a shepherd? Where is a star? Where is an angel?
Is it wood? Why not holy? Is it film? Why stunt only?
Why tears in the eyes? Who awards it as comedy?
Is it a hill? Where is Beverly? Is it a Disney? Who is happy?
Where is gold? Are you kidding? This is Cali? Is it golden? Where is the bridge? I see a wall.
Where is a home? No more sweetness. It is on fire; how to escape? I am on one way only.
Go home. Is it a call from ET? No, add sickness, not to worry?
Where is a friend? Who is on my side? Oh, silent night, no silver line.
Nobody understands. Brain is falling apart, no pill to apply
But I will rise; a star will guide. For now, head home; the pain will die.

On December 31, 1973, I boarded the plane to India. It was the worst new year in my life. I was not welcomed at home either, and nobody had sympathy for me. Why? They wanted me to stay in America so that someday I could sponsor them to come to America. I survived on one verse of the Bible, "I will be your God throughout your lifetime—until your hair is white with age. I made you, and I will care for you. I will carry you along and save you" (Isaiah 46:4, NLT).

How to Kill a Giant at Workplace and at Home?

All you need is a staff on your desk, five stones in your backpack, and a sling on your desktop! Really? Yes, really. It may sound outdated in this digital era, but you can't argue against the proven weapon. Here is how.

You are standing there alone, and you have to push the limit to achieve the gold medal. Goliath is standing on the other side with sharp arrows on his back and a pointed carbon steel spear in his hands aimed towards you. The poison-coated words are spitting out from his ugly mouth in front of your peers and colleagues. This happened to me when I was working at several industry giants: MCA Disco Vision (a subsidiary of Universal Studios), IBM, Pioneer Corporation, a Japanese company, Mattel Electronics, Hughes Aircraft, GM, Boeing, and the Navy.

Believe it or not, bullies are not only in schools, but they also reside in workplaces. The reality is, to win the war you always have to face the Goliath, but the beauty is that there is always a hidden angel behind your back who will protect you and guide you. Out of nowhere, an angel appears and whispers in your ear, "I am here; do not be afraid. Be strong; lift up your staff, go get the sharpest stones you can find, and carry a sling in your backpack. The game is about to be over."

Here is the secret of how it works. Let us get ready with the ammunition.

Collect five stones:

1. Trust.

> "The LORD is my rock, and my fortress, and my deliverer; my God, my strength, in whom I will *trust*; my buckler, and the horn of my salvation, and my high tower" (Psalm 18:2, KJV) (emphasis added by the author).

> "But I am like a green olive tree in the house of God: I *trust* in the mercy of God for ever and ever" (2 Samuel 52:8, KJV) (emphasis added by the author).

"The God of my rock; in him will I *trust*: he is my shield, and the horn of my salvation, my high tower, and my refuge, my savior; thou savest me from violence" (2 Samuel 22:3, KJV) (emphasis added by the author).

"In God have I put my *trust*: I will not be afraid what man can do unto me" (Psalm 56:11, KJV) (emphasis added by the author).

2. Faith.

"And the Lord said, If ye had faith as a grain of mustard seed, ye might say unto this sycamine tree, Be thou plucked up by the root, and be thou planted in the sea; and it should obey you" (Luke 17:6, KJV).

"By faith they passed through the Red sea as by dry land: which the Egyptians assaying to do were drowned" (Hebrews 11:29, KJV).

"By faith the walls of Jericho fell down, after they were compassed about seven days" (Hebrews 11:30, KJV).

3. Meekness.

Do not burn your bridge, but rather build a new bridge every day, even in very hostile circumstances. Control your tongue and remember to be meek; it will pay off in the long term. When I was working at Boeing Satellite, I was transferred from one program to the other because the program came to an end and the government funding was cut off. On the first day of the new program, during a technical problem-solving meeting, one old-timer crazy engineer called me a loser. I swallowed the bitter pill because that morning, the bread for my breakfast was kneaded with the living words,

"But the meek shall inherit the earth; and shall delight themselves in the abundance of peace" (Psalm 37:11, KJV).

"The LORD lifteth up the meek: he casteth the wicked down to the ground" (Psalm 147:6, KJV).

Guess what? Within two weeks, the Navy offered me another job as a chief engineer for the Navy Trident Submarine Navigation Program Office, Anaheim, California, at a Boeing facility. My work was acclaimed in a personal letter by the vice admiral in charge of all nuclear submarines on both coasts. Even after I retired, I still cherish his letter with honor and privilege that makes me humbled. Following the living God's words paid off.

4. Skill.

Always be curious to learn new skills and techniques to sharpen your demand. It is lifelong learning if you want to be a winner. I learned every process of how to make a DVD disk when I was a research engineer at MCA Disco Vision, a subsidiary of Universal Studios in Torrance, California. So, when the time came to put the new product from the lab to the market, the director appointed me as production manager of the pilot production line to manufacture the CDs/DVDs first produced in the world.

When I was working for Mattel Electronics, Hawthorn, California, I studied every scientific publication available to learn about piezo crystals. It paid off. Mattel Electronics sent me to Japan to work with Toshiba to get a license to produce electronic musical instruments in Japan. This knowledge was also useful at Hughes Aircraft Company, El Segundo, California, on the Trident Missile program to determine the failure cause of the ceramic chip capacitors. This skill helped me to determine why the anti-personnel and anti-tank mines failed during the qualification testing at Aerojet, Downey, California. I learned the magnetics from my Jewish guru, Sam Swaz. I was able to design and detect failure modes in transformers used in high-reliability satellites at Boeing Satellite Company. This skill was a great tool when I solved the Navy's nuclear submarine navigation pulse transformer failure at Boeing, Anaheim, California. These were the few skills I learned worth mentioning here to make a point.

5. Courage.

The mantra for success is "Do not be afraid." If you think you are right, you have done everything you can possibly do, and you have made the right decision in good faith, do not be afraid; go for it, no matter how challenging it might be. Look what the living God tells you.

"In God have I put my trust: I will not be afraid what man can do unto me" (Psalm 56:11, KJV).

"And I say unto you my friends, Be not afraid of them that kill the body, and after that have no more that they can do" (Luke 12:4, KJV).

Takeaway: Depression is a disease that may not be cured with a pill made in a test tube in the lab but can be cured with unconditional love and outpouring compassion made in the blood of your heart. Churches all over America, give an altar call. If you know anyone suffering from depression, come out of the four walls of the church and reach out and offer a real pill that will cure the disease. Let us take the real spiritual pill on every military base. Uncle Sam is calling you.

Isaiah 40:31 (NASB), "Yet those who wait for the LORD Will gain new strength; They will mount up with wings like eagles, They will run and not get tired, They will walk and not become weary."

Matthew 11:28 (NKJV), "Come to Me, all you who labor and are heavy laden, and I will give you rest."

---

17. MESSAGE FOR THE IMMIGRANTS

If one of the many great American presidents, John F. Kennedy, were alive today, he would say to immigrants, "Don't ask what your adopted country can do for you, but ask what you can do for your adopted country."

America has attracted the best, brightest, cream-of-the-crop talents and, at the same time, accepted millions of poor and lost souls of the world in search of a better life. This nation has sent more missionaries to every corner of the globe than any other country in the world.

In 1970, Congress opened the door for immigrant visas for superior performance in science, engineering, and technology. Thousands and thousands of immigrants flooded the gates of the Big Apple and the City of Angel. They were bright, filled with entrepreneurial spirit, and go-getters. They turned the free green card into a gold card. How generous this nation is that it also allowed "chain immigration" for the immigrants' children, parents, brothers, sisters, and other relatives.

African Americans arrived and turned the American farms into the food basket of the world. The Asian and South Asian immigrants arrived and turned sand into the golden chips in Silicon Valley. African Americans are woven into the tapestry of the American fabric. Non-Judeo-Christian (NJC) immigrants are still soul-searching. The umbilical cord is so tightly attached to their motherland that it's hard to cut off. Will the third or fourth generation cut the cord and be a part of the American culture with curry or dim sum flavor? Yes, better be yes. This nation has done so much for you, and it is time to repay your debt. Are you proud to be an American, the country that gave freedom, equal opportunity, wealth, and justice for all not possible for the millions you left behind in your own country? If not, follow ET; home, home.

Takeaway: Ask not what your country can do for you—ask what you can do for your country (President John F. Kennedy in his inauguration address).

Isaiah 26:15 (NLT), "O LORD, you have made our nation great; yes, you have made us great. You have extended our borders, and we give you the glory."

Genesis 28:3 (NET), "May the Sovereign God bless you! May he make you fruitful and give you a multitude of descendants! Then you will become a large nation."

What applies to Israel also applies to the USA.

18. IN 1968, MAO ZEDONG GAVE RED CARD TO CHINESE STUDENTS, BUT UNCLE SAM GAVE GREEN CARD TO ALL

Don't ask what your adopted country can do for you; ask what you can do for your willingly adopted country that offered you a new life. If life was so good in your birth country, you might not have adventured in Uncle Sam's territory, and that includes me, also. In a way, we have left our identity behind voluntarily and now have to earn a new identity. For non-European immigrants, it is tougher than the Europeans because of the color of their skin, religion, customs, culture, food, habits, and beliefs in our home country superstitions that don't work here. You have to leave all this heavy baggage on arrival when you land at the airport of the land of honey and milk, a new Canaan. Tough, isn't it? But that is the price you have to pay in exchange for the green pasture called the green card you always dreamed of. Relax, in spite of all our blemishes and shortcomings, this one nation under the living God is so great that she offers hope, a second chance, and opportunity to everyone. This nation puts Jesus Christ's spiritual teaching into practice. The Bible says, "Come unto me, all ye that labor and are heavy laden, and I will give you rest" (Matthew 11:28, ASV).

Don't believe it? Look, so many immigrants, including me, coming from ordinary middle-class families, have crossed the boundary that they could not do in their own homeland and have achieved the dreams of seven colors. That's the magical secret this country has; no other nation can take credit like this. Will this motivate you one day? If you are in America, dream, and dream big because here everything maps out on a grand scale.

Takeaway: This is the land of honey and milk, green pasture and still water. The green card holder's cup is overflowing.

Psalm 23:2 (NKJV), "He makes me to lie down in green pastures; He leads me beside the still waters."

Psalm 23:5–6 (NKJV), You prepare a table before me in the presence of my enemies; You anoint my head with oil; My cup runs over. Surely goodness and mercy shall follow me All the days of my life; And I will dwell in the house of the LORD Forever.

19. GREEN CARD PURCHASED WITH RED BLOOD

How much does it cost to buy a green card? A gallon of pure red blood. A true story.

A migrant called Ephu paid thousands of rupees for a voyage of death from Ahmedabad (India) to Mexico to San Diego. He paid the price of a green card in two gallons of his blood. You can hear in your ears, "It's a small, small world" from Disneyland, not far from the bloodshed site in Anaheim, California. A man in India had a dream to see the happiest place on the earth, only ten miles away from the location where he lost his life before he could visit Disneyland. He left his homeland to leave behind the evil agony of poverty, struggle to get a job, racial discrimination, pain of poverty, casteism, and religious intolerance. This man came to America in hopes of a new life with not a single penny in his pocket.

I thought about my days when I came to America with only a hundred dollars that disappeared in one month. So, a friend and I helped this man run a small, convenient market in a prime area near Disneyland that would allow him to get a green card eventually and stay in this country legally. One day in 1974 turned into the bloodiest day of his life; that has become a norm lately in America, called the deadly madness of gun violence. The man was shot dead behind the cash register by a teenager just for a few bucks. I saw blood all over the floor. He left behind his wife and four-year-old son back in India. The dream died before the flower blossomed.

I could not sleep that night. It was the first time in my life I had seen so much red blood all over the floor. Is it worth it to risk your life in exchange for a green card to stay in America? Go to Texas, the Rio Grande River, or the California-Mexico border. You will see that is the price the migrants of third-world countries pay almost every day at the US-Mexico border.

Takeaway: People bet their lives in search of freedom. How much should we cherish it?

"Freedom is never more than one generation away from extinction" (President Ronald Reagan).

20. A FREE JAR OF NINE VITAMINS FOR A HEALTHY LIFESTYLE GUARANTEED

Life is beautiful. Find it, value it, and live it with nine vitamins.
Life is a panoramic three-dimensional oil painting that reflects different colors depending on what angle you look at it. There are hundreds of names for the creator who created this marvelous, amazing, incredible, miraculous, wonderful piece of an art gallery called life, which He created with His hands out of the mud. Life is an ocean of blessings; don't pollute it. It's a marvelous machine designed by the supreme engineer, the designer and creator of all, the living, loving Lord (LLL, not CLL) of Abraham, Isaac, Jacob, and the Americans. Life is a gift basket; keep replenishing with nine fruits, for you and to share with others around you.

1. Love.

This will shake you up, but it is true. Take it with a grain of salt.

But love ye your enemies, and do good, and lend, hoping for nothing again; and your reward shall be great, and ye shall be the children of the Highest: for he is kind unto the unthankful and to the evil.

Luke 6:35 (KJV)

Love your enemies? Tough to swallow a bitter pill, but you have to swallow bitter pills to kill the headache, don't you?

Revenge is not a tool to win the victory, but love is. Stupidity is an AC current; love is a converter that will convert AC into the DC of *joy*.

2. Joy.

   Be joyful because joy is a sparkling gingerly soda drink that sprinkles peace around you. Joy and peace are twin sisters, and they make a smoothy for you.

   "For the kingdom of God is not meat and drink; but righteousness, and peace, and joy in the Holy Ghost" (Romans 14:17, KJV). Joy brings peace.

3. Peace.

   Let be peace with you all the time because what the great saint Peter offered to the Corinthians also blesses you.

   Listen to Peter, "Finally, brethren, farewell. Be perfect, be of good comfort, be of one mind, live in peace; and the God of love and peace shall be with you" (2 Corinthians 13:11, KJV).

   If you have peace in your heart, *patience* will flow in your blood and keep you calm, cool, and kind.

4. Patience.

   Patience generates kindness. Do you know how many times our God is patient with us? Seventy-seven times seven. Believe it or not, He is a God of patience.

   Listen to this, "Now the God of patience and consolation grant you to be likeminded one toward another according to Christ Jesus" (Romans 15:5, KJV). Patience kindles kindness.

5. Kindness.

   If the blood flows in your heart, kindness should flow in your blood. Why? Because the Word of God says so,

   "And rend your heart, and not your garments, and turn unto the LORD your God: for he is gracious and merciful, slow to anger, and of great kindness, and repenteth him of the evil" (Joel 2:13, KJV). Anger ignites the fire of ruthlessness, but kindness brings the gift basket of goodness.

6. Goodness.

This fruit has its own super sweetener; you don't have to add anything else. It's a smoothy for your health, physical and mental. That's why we say "my goodness" when we don't have a clue what's going on. Be good, and something good will happen to you. Try it. Begin your day with goodness, and it will close with his faithfulness to you. The psalmist said, "To declare Your goodness in the morning And Your faithfulness by night" (Psalm 92:2, NASB).

Did you know that faithfulness is the shadow of goodness? Be good, and His faithfulness will follow you all your life. Don't believe it? Read this, "Certainly, goodness and faithfulness will follow me all the days of my life, and my dwelling will be in the house of the LORD forever" (Psalm 23:6, NASB).

7. Faithfulness.

This is the melody of a successful life. Sing it every morning before you head out to work. "How great is Thy faithfulness. Morning by morning, new mercies are seen. How great is Thy faithfulness, again and again."

I pray every morning, "Oh Lord, I am nothing, but let Thy mercy and faithfulness shape me. I am the clay, and You are the potter; break me and mold me so I can be a child of gentleness."

Faithfulness shapes you to be a person of gentleness. Let us see what His saint has said,

"But you, as a person dedicated to God, keep away from all that. Instead pursue righteousness, godliness, faithfulness, love, endurance, and gentleness" (1 Timothy 6:11, NET).

8. Gentleness.

"Let everyone see your gentleness. The Lord is near!" (Philippians 4:5, NET).

Be gentle to the little ones who need your gentle touch to grow with a smile on their face. Gentleness teaches how to control anger. The control of anger is a synonym for self-control.

9. Self-Control.

Self-control is not a fear but a power. Read this, "For God did not give us a Spirit of fear but of power and love and self-control" (2 Timothy 1:7, NET).

When we lose self-control, the love evaporates. When love evaporates, we become powerless. Reverse the cycle. Love everyone around you; that will teach you self-control, which will make you powerful to fight the devil again.

Takeaway: Read Galatians 5:22–23.

By now, you figured it out: that amazing jar is the Holy Bible, and the nine vitamins are the fruits of the spirit, the words of the living God, that will make your life beautiful and a worthwhile adventure, guaranteed.

Can India Become a World Power?

No, not in the near future. Why India can't become a world power? It is cultural pollution that hinders India from becoming a world power. Inductance flux around India's world power ambition is surrounded by the caste system, racism, religious intolerance, cultural biases, and superstitious practices; there is no mechanical mind, no dirty hand nature of the scientific community, no hands-on education, no tools in the crib, no garage as every house has in America where every American is a mechanic and new inventions are born in these home laboratories. Yes, India's economy will thrive, but India is way, way behind the true democracy, living standards, wealth, health standards, education, technology, military power, and people's aspirations of America.

America is blessed beyond any doubt because she is a Judeo-Christian nation; it is a second promised land.

Takeaway: What is true for Israel is also true for America because both nations are under His umbrella, the Bible, the living words of the living God.

Joshua 1:3 (NLT), "I promise you what I promised Moses: 'Wherever you set foot, you will be on land I have given you.'"

Jeremiah 11:5 (NET),

"Then I will keep the promise I swore on oath to your ancestors to give them a land flowing with milk and honey. That is the very land that you still live in today." And I responded, "Amen! Let it be so, Lord!"

(1/10/2023)

21. IS THERE A GOD? YES, ABSOLUTELY YES

Let me introduce Him to you if you don't believe so.

The universe is controlled by two disciplines: science and beyond the science. Science is understood by physics, chemistry, math, and biology. Few of us exceed in these fields by God's given talents and skills to make the lives of others more beautiful and more enjoyable through new discoveries in science and technology.

Science and technology are the human arena. Human beings constantly, vigorously, and curiously explore this arena. This human nature has led humans from the Stone Age to the moon landing, only in America so far.

Knowledge and wisdom are two different gifts. Wise men and women have both gifts, and they use this discipline for the common good. And they will be blessed, and their talents will be multiplied. The monster might have knowledge but no wisdom and will misuse this discipline, but, in the end, he will be eliminated like Adam and Eve from the garden.

The other discipline, "beyond the science," is given free to all. It does not require scientific knowledge or technological breakthroughs. All it requires is simple trust, faith, and obedience to your inner call to answer the Holy Spirit, yes. It is called pure wisdom; it is manna, and it's free. Once received, believe it or not, it will be replenished every forty years. If you accept it, the knowledge will follow. Things that science and technology can't achieve or offer or understand, called joy and happiness, can be received miraculously. When it happens, it's called a miracle. Believe in an angel, and it will happen.

There are many examples of this spiritual phenomenon throughout history. Moses led the Israelites for forty years through the desert to Canaan. There was no freeway, and Mr. Ford was not born yet.

William Booth, an ordinary British man, reached out to the poor and neglected on the streets of London and founded the Salvation Army, which still reaches out and touches millions and millions worldwide and gives them hope and new life; I am one of them. How did that happen? Because William Booth had "beyond the science" knowledge and wisdom to recognize the call from his creator, the living God.

Mother Teresa, an ordinary nun born to an Albanian family, received a "beyond the science" gift. She walked on the dirtiest streets of Calcutta and restored a new life for millions of homeless, neglected by their own countrymen, blind, aged, and suffering from AIDS/HIV. She learned English and the local Indian language, Bengali, to talk directly to the locals. Nobody has carried out such a mission in India, even today. She didn't go to Harvard or Stanford or MIT, but she had God-gifted knowledge and wisdom; she had a BS degree called "beyond the science."

Dr. Martin Luther King JR. is a larger-than-life example of what determination can do in America. Look what this great man did. From a shackle to the cross to "I have a dream" to finally the president of America, Mr. Obama, "I have a dream" came true in a relatively short time in American history. How did that happen? The spirit of "beyond the science" was gifted to Dr. King Jr. while he was pastoring at Dexter Avenue Baptist Church, Montgomery, Alabama. A man of God, a reflection of Christ on Earth. Before he said goodbye last time from the balcony of room 306 of the Lorraine Motel in Memphis, he wanted to sing,

> I am tired, I'm weak, I am worn
> Through the storm, through the night
> Lead me on to the light
> Take my hand, precious Lord
> Lead me home.

If he were alive today, he would sing,

> When my work is all done, and my race here is run,
> Let me see by the light Thou hast shown
> That fair city so bright where the land is the light
> Take my hand, precious Lord, lead me on
> Precious Lord, take my hand.

There is strong evidence of what a man can do when he believes, trusts, and obeys that there is power "beyond the science" granted free by the living God, Jehovah Jireh (Genesis 22:14).

The greatest president the world has ever seen didn't attend any university, and yet, my hero recorded the most appealing, vibrant speech to Americans ever addressed,

"This nation, under God, shall have a new birth of freedom—and that government of the people, by the people, for the people, shall not perish from the earth" (Abraham Lincoln, November 19, 1863).

How did he get such amazing knowledge and wisdom? From the Spirit of the Lord, Almighty God. As he has referenced in his several speeches, it is a "beyond the science" free gift granted to him.

What is the common thread among all these high achievers? No degree in science and technology can grant you or explain to you the superpower of knowledge and wisdom, but you can receive it free by simply trusting and obeying your creator, the living God, Jehovah Jireh (Proverbs 3:5).

"If they obey and serve him, they shall spend their days in prosperity, and their years in pleasures. But if they obey not, they shall perish by the sword, and they shall die without knowledge" (Job 36:11–12, KJV).

Takeaway: Not today, but 2000 years ago, Paul told Timothy, his pastor, "Don't believe those who say they are a master of science but don't see God." Read this,

O Timothy, keep that which is committed to thy trust, avoiding profane and vain babblings, and oppositions of science falsely so called: Which some professing have erred concerning the faith. Grace be with thee. Amen.

1 Timothy 6:20–21 (KJV)

In other words,

Timothy, protect what has been entrusted to you, avoiding worldly, empty chatter and the opposing arguments of what is falsely called "knowledge" [science]—which some have professed and thereby have gone astray from the faith. Grace be with you.

1 Timothy 6:20–21 (NASB)

My God is so big that you can't find Him by your small piece of science. But, "I love those who love me; And those who diligently seek me will find me" (Proverbs 8:17, NASB).

22. ONLY A PERSON OF JUDEO-CHRISTIAN FAITH SHALL GOVERN FIVE EYES NATIONS

Five Eyes nations are ordained nations by the living God and flourished into the lands of honey and milk. They are Jews and Gentiles, sons and daughters of Jacob; everybody else is the invited guest to the party, with a hope that they will melt into the Judeo-Christian faith. It is a historical fact that Five Eyes are Judeo-Christian nations, and so the governors of these nations at all governing levels have to be of Judeo-Christian faith because our cornerstone Bible warns us,

"They decided to abandon the Temple of the LORD, the God of their ancestors, and they worshiped Asherah poles and idols instead! Because of this sin, divine anger fell on Judah and Jerusalem" (2 Chronicles 24:18, NLT).

Five Eyes, Jacob's descendants, do not abandon the temple of the Lord, the God of our ancestors, who built your nations. If you do, the divine anger will fall on your nation and its capital. It is a historical fact that America is a Judeo-Christian nation, different than any other nation in the world. However, we love and be compassionate to all other nationalities because the basic teachings of the Bible are love, mercy, forgiveness, kindness, joy, and peace.

Takeaway: No world power ever will touch any nation of the Five Eyes because the words of the living God say so; you are the apples of His eye, Israel included, as long as the Bible remains your centerpiece on the tabernacle of your capitals.

Zechariah 2:8 (KJV), "For thus saith the LORD of hosts; After the glory hath he sent me unto the nations which spoiled you: for he that toucheth you toucheth the apple of his eye."

23. HOW TO WIN HUMBLY AND LOSE GRACIOUSLY?

Sometimes you win, and sometimes you lose. Life is a maze; you can't navigate the way out with your physical eyes. But I would take a calculated risk rather than sit at the bay and stare at the waves. Either I will win or lose if I take a risk to follow my dream. If I win, I will praise Him and pray to make me humbler. If I lose, I will accept my shortcomings graciously, close my eyes, and ask the Almighty to grant me the knowledge that I don't have and the wisdom to make the right choice to plan the next strategy. This way, the hard rock sorrow of losing the game will turn into a snowball and will melt away. Listen, my friend, if He can die on the cross for me on Friday and rise from the grave on Sunday, He can move the mountain for you and me every day. The question is, do you know Him? Make Him your friend; take a risk and see what happens.

He has a hundred names, His 800 number is open twenty-four seven, and His prayer channel is free. If anybody laughs at your failure, pick up the 800 number prayer phone and say Abba, engineer of the universe, show me the next move; here I am.

You will be amazed at what happens next. That's what happened to me on that dark night when I decided to end my life when all my relatives and friends left me alone and laughed at me when I took a risk and failed. Miraculously, what I thought to be the end of my life turned out to be a victorious celebration of winning when He lifted me. I recalculated my strategy and adventured on a second risk. I would rather take a risk and die instead of simply sitting on the rock and crying, living on someone's mercy, and being sad my whole life. Remember, only a few are born with a silver spoon in their mouth; all others have to take a risk to achieve a golden spoon. So, get up from the rock and jump into the ocean, fight with the waves, and your dream will come true. If you want to win a prize, you have to take a risk and be courageous even in a time when all look so gloomy and people around you put you down because the reward is hidden behind the risk for you, not behind the people around you. Listen to what the words of the living God say.

Takeaway: "But you, be strong and do not lose courage, for there is a reward for your work" (2 Chronicles 15:7, NASB).

(1/13/2023)

24. INVEST YOUR TALENTS, DON'T BURY THEM

Did you know someone opened a free savings account when you were born and deposited five talents in it? If you don't believe it, read Matthew 25:14–29 (NKJV). Everyone is given five denarii. Why? Do not waste your God-given talent, skill, knowledge, and wisdom. Your creator has blessed you to be wise, healthy, and wealthy so that you can be a blessing to others.

The eleventh commandment was not chiseled on two stones but was spiked in your DNA because you are a child of God. Get out of the Sinai desert. He has planned a promised land covered with green pasture where your cup will overflow with milk and honey you have never tasted before in your life. Can you read your DNA? The eleventh commandment is: Invest, invest, and invest, and don't forget 10 percent is His as He directs to you. This is true spiritually, and ironically, it also applies to responsible financial living.

Takeaway: Save every penny and invest every penny. It's not how many pennies you put in the jar; it teaches you how many jars you will need to buy a home and a car and support your kids for college.

The secret of multiplying your God-given talents is: do not bury your denarius. The question is, are you investing your talents or burying them?

The servant who received the five bags of silver began to invest the money and earned five more. The servant to whom he had entrusted the five bags of silver came forward with five more and said, 'Master, you gave me five bags of silver to invest, and I have earned five more.'

Matthew 25:16–20 (NLT)

---

25. TEN MANTRAS TO BE SUCCESSFUL

In the old days, when a student graduated from a school of high learning, the guru would whisper a mantra in his ears. The secret mantra was meant to guide him to a prosperous future. Here, I am giving away mantras to be successful, freely and openly. Open your ears.

1. Get up before the sun gets up. "But seek ye first his kingdom and his righteousness and all things shall be added unto you (Matthew 6:33, ASV).
2. Don't hit the sack before the sun says goodbye for the day
3. If there is a lion, there is a Daniel; if there is a Goliath, there is a David. Dare to be Daniel and David.
4. There is no such thing as failure; it is just that you forgot to reset the success button.
5. If you win, celebrate your victory with a grand party. If you fail, hold a grand opening ceremony to celebrate a new venture under new management. Celebrate either way.
6. There is no *cul-de-sac* street in adventure; you just forgot to take off the blindfold mask of your eyes. Get a new spectacle and keep going.
7. Add today's plan to your breakfast cereal, review it at bedtime, and revise it as the day goes by. If you don't have a plan, you don't know where you are going.
8. Aim high, higher than Everest; deep dive, deeper than the ocean; dream colorful, more spectacular than the seven-color spectrum; go where nobody has gone yet, beyond the limit of the sky.
9. Remember, the carpenter's Son is always with you. Do not be afraid. You can carve the diamond hidden in the rock and sharpen your chisel and hammer with knowledge and wisdom.

"Teaching them to observe all things that I have commanded you; and lo, I am with you always, even to the end of the age" (Matthew 28:20, NKJV). Amen.

10. Plant a seed in fertile soil; don't hide it in a jar.

All you need is one fertile apple seed that will grow and bring a bountiful truckload harvest of Gala apples. That's what Dr. Cook, a Salvation Army missionary from New Zealand, did in a small town called Anand, Gujarat state, India. (By the way, Gala apples originally come from New Zealand.) He turned a missionary hospital into a medical miracle for thousands of poor and needy seeking medical help in hundreds of surrounding villages. After a hundred years, this hospital is still serving the same mission and thriving.

Two-thousand-year-old seeds were found inside a jar by an archaeologist in Masada, in southern Israel. The jar had been sitting in someone's cabinet for years, doing nothing. One scientist got an idea and planted the seeds in fertile soil. Today, an ancient date tree has grown out of these seeds in the desert beyond anybody's expectation.

"Plant your seed in the morning and keep busy all afternoon, for you don't know if profit will come from one activity or another—or maybe both" (Ecclesiastes 11:6, NLT).

When the monster storm arrives, shakes your wooden door, and knocks on your chest, hang on to the cross. Be calm, close your eyes, and pray. You will see a ladder descending from the heaven. It's the ladder of hope, an encouraging spirit to stand up, rise, and fight. It's a matter of time; wait. The storm has a short life because it is made of air bubbles; it will burst soon, but you will survive because you are leaning on the rock. Rejoice and smile; plan your next move. If you are God's child, your last name is success.

What is success? Wealth, fame, a mansion, gold, diamond, a position? The answer is "yes" if it is His plan, if you share it with others, if you use it wisely, and if you don't hide it but multiply it so others can benefit from it.

For most of us, success is to set the highest possible goal, block all the destructions, aim high, be positive, and shoot the arrow every day at the center of the five concentric circles.

Takeaway: My living God, if He can make the blind to see, lame to walk, deaf to hear, dead to be alive, and He also rose from the grave after three days, how can He not protect you from the storm today? It may seem like the storm will never end, but He is always on time—in His time.

Cross is a crossing point where the meanest, cruel, torturous, and brutal nature of humankind is nailed down with the greatest example of love, mercy, sacrifice, compassion, kindness, generosity, and forgiveness.

26. BELIEVE IT OR NOT, HITLER IS STILL ALIVE, AND HIS NAME IS CASTELER

A study by the Henry Jackson Society in the UK found that Hindu pupils are being "held responsible" for the actions of India and facing xenophobic slurs from white pupils.

Researchers also found evidence of xenophobia, including from Christian pupils, with one child saying, "Jesus will send your gods to hell."

Fostering Discrimination

The report found that religious education was "fostering discrimination" against Hindus with inappropriate references to the Indian caste system and misconceptions over the worship of deities, which students felt made "a mockery of them."

He said that as well as discrimination taking the form of anti-Hindu slurs, there was "a problematic approach to teaching Hinduism, which may be feeding into prejudice, and whether incidents of bullying and discrimination are being adequately dealt with by each individual school" insulting staff's work and using profanity.

Casteism is a social concentration camp in India to demoralize innocent human beings even before they are born to maintain an artificial supremacist ideology that has existed only in India. What is surprising is that highly educated Indian immigrants living for years in Five Eyes Judeo-Christian nations still bring this mental disorder into the civilized world without any shame!

Hitler misused the cross; he bent the four ends of the cross and ended up in the genocide of two-thirds of the twelve tribes of Jacob in Shoah, and the world remained silent for a long time. The cross is the symbol of love, joy, peace, forgiveness, new life, and dedication to humanity, not of the destruction of human beings. All are equal under the cross and invited to the party of celebration of the resurrection of Christ, my Savior and Lord, no matter what your skin color, nationality, social or political status, caste, or race is. The message of Judeo-Christian Five Eyes nations is, **"Don't twist the cross; the teaching of the cross is very straightforward."**

"Come unto me, all ye that labor and are heavy laden, and I will give you rest" (Matthew 11:28, ASV).

The caste system and religious intolerance in India are a social COVID-2000 because it has roots more than 2000 years old. Let us hope and pray and project the love, forgiveness, mercy, and grace that flows from the cross so that the new generation of India will eradicate this disease soon. There is a vaccine for COVID-2000, which was offered free to the world by Jesus Christ, my Lord and Savior, 2000 years ago,

> For we dare not class ourselves or compare ourselves with those who commend themselves. But they, measuring themselves by themselves, and comparing themselves among themselves, are not wise.
>
> 2 Corinthians 10:12 (NKJV)

Then, who can take credit as an elite class? The answer is in the Bible.

> Woe to those who live in ease in Zion, to those who feel secure on Mount Samaria. They think of themselves as the *elite class* of the best nation. The family of Israel looks to them for leadership.
>
> Amos 6:1 (NET)
> (emphasis added by the author)

Who is a Zion nation in the modern world? It is a family of Five Eyes nations. Why? How? Look, all Asian, South Asian, and Middle East nationals want to immigrate to any of these Five Eyes nations. Go to India and randomly ask anybody, "If an immigrant visa is granted to you today, will you consider moving to any of the Five Eyes nations this week?" Ninety-nine point nine percent of them will say yes. Why? The Five Eyes are the most blessed nations in the world. America will remain the dreamland where the Wisconsin cheese is spread on every street, hot dogs and hamburgers are grilled on every plaza, the aroma of pepperoni pizza is in the air from every hut, and the Americans don't know it, but the immigrants are craving for it every day.

(2/2/2023)

In a small, little, dusty town called Napad, Gujarat state, India, my parents, Salvation Army officers, put me there with my grandparents, also retired Salvation Army officers, house. I attended primary and secondary high school in this town and had lots of Hindu and Muslim friends. India is a Hindu majority-dominated country; roughly 85 percent of the population is Hindu. Most Hindus and Muslims are loving, caring, good Samaritan people as individual human beings, like those in any other country in the world. But there are about ten percent jealous, extremist, extreme far right, racists, religiously intolerant, polluted with the Stone Age caste system, fanatics, and bad apples that ruin the community. They spark fear and lies, spread unfounded rumors mixed with a poisonous religious tone, and ignite the fire of communal riots. The beautiful, peaceful community now takes over the personality of a terrorizing storm overnight. The friend is no longer a friend. One who was a decent human being yesterday, all of a sudden, turns into a monster. The story of Jekyll and Hyde comes alive.

Communal tension breaks out between Hindus, Muslims, and, lately, Christians in the northeast corner. Every street corner is burned by the mob. Unexplainable, but it is true; I have seen it with my own eyes. Murder, rape, destruction of public properties, and homes turned into a pile of ashes overnight. Unbelievable but true.

Takeaway: Hate is not a cure to end the fire of dispute, but it is a fuel to ignite more. Offer love and watch a miracle happen; the fire turns into the fountain of friendship, and you and your enemy will cherish each other for generations to come.

Takeaway: "You shall not hate your fellow countryman in your heart; you may certainly rebuke your neighbor, but you are not to incur sin because of him" (Leviticus 19:17, NASB).

"But I say unto you, Love your enemies, bless them that curse you, do good to them that hate you, and pray for them which despitefully use you, and persecute you" (Matthew 5:44, KJV).

27. VICTIMS OF CASTEISM IN INDIA

One day, in my hometown, Napad, I was standing at the small snack house, the Indian version of McDonald's. This was my favorite place to munch vadas, a spicy potato ball deep fried in oil, a vegetarian version of hamburger.

A dirty, filthy gangster named Kalio always wanted to hurt me. He saw me and started spitting out dirty, nasty, derogatory language because I was Christian and an excellent performer in the school. He pushed me and threw me on the ground. He shouted again and again, "You, Christian, are not first class; you are L class. I hate you. Go to hell."

I went home; blood was all over my face, hands, and legs, and I had tears in my eyes.

Grandpa asked, "What happened?"

I told him what had happened.

He pulled out his old, rusted dagger, turned on the giant dagger sharpening machine in the attic, and began to whet its blades in even, rhythmic strokes. I could see the fiery sparks flying all over the attic. He was originally from the Hindu Rajput class, came to know Christ through a missionary, and hid a dagger in the attic, a customary ritual from his old culture.

He came down from the attic and opened and closed the Bible three times. I didn't know why three times, but now I am thinking what might have happened like this:

First time,

"But Jesus said to Peter, 'Put your sword back into its sheath. Shall I not drink from the cup of suffering the Father has given me?'" (John 18:11 NLT).

He closed the Bible and opened it again. Second time,

"Then Jesus said to him, 'Put your sword back in its place! For all who take hold of the sword will die by the sword'" (Matthew 26:52, NET).

He closed the Bible and opened it a third time,

"O sword of the Lord, how long will you have no rest? put yourself back into your cover; be at peace, be quiet" (Jeremiah 47:6, BBE).

He quieted down and went back to the attic. I heard him crying in his prayer.

The next day, all my friends, Raman Patel, Jagdish Patel, Ismael Vohra, Vipin Shah, Raman Darji, Babu Thakor, and many others who were Hindus, Muslims, and Jains, cornered Kalia and beat him up in the dark alley and told him, "If you ever harass Bram again, we will cut off your tongue." I never saw Kalio again.

Yosef Modan, a Muslim friend of mine, was a physics teacher at VP Science College, Vidyanagar, Gujarat, India. He was a colleague and a super close friend. That day, a Hindu vs. Muslim riot broke out. The rumor was a Hindu monk was beaten up by a Muslim person because a Hindu cow vigilante beat another Muslim for slaughtering a cow or might have used some words against Hinduism. That week, he did not return to college because he was afraid that the Hindu students he was tutoring free would kill him on the way to college for no reason.

In 1967, an American Peace Corps volunteer, a professor from the University of Arkansas, arrived in Vidyanagar, Gujarat state, India. This was the first experiment to introduce the American physics, math, and chemistry textbooks in Indian universities. Before this time, only British textbooks were used, and mainly general theoretical physics was taught. American textbooks are geared toward not only theory but on real-world application.

For example, I taught first-year physics 101 students at VP Science College, Gujarat state, India, in 1968 about how much power from a rocket would you need to place a satellite in a geo-synchronized orbit. In those years, Indians didn't know what a satellite looked like, but it was all laid down in the American textbooks. Thanks, America. I am a living witness.

The S. P. University, Vidyanagar, Gujarat state, was the first institute to have the initiative of American physics and chemistry textbooks teach-

Bramvel Christian

ing at the university level in India. The American professor conducted a physics seminar for the physics faculty on how to teach the American physics textbook introduced in India first time in this university. I was appointed as his teaching assistant to prepare and demonstrate the supporting experiments for each lesson. I was very successful and became very popular among the staff and students.

One of the participants was a Patel professor with a PhD degree from another local college in Anand, Gujarat state, India.

One day, at quiz time, the American professor asked, "What is the name of the latest element on the periodic table?"

I was the only one who answered correctly—rutherfordium. I remembered it because in 1967, this element was discovered, and that year, in my town, Anand, Gujarat state, India, an Irish missionary doctor was very popular, and his name was Rutherford.

After the break, I was going down the stairs with all the other seminar participants, and this jealous Hindu professor just behind me shouted, "The name of the latest element is low casteism." He spitted out the dirt of racial slurs from his agley mouth for me because I was Christian. And he bent backward and laughed at me, and all others joined him to make a mockery of me. All were friends and praising me all these days, and now, what happened all of a sudden? I was shocked and insulted. My morale broke down to teach physics anymore. I couldn't say a word. The American professor wouldn't understand this anyway, so there was no point in telling him.

The truth is, a PhD degree doesn't make a man wiser; the rotten brain can't be revitalized by textbooks only but by the knowledge and wisdom that will be gifted to the meek and gentle followers of the living God by His grace, unconditional love, and unsurpassed mercy. This happens in India every day; those self-proclaimed upper-class jealous Hindus take advantage of the socio-economic victims, but life goes on. The two-thousand-year-old caste system cobra is still alive in some of the ignorant, stupid hearts and spits out racial poison to destroy the aspiration of emerging brilliant stars out of darkness before they can rise and shine.

"The tongue of the wise useth knowledge aright: but the mouth of fools poureth out foolishness" (Proverbs 15:2, KJV).

"The lips of the wise disperse knowledge: but the heart of the foolish doeth not so" (Proverbs 15:7, KJV).

Why do our closest friends, when we need them most on our side, turn around 180 degrees on our enemy's side? The answer is simple: that is the difference between Christ and human beings. Look at what Christ's closest disciple, Peter, sitting on His right hand at the dinner table in the upper room for the Last Supper, did to Him when they wanted to crucify Him.

"Again, Peter denied it, this time with an oath. 'I don't even know the man,' he said" (Matthew 26:72, NLT).

Are you surprised?

Learning and knowledge are two separate pathways, a thousand miles apart. Learning teaches how to read the book, but knowledge teaches how to extract wisdom from the book. You may have a PhD degree, but if you didn't receive the knowledge and wisdom that comes from the Holy Spirit and not from the books, you are still the most stupid, ignorant person at the bottom of the list who can only read the books but does not gain the wisdom and knowledge that come from above. You don't need to be smart but meek and humble to be gifted with knowledge and wisdom from above. Read this,

> But the wisdom from above is first of all pure. It is also peace loving, gentle at all times, and willing to yield to others. It is full of mercy and good deeds. It shows no favoritism and is always sincere.
>
> James 3:17 (NLT)

(8/5/2023, Saturday)

Even though some Indian leaders, after visiting the Western world, have attempted to break the senseless caste tradition, it continues to be practiced in most villages and behind the door in towns and cities. These dogmas and the social rules framed by the so-called upper class to suit their convenience actually demean the whole country. Such a demonizing custom should never continue in a civilized society governed by the rule of law, but it does in India.

Takeaway: If you are a Christian and a devil puts you down, what will you do?

Matthew 5:16 (KJV), "Let your light so shine before men, that they may see your good works, and glorify your Father which is in heaven."

You are on the path of a rising star, but the devil will drop out when the bright day turns into a dark night; watch out.

If you are a Christian, you belong to the highest class among any class, race, tribe, or kinfolks because the words of the living God say, "So, God created man in His own image, in the image of God He created him; male and female He created them" (Genesis 1:27, NKJV).

(2/3/2023)

28. IN THE NAME OF RELIGION IN INDIA

The country that claims that "we are the nation of hospitality" in recent years has become a nation of hostility toward the freedom of religion, speech, and press. The cruelty, hate, and violence against Christians are spread in many areas, specifically in northeast corner states. Some states in India have passed controversial anti-conversion laws, which can be adversely used to persecute and harass Christians and other minorities, as the US Commission on International Religious Freedom has expressed concerns and called for the laws' revocation. In spite of landing a spacecraft on the moon, there are millions and millions of Indians living below the poverty level in India. Eighty percent of the population still live in small villages, and there is no running water in the homes, no electricity in all villages, no schools with cafeterias or no gymnasium, no lunch provided to the poor kids, no hospitals within twenty miles area, and no hygienic toilets in the school or home or in the public places. They still sit on the floor and eat with their hands, nobody teaches hygiene and good health practices, and the list goes on about what we take for granted in the Western world.

Instead of going to the moon, India needs to land on the hearts of the common people first to bring their living standards to the level of the Western world. That is a real index of economic progress to compare with the Western world. The free knowledge from American institutes and free inventions from American brains of high-tech industries given away to other nations should be utilized to make the life of the common people more enjoyable, more affordable, and healthier with a high-flying flag of freedom and justice for all on the heartland rather than on any other planet.

Why does India need to protect Hinduism? Light does need to be protected; if it is a light source, it will shine by itself forever without any human hand like a God-made sun, or, eventually, it will extinguish like a manmade candle. Religion is not a personal or national property that you are entitled to own and protect, but rather, it is a gift, the internal will of humankind, a humanitarian virtue, and, above all, a universal human right protected by international human rights agencies.

Change is inevitable for progress. Let progressive human beings be allowed to decide and accept change if they determine that said change will uplift their lives and lead into the light, out of the darkness.

The paradigm of religion is a hope and dream center for humanity of six Ps that grant you the universal human rights to practice, preach, proclaim, pardon, be a partaker, and let peace be with you. That's what Christian missionaries from around the world did in India.

Missionaries from around the world left the comfort of their homeland and hugged India with open arms and no bias by opening up schools, colleges, hospitals, homes for women, alcoholics, and children, and shelters for those who were left behind by their own countrymen, neglected, called by lower names, victims of the lowest level of bigotry and callousness, forgotten in dark places. Why? Because we are told, "Greet ye one another with a kiss of charity. Peace be with you all that are in Christ Jesus. Amen" (1 Peter 5:14, KJV).

Why? Because it is our mandate from Jesus Christ to share the good news and make life more enjoyable for those who are left behind and marginalized by the so-called selfish upper class, socially, monetarily, racially, or politically. We bring good news to these victims of social injustice to comfort them and lift them to a higher ground. Why?

Takeaway: Why do we do what we do and will continue to do? Because the Bible says, "And he said unto them, Go ye into all the world, and preach the gospel to every creature" (Mark 16:15).

"Greet ye one another with a kiss of charity. Peace be with you all that are in Christ Jesus. Amen" (1 Peter 5:14, KJV).

Christians love everybody because that is what Christ has taught us: Love, joy, peace, patience, kindness, goodness, faithfulness, gentleness, and self-control are our core tenets.

My friends, read the Bible in Galatians 5:22–23.

---

29. WELCOME ALL, BUT REMEMBER THIS IS A JUDEO-CHRISTIAN NATION CALLED AMERICA

It is a historical fact that this land is a Judeo-Christian nation built on the solid rock of the ten commandments. The president, vice-president, governors, Lt. governors, mayors, school superintendents, and all other leaders of the governing bodies have to be of Judeo-Christian faith, no exception.

Why? Take a look at the first two commandments:

1. Though shalt have no other gods before me.
2. Though shall not make unto thee any graven image.

"And he declared unto you his covenant, which he commanded you to perform, even ten commandments; and he wrote them upon two tables of stone" (Deuteronomy 4:13, KJV).

We worship the living God and have to follow His commandments. That's why America is blessed and has become a dreamland for all other nations. That's why America has become a magnet for the techies of the world. That's why America has become a Wall Street of the world's economy. That's why America wins gold after gold in the Olympics. That's why America achieves Nobel Prize after prize. That's why ninety percent of American universities are listed as world-class institutes of higher learning. That's why Americans invent marvelous technological breakthroughs, wonders after wonders, and give away free to the world.

Caution: The day we ignore the first two commandments, America will enter into forty years of wilderness and will need another Moses to come out.

Recently, our Hindu immigrant friends have been getting their feet wet in politics. Most Indian Hindus are nice, loving, friendly people, but many still have arrived with their old, dirty luggage wrapped in a two-thousand-year-old stinky fabric of casteism. That mentality of hatred, discrimination, and illusion of self-stamped upper-caste status hidden inside their luggage leaks out in public life. My Hindu friends, we love you as Christ loved us, but we need to tell you the truth: America, the Judeo-Christian nation, is built upon two rock commandments. American Christians, you need to witness more prayerfully and aggressively to our new generation of Hindu immigrant friends. The mission field has arrived at our doorsteps. There is no place for any extremist group in America that has ties to a violent ideology and hate for minority victims of religious persecution in their homeland.

The Parliament of the World's Religions conference, held in August 2023 in Chicago, USA, has quietly removed Hindu religious leader Nivedita Bhide as one of the speakers on Hinduism at the conference after several participants raised concerns over her ties to Hindu extremist groups.

It has been reported by the news media that there are Hindu extremist groups in the USA that promote the propaganda of extreme ideology of supremacy and still believe in the caste system. Such far-right Hindu nationalist groups are a concern. Americans need to take the gospel to these sneaky far-right Hindu groups. The rise of right-wing fascism in India or in any other country or in America is a danger for a Judeo-Christian nation.

Hello, American pastors. This is a new era in America. Now, the mission field has arrived at home, and the church bell is ringing and asking, "Who is on my side? Who will go for me? Are you awake, my child? Are you listening to me? The mission I want you to go to is here now."

Remember what the Lord Jesus Christ has said, "Do not be afraid; I will be with you until the end of the earth."

"Do not fear, for I am with you; Do not be afraid, for I am your God. I will strengthen you; I will also help you; I will also uphold you with My righteous right hand" (Isaiah 41:10, NASB).

The missionaries that answered this call went to far lands and shared the good news. Now is the time to act within the Five Eyes nations to invite all our Hindu immigrants to our churches and let them test the love, joy, peace, mercy, generosity, and friendship of Jesus Christ. We need to win their hearts and minds to spread the good news of the gospel.

When my friend says, "I am Hindu, but I believe in Christian values," my friend, the Bible says you cannot serve two masters.

"No man can serve *two masters*, for either he will hate the one, and love the other; or else he will hold to the one, and despise the other. Ye cannot serve God and mammon" (Matthew 6:24, KJV) (emphasis added by the author).

In Gujarat state, India, where Mr. Mahatma Gandhi was born, there is a saying that goes like this, "You cannot place your foot in milk and yogurt at the same time," meaning you cannot serve two masters. How true!

My Hindu friends, come out of the closet; do not be afraid. Witness to others the new love, joy, peace, and tranquility you have found in Christ Jesus. Share the good news of Jesus Christ with your fellow countrymen and women. Jesus Christ loves you, and so do we, no matter where you came from and where you are going.

I honestly pray that if Saul can become Paul, one day Swamy will become Jesuswamy.

All Americans, including me, earnestly and lovingly will continue to pray for my Hindu friends so one day you will see Christ face to face and touch His nailed extended hands, and He will perform miracles through you. Come, we welcome you.

Those who are left behind in India are victims of socioeconomic and religious persecution. Mr. Gandhi named them God's people. He had a good intention, but the term he used sounds like a mockery of human beings, a joke, a sarcastic name. The Indian government made the same mistake and labeled them as "backward class," "scheduled caste," or "*dalits*." Wake up, India. This is the twenty-first century, and you want to send Indians to America on H1 visas as an export commodity but use such negative language purposely for those left behind? Before you arrive in America, your country needs to dismantle the cruel ideology of casteism that will help to improve UNO's human rights rating for India and promote equal opportunities for all in India, just like you have experienced here in the USA. That is what America stands for. You have to melt in the American ideology if you want to accept this nation as your new home.

The vast marginalized population of India should be called victims of ideology persecution (VIPs), not any other terms that degrade God-made human beings.

Takeaway: Can immigrants from Asia, South Asia, and the Middle East sing the songs of immigrants on the Fourth of July as sung by the Israelites as they ascended to Jerusalem (Zion) to worship God during annual feasts?

When the Lord brought back His exiles (immigrants) to Jerusalem (America) it was like a dream! (Psalm 126:1–2, NLT) "Read Psalm 120–134" should be printed on the back of the green card to remind the Song of Ascent from their homelands to America to celebrate the Pilgrimage (Immigrant) Festival (Deuteronomy 16:16). Praise the living God, not the figurines.

(02/13/2023)

30. IS THERE A VITAMIN PILL FOR STRENGTH AND ENCOURAGEMENT?

The answer is yes, and surprisingly, it is free. The problem is that not many people are willing to try it because it requires strength and courage to take the first step. Of course, it has a very high price tag. The price you have to pay is the full dedication to give it all, discipline yourself to resist negativity, do not be afraid of any adventure, and go alone where nobody else has dared to go; trust and obey your inner voice inspired by your creator, the Almighty, the living God, who is greater than any living creature in the universe.

Listen to what the Bible has to say,

"You are from God, little children, and have conquered them, because the one who is in you is greater than the one who is in the world" (1 John 4:4, NET).

It is hard to take the first step believing that the one in you is greater than the one in the world. If you are in search of a diamond, remember the diamond is buried and hidden miles and miles underneath the tough rocks to be chipped out first.

I, a Salvation Army officer's kid, living on five pitas like millet bread and curry made with two potatoes most of the time, graduated from high school in India with distinction rank. My grandfather had a great sense of humor. He would read at the dinner table this passage from the Bible,

> One of his disciples, Andrew, Simon Peter's brother, saith unto him, there is a lad here, which hath five barley loaves, and two small fishes: but what are they among so many? And Jesus said, Make the men sit down. Now there was much grass in the place. So, the men sat down, in number about five thousand. And Jesus took the loaves; and when he had given thanks, he distributed to the disciples, and the disciples to them that were set down; and likewise of the fishes as much as they

would. When they were filled, he said unto his disciples, gather up the fragments that remain, that nothing be lost. Therefore, they gathered them together, and filled twelve baskets with the fragments of the five barley loaves, which remained over and above unto them that had eaten. Then those men, when they had seen the miracle that Jesus did, said, this is of a truth that prophet that should come into the world.

John 6:8–14 (KJV)

This is exactly what happened in my childhood in 1939–1945, during World War II time. I had little to eat, being a Salvation Army officer's child in a far, remote, small town, surviving on a monthly paycheck to paycheck of about twenty dollars a month given to my retired grandfather. But I was always happy, healthy, and smart and maintained A grades throughout my high school years and tutored other kids in science and math free of charge.

Yes, how true! "Therefore they gathered them together, and filled twelve baskets with the fragments of the five barley loaves, which remained over and above unto them that had eaten" (John 6:13, KJV).

My state board high school final exam certificate remarks, "Passed with distinction." Yes, five pieces of millet bread and two potatoes performed a miracle because I put my trust in Him, the living God. And so, my friends, I strongly urge you to try it; you will be glad you did it.

My next adventure was to attend a college with a few pennies in my pocket in 1957. I looked at the college bulletin board. There were loans, grants, scholarships, and free money for higher education for red Patels, high Patels, bitter Patels, fourteen villages Patels, Shah, Agrawal, Murthy, Narayan, Ramanujan, and hundreds and hundreds of Hindu last names, but not a single fund for a Christian student. And I laughed. What if I change my last name from Christian to Patel? India is plagued by casteism, a cancer that has prevailed for the last 2000 years, and there is no cure so far. Will it take another hundred years to find a cure?

So, I started a night job as a test lab technician at Amul milk factory, the largest milk products producer in India in Anand, Gujarat state, and attended science college during the day time. Achieved BS in physics and math with an A grade. I continued the night shift at the same milk factory and tutored private classes to get enough money to pay for my

Bramvel Christian

tuition and books. I achieved an MS in solid-state physics from the S. P. University of India in Gujarat state.

How did that happen with very little in my pocket? The answer is in this biblical verse, "Teaching them to observe all things whatsoever I have commanded you: and, lo, I am with you always, even unto the end of the world. Amen" (Matthew 28:20, KJV).

Now what? I read the daily newspaper. It was a simmering, steaming, super hot summer in the months of June and July when the temperature rises as high as 120 degrees Fahrenheit in the air. I flipped through the newspaper advertisement sections, full of announcements—going to the USA for further study Mr. Red Patel, high Patel, bitter Patel, fourteen villages Patel, Shah, Agrawal, Murthy, Narayan, Ramas, and Krishnas, and many Hindu last names, but not a single Christian name. And I laughed again. Is the USA a land for red Patels, high Patels, bitter Patels, fourteen villages Patels, Shah, Agrawal, Murthy, Narayan, Ramas, Krishnas, and many Hindu last names, but not a single Christian? And I laughed again.

"I have a dream"—I read about a great Christian man, Dr. Martin Luther King. I used to tell my friends, "I have a dream to go to the far, far away nation where the dream comes true; it's called America."

I read about the greatest of the great presidents the world has ever seen, President Abraham Lincoln and his inspiring words, "This nation, under God, shall have a new birth of freedom."

I wanted to see a nation that acclaims to be one nation under God.

I read about George Washington, "If freedom of speech is taken away, then dumb and silent we may be led, like sheep to the slaughter."

What's the difference between a thief and a corrupt politician? It's how the money is pocketed: one steals public money and puts it in his pocket, and the other teaches someone else how to steal government money and transfer it to his pocket. If you make a joke like this in India, you may end up in jail for six months. Actually, that happened to one of the politicians in India.

I decided I wanted to go to a nation where the freedom of speech and practicing Christianity is still alive, respected, and held high as a model for democratic nations, where the Statue of Liberty not only proclaims justice and freedom for all but is practiced every day. The justice of the ten commandments is shining in her hands under the lamp of freedom.

I was standing at the Gateway of India, where the freedom of practicing Christianity and justice for minorities is a mockery, and heard the sound of the beacon coming from Elis Island in New York.

"Come to me, all you who labor and are heavily burdened, and I will give you rest" (Matthew 11:28, HNV).

That's the place millions and millions of immigrants around the world, including India, want to go at any cost.

When Mr. Mahatma Gandhi was pushed out of the train first-class compartment because of the color of his skin in South Africa, he said, **"Throw away my luggage, can't throw away my dream," but that's exactly what his countrymen do in his own country.**

And so, when one of Gandhi's great-great-grandsons pushed me off on the staircase of the S. P. University, Gujarat state, India, because I was Christian, my dream to go to America was still alive.

One day, my inner soul said, "Yes, you can do it; you can go to America." The next day, I checked my bank balance, and the devil said, "How can you? You don't know anybody in America. How can you? Forge it. Don't even think about it."

And the angel whispered in my ears, "God selected Moses, in spite of his speech impediment, and he led six hundred thousand Israelites out of Egypt and the wilderness. God can do a miracle for you. If the devil asks you, 'Who can send you to America?' Tell him His name is 'I AM.'"

"And God said unto Moses, I AM THAT I AM: and he said, thus shalt thou say unto the children of Israel, I AM hath sent me unto you" (Exodus 3:14, KJV).

So, I will go in the name of the Lord, Jehovah, whose name is, "I AM THAT I AM."

The first Israeli president, Hilda, called in the middle of the night to wake up the most brilliant president in foreign policy the world has ever seen, Nixon. His diplomacy opened the door to communist China, which nobody else could do.

The wheels came off, tumbling down the chariots of Egyptians, Jordanians, and Syrians when they heard the roaring mighty American jet fighters on Jerusalem's skyline. Moses' time history was repeated.

To earn extra money for my travel to the USA, I tutored Dr. Kurian Varghese's daughter. This Christian man caused a milk revolution in India by creating several milk products from domestic buffalo milk for the first time in the world after India's independence in 1947. His biography says,

> **"Tough times, closed doors, and a whole lot of rejections helped me get where I am today," Varghese said. "Instead of letting setbacks define me, they drove me to work harder. Circumstances forced me to find my own way and develop a unique perspective, one that allows me to see possibilities where others sometimes see roadblocks."[1]**

How true!

(2/17/2023)

My inner soul was knocking on my heart and telling me, "Do not worry. Turn your worry into curry; your critics will stop by your doorsteps to test the aroma."

All you need is a mix of a little bit of ginger, garlic, and red chili peppers. I'll tell you the rest of the recipe.

When a problem arrives, the first thing that happens to us is, "Why me? What do I do now? How can I cope with this? Where do I go? Who will help me? What did I do wrong?"

Relax. The sky is not falling down, even though it might look like it. What you think is a 9.0 earthquake on the Richter Scale might be five-pound hot potatoes on the bathroom scale. And even if it is a 9.0 earthquake, there are ways you can break it down into small potatoes. How? That's where the ginger, garlic, and red chili pepper recipe comes in handy. Let us talk about it.

Did you know most airlines carry ginger ale?

There are two main types of ginger ale—the golden style and the dry style (also known as the pale style). It doesn't matter which type of ginger ale you may like, but the fact remains it effectively works as a home remedy for indigestion and motion sickness, and it also soothes coughs and sore throats.

If you haven't tried it before, the next time you fly, try it. **In real life, ginger ale is self-control, coolness, and calm. President Theodore Roosevelt said, "Stay calm and carry a big stick."**

---

1. "Verghese Kurien." Wikipedia, n.d. https://en.wikipedia.org/wiki/Verghese_Kurien.

Say, "Oh yeh, are you gonna destroy me? Make no mistake; you don't know what you are up against." Remember, there is someone greater in front of you than the one hiding behind you.

"You, dear children, are from God and have overcome them, because the one who is in you is greater than the one who is in the world" (1 John 4:4, NIV).

Take a deep breath. Be assured that if there is a problem, there is a solution. Find the right formulae, plug in all variables, and bingo, the solution will emerge. All the options you have are variables. Your past experience, advice from your trusted friends, and prayer to the Almighty, creator of all, the living God, will generate a formula for you. It might happen right away, or it may take some time, but it will happen in His time. Keep chucking ginger ale.

Many people don't like garlic, although they feast on garlic pizzas. Turn garlic of bitterness into a party of pizzas. Revenge is not a win, but the middle path of consensus cools down war into peace. Sometimes, insults smell like garlic; swallow it, and, in the long term, it will turn into a sweet vanilla ice cream.

Now comes chili peppers. Red, hot, 400 degrees Celsius hot! Harsh words from your well-wishers. Are they? A sword of derogatory language sears you in half. The Bible says,

"There is one who speaks like the piercings of a sword. But the tongue of the wise promotes health" (Proverbs 12:18, NKJV).

"Watch your tongue and keep your mouth shut, and you will stay out of trouble" (Proverbs 21:23, NLT).

So, always watch the words coming out of your mouth; don't spread hot chili peppers but the flowers around you. In the long run, you will be glad you did. On the other hand, the corrective words to guide someone, as I have spread in this book, might taste like hot chili but are necessary, just like in Kung Pao chicken.

So, be careful how you use chili words. Are you correcting, encouraging, raising up someone, or tearing apart someone?

Takeaway: A dream is like a butterfly. It does not fall on your hands; you have to catch it. Mend your net first, and get all negative thoughts out.

Ten people may discourage you, but all you need is good news from two. Go for it, march on; that's the sign of victory waiting for you. Take a first step as Joshua did.

Those men who brought the bad report of the land also died by a plague in the presence of the LORD. But Joshua the son of Nun and Caleb the son of Jephunneh remained alive out of those men who went to spy out the land.

Numbers 14:37–38 (NASB)

(2/18/2023)

31. HOW DID I BECOME A SUCCESSFUL ENGINEER?

To become a successful engineer, you have to accept a challenge. You have to solve the technical problems nobody else dares to tackle. You have to go alone if nobody else walks the path it takes to solve the mystery. Here are some challenges I had to face to finish the marathon. How did that happen? Here is the key, "And the spirit of the LORD shall rest upon him, the spirit of *wisdom* and *understanding*, the spirit of *counsel and might*, the spirit of *knowledge* and of the *fear of the LORD*" (Isaiah 11:2, KJV) (emphasis added by the author).

Here are my seven color successes:

I was the manager of the pilot production of the CD/DVD discs produced for the first time in the world in Torrance, California, by MCA Disco Vision Company, a subsidiary of Universal Studios, in 1974.

I had to figure out how to solve the problems for a product never produced before. Amazing!

Resistors failed in the critical sensors of the Trident missile; nobody in Hughes Aircraft Company, El Segundo, California, could figure out why, but I did.

The transformer core cracked and failed on the circuit boards of the Air Force satellite, DirecTV Satellite Company, El Segundo, California. I resolved the problem.

How to maximize the sound performance of the piezo crystals in electronics-simulated musical instruments? Mattel Electronics, Hawthorne, California. I invented a technical solution, and Mattel sent me to Japan to implement the plan in their factory at Toshiba.

When antitank and antipersonnel mines failed, nobody was willing to go near the failed mines and figure out why. I did this at Aerojet Company, Downey, California.

Why did the pulse transformers keep failing on the navigation board of the nuclear-missile-loaded Trident submarine? I figured it out at Boeing, Anaheim, California.

Why did the interconnecting module of the submarine navigation system fail to send critical signals? Nobody knew; I figured it out at Boeing, Anaheim, California.

Was there a ghost in USA Navy submarines? The answer is yes, in technical terms. The submarine navigation command module was off, and all of a sudden, entered into the navigation mode. These young, bright, brave sailors, eighteen years old, who give their best prime time age for the country's sake, don't have to deal with ghosts at sea. Who will kill the electronics ghost? I did. They are safe now.

I was a chief engineer at Boeing, Trident Submarine Navigation Program, Navy Office, Anaheim, California. The Navy wanted to move submarine navigation sensor production and testing from West to East. It was one-of-a-kind sensors with state-of-the-art, cutting-edge technology no one in the world could make. Each sensor was a piece of gold. National security depended on these sensors. Each test station weighed two tons, and there were ten of them. How to move this most critical equipment from the East Coast to the West? Who would take leadership and manage the move for the Navy? I did at Boeing, Navy Program Office, Huntington Beach, California.

The secret of technical success is not in the textbooks but in your head, heart, mind, and two hands; you need to bow down in prayerful meditation. The Almighty living God asked the sons and daughters of Jacob to pray early in the morning, in the afternoon, in the evening, and at all times when they were traveling from the land of slavery to the land of honey and milk, the promised land.

Today, Israel, with a size less than New Jersey, thrives as the fourth most successful economy among developed countries in 2022. The IMF estimated Israel's GDP at US$564 billion and its GDP per capita at $58,270 in 2023 (thirteenth highest in the world), a mark made in a very short time after 1948. How did that happen? The key is listed above.

Takeaway: How could I solve the most difficult technical problems that other highly educated, experienced engineers could not? I don't know, except for one thing, "As for these four children, God gave him knowledge and skill in all learning and wisdom: and [Bramvel] had understanding in all visions and dreams" (Daniel 1:17, KJV).

Just kidding.

32. SAME TRAIN STATION, TWO DIFFERENT CROWDS

In April 1967, I left India for graduate studies in physics at UCLA. Amazing! With my handwritten application, I was accepted at UCLA. The whole town, my students, and college teaching staff came to Anand railway station, Gujarat state, India, to bid me farewell. Lots of cheers in the sky and tears in the eyes, heavy, awesome flower garlands around the neck, and kisses on the cheek. Unbelievable for a native son, a popular physics teacher in the science college going to America.

The train arrived, and the cheers were so loud that the whole town could hear; tears ran down the cheeks in everyone's eyes. I was showered with rose petals and garlands, and I was told, "Goodbye. Wish you all the best, and God be with you." And the dear missionary sang, "I will go, I will go, in the strength of the Lord." A long whistle, and the train departed. All was calm, all was bright, and I was stepping into a new era.

In December 1968, right after the first-semester final, I came down with homesickness that turned into depression. It was hard to describe. I missed my home; it was Christmas time. Home alone in Westwood, near the UCLA campus. All apartments were empty, and it looked like a ghost town or a graveyard. I couldn't take it anymore. It was a disease, and it was killing me. Homebound ET. Home, home.

On New Year's Eve, I headed home.

The train arrived at the same railway station. It was an early, foggy morning, and nobody was there. Where were my friends? Where were my relatives? Where were my well-wishers? The sun was rising, but it was all dark to me. It felt like the world was coming to an end. I picked up an old, rugged suitcase.

I heard in a distant corner, "On a hill far away stood an old, rugged cross. The emblem of suffering and shame."

My return without reaching the finish line was declared in the town as a failure and shame. Tears ran down my cheeks. *Oh Lord, what did I do? What will I do now? No one, no one, will support me or welcome me.* I came out of the train station by myself, and there was that same missionary waiting for me. He hugged me.

The Salvation Army officer said, "Don't worry, I understand. Let's go home."

I felt like what Isaiah says in Isaiah 13:10 (NLT), "The heavens will be black above them; the stars will give no light. The sun will be dark when it rises, and the moon will provide no light."

And Job says in Job 3:9 (NLT), "Let its morning stars remain dark. Let it hope for light, but in vain; may it never see the morning light." And in Job 16:16 (NLT), "My eyes are red with weeping; dark shadows circle my eyes."

The missionary took me to his home. He offered me hot black tea with sugar and milk, and then he read the Bible,

"Hope deferred makes the heart sick, but a dream fulfilled is a tree of life" (Proverbs 13:12, NLT).

"I pray that God, the source of hope, will fill you completely with joy and peace because you trust in him. Then you will overflow with confident hope through the power of the Holy Spirit" (Romans 15:13, NLT).

> The sounds of joy and laughter. The joyful voices of bridegrooms and brides will be heard again, along with the joyous songs of people bringing thanksgiving offerings to the LORD. They will sing, 'Give thanks to the LORD of Heaven's Armies, for the LORD is good. His faithful love endures forever!' For I will restore the prosperity of this land to what it was in the past, says the LORD.
>
> Jeremiah 33:11 (NLT)

Ironically, the same missionary wrote that same verse on my wedding greeting card four years later. He was right then, and he is right now because the Bible says, "Therefore do not worry about tomorrow, for tomorrow will worry about itself. Each day has enough trouble of its own" (Matthew 6:34, NIV).

I heard a voice beaming from the Crystal Cathedral, Garden Grove, California, "Tough times will not last, but the tough people do. Be strong, stand up, and go in the strength of the Lord again."

Joshua 1:9 (NLT), "This is my command—be strong and courageous! Do not be afraid or discouraged. For the LORD your God is with you wherever you go."

Psalm 31:24 (NLT), "So be strong and courageous, all you who put your hope in the LORD!"

Ephesians 6:10 (NLT), "A final word: Be strong in the Lord and in his mighty power."

These heavenly, inspiring subliminal messages kept knocking on my heart, mind, and brain. I was dead morally but became alive by His words and love of the missionary, and I headed out to seek the job.

Mr. R. P. Patel, head of the physics department, was a very brilliant Hindu man living Christian values. God used him as an instrument to grant me the same job I had before, teaching physics at V. P. Science College, Vidyanagar, Gujarat state, India. He understood what was going on in my heart. Up until now, nobody knew that if I didn't get a job within a month, I had a plan to end my life because those who didn't do a thing for me were criticizing me with sharper-than-knife words; I could not take it anymore. Seriously, if he had not helped me, I might have ended my life. All staff members were very supportive, and I came out of depression. God bless all my Hindu friends; I wish I could do more to win their hearts for Christ.

Takeaway: "Then spake Haggai [Mr. R. P. Patel] the LORD'S messenger in the LORD'S message unto the people [to me], saying, I am with you, saith the LORD" (Haggai 1:13, KJV).

"Give ear, O Israel: today you are going forward to the fight; let your heart be strong; do not let uncontrolled fear overcome you because of those who are against you" (Deuteronomy 20:3, BBE).

"In God have I put my trust: I will not be afraid what man can do unto me" (Psalm 56:11, KJV).

(2/28/2023)

33. MY EARLY LIFE

A small town called Anand on the west coast of India, Gujarat state, became the capital of dairy products in India after achieving independence from the British in 1947. From this town, India's milk industry was revolutionized by a South Indian Christian man named Kurian Verghese. Today, this town, Anand, is known as the Wisconsin of India. This man with a degree in mechanical engineering from Michigan State University and knowledge of dairy science from Australia, in those early days, engineered a giant dairy project called Amul Dairy, along with another local hero, Tribhovandas Patel, who organized all farmers of the surrounding villages for the first time in the history of India.

I had the privilege to tutor the daughter of Mr. Kurian V. and the son of Mr. Shah, the vice president of operations of Amul. Not far from this town, there is a university town called Vallabh Vidyanagar, meaning a town of knowledge. There, I got my bachelor's degree and my master's degree in solid-state physics and taught physics at the same university.

(3/1/2023)

I was raised in a small, dusty town in Gujarat state, India. One of the greatest poets of this state was by the name Uma Shakar Joshi. He was also the vice-chancellor of the Gujarat University. He visited the USA around 1957. When he returned, he wrote a poem titled "*Paschim na vira vaya, Uthne Ukarada Joto Nathee*" (in the Gujarati language). A meaningful English translation would be something like this, "The wind from the west is blowing hard. Oh nation of buffalo dung, rise up now. How can you not see what's so obvious to me?"

This is what Indian villages looked like to him in those days.

My parents were Salvation Army officers. They were being transferred from one town to another almost every year. Some towns did not have a primary school either. So, my parents decided to send me to my grand-father's home in Napad, a small village. My grandfather was a retired Salvation Army officer.

In a small town called Anand, my grandpa, my family, and I were at the railway station. I was five years old and did not know much about what was going on. The train arrived. My grandpa pushed me into the train compartment. I didn't want to go. I was crying. Tears were running down my white shirt with Sunday school blue S embryoid on my shirt lapels. The train was crowded. Everybody was looking at me. I was embarrassed, and I became quiet.

It took me a while to get used to a new reality. I started middle school on the top of a hill. I made new friends, Hindus and Muslims. Amazingly, I became very popular in the town because I turned out to be a first-class top student in every grade. I was the only one in the town who knew a few English words, which I had learned from the missionaries at that age. I tutored students in math, science, and English in exchange for homemade snacks and a trip to their mango farms.

On the first day of each month, Grandpa would go to Anand, Salvation Army headquarters, to attend the monthly meeting and collect a monthly salary. He would bring Indian pastries called "jalebee" and "vada" on the trip back. I would stand at the bus stop, waiting for this monthly treat. Most of the time, I could read his face: no payday at this time; MoneyGram did not arrive from London headquarters. No feast this month.

Grandpa would read from the Bible,

> Then he took the five loaves and the two fishes, and looking up to heaven, he blessed them, and brake, and gave to the disciples to set before the multitude. And they did eat, and were all filled: and there was taken up of fragments that remained to them twelve baskets.
>
> Luke 9:16–17 (KJV)

Grandpa said, "We will survive by five *roties* (Indian bread, like a tortilla) and two potatoes." He laughed, and I joined him. What a sense of humor he taught me!

Takeaway: "But he answered and said, It is written, Man shall not live by bread alone, but by every word that proceedeth out of the mouth of God" (Matthew 4:4, KJV).

(03/10/2023)

34. THE WORLD OF STATISTICS, THE PART OF AMERICAN LIFE

Every engineer, financial personnel, marketing person, contract administrator, manager, CEO, CFO, and government personnel should know how statistics can cheat you, misguide you, and make you lose money. The numbers that paint a rosy picture of your project can turn the project upside down depending on which statistical mirror you use to see the big picture. American industry, daily lifestyle, medical practices, education, job market, government planning, and even the entertainment industry run on statistics. In America, our life is controlled by numbers. Every person has a number called SSN. That SSN demands statistical analysis. Math and statistics are great tools. The nation with expertise in math will have a leading edge in computer science and will lead the twenty-first century. That nation will also thrive economically, scientifically, and politically in years to come because math is a magic number for all sciences.

However, the same tools with a deceiving mind can be used for selfish motivations. It is a double-edged sword. This happens in the industry all the time. So, if buck stops at your desk, you need to know how to draw a line between the grey and dark colors of a statistical cloud of numbers.

Takeaway: The statistics that can paint a rosy picture, presented by different techniques, can paint a gloomy outcome. So, if you are a decision-maker, learn how to read statistics both ways. I learned this lesson when I became a Six Sigma Master Black Belt certified by Boeing and the International Quality Organization.

(03/15/2023)

35. WELCOME TO THE LAND OF MILK, HONEY, BURGER, AND DOG

I landed at LAX. Actually, I was very afraid of coming to America for the second time, one year after I got married. The nightmare vision was still fresh and alive and was frightening me. But the dream was also still alive because the only way to thrive and be all you can be against the Indian philosophical, cultural, rituals, and socio-economic casteism was to throw away everything that was frightening me and fight against every odd.

The shadow was telling me, "No, don't go. You will be sorry again."

The voice from Mount Sinai was punching my heart and telling me, "Yes, you must go. There is no other hope around you here in India. This community will not let you live your normal life. See the big picture. The diamond has to go through about a hundred thousand times the normal pressure and more than eight thousand degrees Fahrenheit temperature to turn into liquid form so that it can flow and turn into a beautiful jewel to shine on her gorgeous neck."

I kept hearing in my ears, "You are a solid-state physicist. You know that. So, get up and go. Go to the unknown and the known will be revealed unto you by I AM WHO I AM. Aim high and look into the eyes of the one who has created you, and do not be afraid of the dark shadow of the ugly monster." That was it, and I left India for good.

When I arrived at LAX, the Salvation Army officer and his wife were waiting in the luggage area. "Welcome to America, Bram. How are you?"

What a joy and relief to know that someone was there to receive me! It was nighttime. The glamor of LAX! I had never seen such a show of dancing shining bright light studded with reflectors on the six lanes of the 405 Freeway. It was shocking. Six lanes on both sides; it was equal to ten national highways in India. I never saw such an electrifying light show in India. I was stunned and silent. What a city, what will I do?

The officer dropped me off at Harmony Hall, a recovery home for alcoholics near USC in Los Angeles.

Takeaway:

I have a dream today. I have a dream that one day every valley shall be engulfed, every hill shall be exalted and every mountain shall be made low, the rough places will be made plains and the crooked places will be made straight and the glory of the Lord shall be revealed and all flesh shall see it together.

Martin Luther King, Jr.
I Have a Dream Speech (1963)

(3/16/2023)

36. THE GLAMOR AND REALITY OF AMERICA START THE NEXT DAY

The Salvation Army officer dropped me off and said, "Good luck; you are in good hands."

The officer in charge, Colonel Wiseman, was such a nice, loving, and caring man. He put my bag in a small little room. Another nice man took me to a dining room. Steam-cooked canned beans, vegetables, bread, peanut butter, jam, and coffee. I was not used to this kind of food. But thank God, I had a roof on my head and food on my plate in a new country where I didn't know anybody. I enjoyed peanut butter, jam, and jelly sandwiches for breakfast, lunch, and dinner. I had only one hundred dollars and had to survive until I found a job.

I was shocked to find out the America I did not know about and that most Americans still don't know. The other side of Uncle Sam's empire was not as full of glory as I had thought. The residents were Vietnam, Korean, and WWII veterans, war heroes, engineers, watch repairers, mechanics, businessmen, teachers, and ordinary Joe and his brothers. The nation for which they gave everything they had to offer neglected them when they returned from the war zone. In exchange for their sacrifice and dedication, the devil called "depression" filled their cup with alcohol to the brim. Thank God, there is a church that runs on the biblical principles quoted in Matthew 25:35–40 (ASV),

> For I was hungry, and ye gave me to eat; I was thirsty, and ye gave me drink; I was a stranger, and ye took me in; naked, and ye clothed me; I was sick, and ye visited me; I was in prison, and ye came unto me. Then shall the righteous answer him, saying, Lord, when saw we thee hungry, and fed thee? or athirst, and gave thee drink? And when saw we thee a stranger, and took thee in? or naked, and clothed thee? And when saw we thee sick, or in prison, and came unto thee? And the

King shall answer and say unto them, Verily I say unto you, Inasmuch as ye did it unto one of these my brethren, even these least, ye did it unto me.

Now, they are sober and trying to get their life back again.
They kept asking me, "Why did you come to this country?"
I said, "For better opportunities."
They would laugh. "What better opportunities? Where? Let us know if you find one."
That scared the heck out of me.
The dark shadow came back, "I told you. Aha! Aha! Aha!"
How nice, we received Los Angeles Times every day. I marked up ads of interest and called the companies from the front desk. I didn't know where all these weird places were—San Gabriel, San Fernando, Los Angeles, Santa Monica, Santa Ana, Santa Barbara, and hundreds of other Santas, but no real Christmas Father (the name for Santa in India) came to help me. I would mark the places on the map, walk miles and miles to save every penny I had left, and take one bus to the other in search of a job, factory to factory, school to school, but there was no job in sight, and I was either disqualified or overqualified.

In spite of the disappointment of not finding a job, one thing that kept me going was, "Jehovah is my strength and song; And he is become my salvation [at Salvation Army in Los Angeles]" (Psalm 118:14, ASV).

Finally, I—a man with a master's degree in solid-state physics—accepted a labor job for $1.50 per hour at the Salvation Army alcoholic rehabilitation centers (ARCs) in Santa Ana, California, in April 1973. After working five months there, I continued looking for a professional job and was hired as a physics, chemistry, and math teacher at Cantwell High School, Montebello, California, in September 1973.

Takeaway: How could I do this? The answer is: My strength comes from above, from I AM WHO I AM, not from manmade figurines.

Psalm 61:2 (CSB), "I call to you from the ends of the earth when my heart is without strength. Lead me to a rock that is high above me."

---

37. TEN QUESTIONS THAT WILL DETERMINE YOUR FUTURE

If you are looking for a professional job, be prepared to answer the following common questions in your interview that will make or break your future.

1. Tell us a little bit about yourself. What is your professional background?
2. Why do you want to work for us? Do you know what business we are in? Do you know about the product we make?
3. What is your hobby? What do you do in your spare time? (Don't say, "I play Lego.") What is your favorite TV show?
4. Do you volunteer for any organization?
5. Which book have you read recently?
6. What's the difference between Test Instruction and Test Plan?
7. Do you have any statistical quality control training? Or, Green Belt, Black Belt, Continuous Improvement training?
8. Do you know who is our president?
9. What are your strengths and weaknesses?
10. What is your faith? How do you relax or entertain yourself? How is your family or social life?

One final piece of advice: Provide the strongest references you can, smile, keep a positive attitude, dress up professionally, be on time, present evidence of your highly acclaimed achievements at the end, even if not asked, shake hands and say, "Thank you very much for your time and giving me an opportunity."

Takeaway: The best employee is the one who considers the company he/she works for as his/her. How the company will do depends on how he/she will do.

To protect the environment, we are encouraged to recycle goods as much as possible. One thing I learned at ARC: Can you protect human beings by recycling humanity? The answer is yes. That's what I observed with my own eyes by living with the victims of alcohol and drugs at the Salvation Army alcoholic rehabilitation centers (ARCs) in Santa Ana, California.

38. AMERICA FIRST

Dali Lama missed the point when the voice of America proclaimed, "America first." Look around the giant world from your small window. You will be convinced, indeed, that "America is first." Who stepped on the moon first in the world? America. Who invented stethoscopes? Who first sparked the earth with electricity? Who said, "Hello? Hello!" on the horn first? Who invented the steam engine and locomotive? Who "got going" on automobiles? Where did the computer come from? Who filled every pocket with a melody ringing tune called cell phone? Who invented the chip that converted silicon in Silicon Valley into gold in the Golden State called California? Are you emailing from Tibet to Toronto? And the list goes on.

Dear Mr. Dalai Lama, America is first and will remain first because she is a Judeo-Christian nation blessed by the living God; I AM WHO I AM. "There shall be no other god before me" is written on a rock tablet replica given to America.

Ask any Gandhian in the Big Apple, "Where are you from, Mr. Gandhi?" And the majority will say Bombay.

Ask him again, "Do you know Trombay?" He would think you are mocking him. But the first atomic reactor given by America is still in Trombay near Bombay. Most of India was dark in 1947. So, the atomic reactor was a goodwill gift to a newborn nation. It was gifted with an understanding that it would be used for peaceful purposes only to light up Bombay. If you know how to operate an atomic reactor, you can start the first step to building rockets and missiles. Ask any rocket scientist. That is exactly what happened. Nobody asked, "Where is your peace and tranquility mantra, Mr. Nehru?"

Go to Ahmedabad, Gujarat state, to an area called Satellite. There, you will see a satellite tracking station. Go a little bit closer, and you will see the American flag and "USA" embossed on the multi-million satellite and tracking monitoring equipment, gifts from the NASA. I know this because I spearheaded a tour of physics major students from S. P. University, Gujarat state, India, to this facility on a science and technology trip as part of learning applied physics. I introduced such an industry tour for the physics students for the first time in this university.

Do you know that near LAX, Boeing Company (formerly Hughes Aircraft in El Segundo, California) built the world's first commercial satellite? India ordered the GRANY satellite. I created magnetics specifications for this satellite. All of a sudden, something happened, and India canceled the contract. Now, India builds its own satellites. My beloved India, Bravo Zulu, but remember, America was first.

Takeaway: How can a nation be first? The answer is in the Bible.

Matthew 6:33 (KJV), "But seek ye first the kingdom of God, and his righteousness; and all these things shall be added unto you."

America, seek ye first the living God, not the man-made figurines, and you will remain first in the world, ironclad guaranteed.

Your senator, congressman, mayor, governor, and president, do they seek first the kingdom of the God of Moses, Abraham Lincoln, and Martin Luther King?

(03/17/2023)

39. THE VOICE OF AMERICA

The voice of America is a voice of sharp-edge zeal for patriotism, tenacity of inner strength of Christian faith, remarkable intelligence to invent, and titanium perseverance to break the barrier of poverty, cross the desert, swim the oceans, climb beyond the Everest, and jump higher than the Himalaya until the bamboo breaks. That's the spirit of America, still well and alive. Will it remain alive forever?

Why can't other nations compete with America? It is because their progress is pushed back by self-centered, socially selfish, spiritually blind, intellectually of low IQ, modern standard dummy caste system, and self-proclaimed upper class without any upper-class credentials.

The voice of America is one trumpet tune of the sons and daughters of Moses, Jews and Gentiles from every nation of the globe. Each day, they arrive on the East and West Coast of America, even today. The Spirit of God descends through the Lady of Liberty on Elise Island, proclaiming, **"Then Jesus said, 'Come to me, all of you who are weary and carry heavy burdens, and I will give you rest'"** (Matthew 11:28, NLT).

All my immigrant friends, open the Bible and place your green card on this verse, and we will pray for you.

This Lady of Liberty is so generous that she not only welcomed Moses' children but also millions of others like Hindus, Muslims, Buddhists, Jains, Sikhs, and list goes on, with a hope that they will harmonize in the tapestry of American values and culture and spread the flavor of new, beautiful, bountiful life to their new homeland. Sadly, that did not happen. They still want to cling to their old bones no matter how much calcium they might have left.

In the last fifty years, the highest number of immigrants coming to America are from India and China. But the American churches have failed to win these beautiful souls for Christ.

Matthew 9:37 (NLT), "He said to his disciples, 'The harvest is great, but the workers are few.'"

America, wake up; the mission field has arrived in our own backyard. There is an urgent need to reach out to this bountiful crop right here from Boston to Honolulu and from Anchorage to San Diego.

Did you know that in California and many other states and in the UK, the churches are empty and converted into Hindu temples and mosques?

Do you remember what Jesus said?

John 2:16 (NASB), "And to those who were selling the doves He said, 'Take these things away from here; stop making My Father's house a place of business!'"

American churches, wake up; we need to reach out to these beautiful doves with love, compassion, mercy, and generosity to follow the profound command of our living God.

Mark 16:15 (NASB), "And He said to them, 'Go into all the world and preach the gospel to all creation.'"

Now, the world has arrived at our doorstep. Church, wake up; go and win these beautiful souls for Christ; no need to cross the Pacific or Atlantic oceans. If you don't, what happened to Israel before 1948 will happen to all the Five Eyes nations.

Hosea 13:6 (NASB), "As they had their pasture, they became satisfied, And as they became satisfied, their heart became proud; Therefore, they forgot Me." Has America forgotten Him?

Hosea 2:13 (NLT), "'I will punish her for all those times, when she burned incense to her images of Baal, when she put on her earrings and jewels and went out to look for her lovers but forgot all about me,' says the LORD." Again, America, did you forget the living God and place Baal in your precious heartlands?

These American heroes who lost limbs in wars fought by America are like coconuts, tough like a rock outside but mellow and hearty like Jell-O inside, full of sweet aqua but still thirsty for the living water. Let their sacrifice not go in vain; they died on the battlefield yesterday so we could play on the baseball field today.

John 4:14 (KJV), "But whosoever drinketh of the water that I shall give him shall never thirst; but the water that I shall give him shall be in him a well of water springing up into everlasting life."

Takeaway: American churches, it's your call to pour the living water into their pots.

I am one of the recipients of the voice of America depicted above. Are you? If so, raise your voice to synchronize with the voice of America. Tell your motherland, which you left behind, not to burn the houses of worship of the living God but build the bridges to cross the ocean so you can hear the voice of America.

(03/20/2023)

40. AMERICA, THE MAGNET OF THE WORLD

America is not only the Disneyland of the world but the magnet of the world. America inspires a dream and offers options to fulfill the dream. America is a land that is not comparable to any other land that exists to this date. America is a hope, a dream, a voice of weak and desperate, a melody of success and triumph, and a gold medal of aspiration; it's a land where eagles dare and heroes throw arrows beyond the skyline to win the Olympic golds year after year.

If that does not impress you, look at this: America is a mysterious lab where the world's ninety percent of global Nobel Prize winners are born year after year. If you are still skeptical, listen: America has sent more missionaries than all nations combined on the earth. If you are still not convinced, read the greatest book gifted from your creator and given free to every man on His own creation called the earth. Listen,

"And the name of the city of My God, the new Jerusalem, which comes down out of heaven from My God, and My new name" (Revelation 3:12, NASB).

> Him that overcometh will I make a pillar in the temple of my God, and he shall go no more out: and I will write upon him the name of my God, and the name of the city of my God, which is new Jerusalem, which cometh down out of heaven from my God: and I will write upon him my new name.

Revelation 21:2 (KJV), "And I John saw the holy city, new Jerusalem, coming down from God out of heaven, prepared as a bride adorned for her husband."

Takeaway: My engineering analysis indicates that the new Jerusalem is Washington, DC. America is His bride. When Christ comes again, with the sound of the trumpet, He will descend at the Lincoln Memorial. The seven monuments of Washington, DC, are seven trumpets.

41. WILL CHRIST COME A SECOND TIME IN WASHINGTON, DC?

My engineering analysis certainly indicates so. Have a look.

After the Second World War, God prepared America for His second coming, step by step. How? First, listen to what Isaiah has said, "All ye inhabitants of the world, and ye dwellers on the earth, when an ensign is lifted up on the mountains, see ye; and when the trumpet is blown, hear ye" (Isaiah 18:3, ASV).

How can all dwellers of the earth see and hear simultaneously the seven angels blowing seven trumpets? In order for it to happen, America has invented marvelous inventions one after the other progressively by God's grace, gifts, talents, skills, knowledge, and wisdom granted to our pioneer Judeo-Christian settlers and their descendants. Have a look:

Takeaway: From the telegraph to the telephone to the radio to the TV to the computer to the Internet to AI, all are invented in America. A step-by-step progress is leading to a point where a new technology will be perfected in America. The people of the world will be able to see and listen to Christ when He stretches out both His hands and proclaims good news from the balcony of the Capitol building of Washington, DC.

Isaiah 48:16 (KJV), "Come ye near unto me, hear ye this; I have not spoken in secret from the beginning; from the time that it was, there am I: and now the Lord GOD, and his Spirit, hath sent me."

42. SEVEN TRUMPETS PROPHECY LOCATION IN WASHINGTON, DC

T	Revelation		Angel Location
1	8:7	Hail, fire, blood from the sky. Burns a third of greens and trees.	Arlington National Cemetery (green grass and trees).
2	8:8–9	Asteroid falls into the sea and turns a third into blood, a third of the sea creatures are killed, and a third of the ships are destroyed.	Smithsonian Museums.
3	8:10–11	Another asteroid, this one called Wormwood, turns a third of the freshwater bitter; many die.	Lincoln Memorial Washington Monument. Jefferson Memorial.
4	8:12–13	The sun, moon, and stars are struck, and a third of the light turns dark.	US Capitol.
5	9:1–12	A star falls on Earth, opens the Abyss, and releases locusts like scorpions from the pit to torment men, torturing the unsaved for five months. Military power.	White House.

| 6 | 9:13–21 | A brutal army of 200 million led by four angels kills a third of mankind. | Pentagon. |
| 7 | 11:15–19 | Second coming of Jesus Christ, wicked destroyed, righteous rewarded, temple opens, reveals the ark of the covenant. | Washington National Cathedral. |

Trumpet #1: Arlington National Cemetery is covered with green grass and trees.

Trumpet #2: The Smithsonian's National Museum of Natural History will allow the public to see a sample of Bennu, a carbon-rich, near-Earth asteroid, on Friday, November 3, 2023.

Trumpet #3: Lincoln Memorial, Washington Monument, Jefferson Memorial, and all other memorials are on the banks of the Potomac River, which provides the drinking water in the District of Columbia.

Revelation 8:10 (NLT), "Then the third angel blew his trumpet, and a great star fell from the sky, burning like a torch. It fell on one-third of the rivers and on the springs of water."

Trumpet #4: The bronze Statue of Freedom, facing east over the central entrance of the Capitol, points to the sun. Two symbols found at the US Capitol, the eagle and the Union Shield, represent the stars and the moon.

But even before Jefferson's proposal was approved, the US Capitol building was being used for *church services*. A 1795 newspaper in Boston reported that in "our infant city (Washington, DC). Public worship is now regularly administered at the Capitol every Sunday morning at eleven o'clock by the reverend."

Trumpet #5: The White House represents the powerhouse of the world's economy and also military might.

Exodus 16:31 (KJV), "And the house of Israel called the name thereof Manna: and it was like coriander seed, white; and the taste of it was like wafers made with honey."

The White House is the fifth trumpet because America has shared plenty of food (manna) with all nations of the world. I remember tons and tons of cheese and milk powder arrived free from America through the Salvation Army to the Emery Hospital in my little town called Anand, India, in 1950, right after World War II ended and sugar and other commodities were under rationing.

Trumpet #6: The Pentagon represents the world's most powerful army, navy, air force, and now space force.

Trumpet #7: The Washington National Cathedral is a symbol of a new era where every new president attends prayer service for guidance and wisdom for the new presidency about to begin. Washington, DC, is a new Jerusalem. See what the Bible says,

---

Takeaway: Revelation 3:12 (KJV), Him that overcometh will I make a pillar in the temple of my God, and he shall go no more out: and I will write upon him the name of my God, and the name of the city of my God, which is new Jerusalem, which cometh down out of heaven from my God: and I will write upon him my new name.

Revelation 21:2 (KJV), "And I John saw the holy city, new Jerusalem, coming down from God out of heaven, prepared as a bride adorned for her husband."

Next, you will see the proof of why America is a new Jerusalem.

---

43. CUTTING-EDGE TECHNOLOGICAL BREAKTHROUGH, AMERICAN INVENTION HISTORY FROM 1891 TO 2023

Incandescent lamp—Thomas Edison's (1891).
Keypunch—Herman Hollerith (1901).
Hearing aid—Miller Reese Hutchison (1902).
Cyclotron—Ernest O. Lawrence, University of California at Berkeley (1929).
Thermistor—Samuel Ruben (1930).
PH meter—Arnold Orville Beckman (1935).
Compact fluorescent lamp—George Inman, Edward E. Hammer (1936).
Digital computer—George Stibitz (1937).
Nylon—Wallace H. Carothers at E. I. du Pont (1938).
Automated teller machine—Luther George Simjian (1939).
Microwave oven—Percy Spencer (1945).
Space observatory—Lyman Spitzer (1946).
Credit card—John C. Biggins (1946).
Transistor—John Bardeen, Walter Brattain, and William Shockley at AT&T Bell Labs (1947).
Supersonic aircraft—United States Air Force (1947).
Instant camera—Edwin H. Land (1947).
Video game—Thomas T. Goldsmith Jr. and Estle R. Mann (1948).
Cooler—Richard C. Laramy of Joliet, Illinois (1951).
Barcode—Norman Joseph Woodland (1952).
Artificial heart—Dr. Forest Dewey Dodrill, Dr. Robert Jarvik (1952).
Voltmeter (digital)—Andrew Kay (1953).

Synthetic diamond—Howard Tracy Hall, GE Research Laboratory (1954).

Radar gun—Bryce K. Brown (1954).

Nuclear submarine—Admiral Hyman Rickover, Naval Reactors Branch of the Atomic Energy Commission (1955).

Hard disk drive—Reynold Johnson, IBM (1955).

Industrial robot—George Devol and Joseph F. Engelberger (1956).

Videotape—Charles Ginsburg and Ray Dolby (1956).

Laser—American physicist Gordon Gould (1957).

Integrated circuit—Jack Kilby (1958).

Global navigation satellite system—Johns Hopkins University Applied Physics Laboratory under the leadership of Richard Kershner, for US Navy (1960).

Communications satellite—American aerospace engineer John Robinson Pierce, NASA (1962).

Light-emitting diode—Nick Holonyak (1962).

Computer mouse—Douglas Engelbart, Augmentation Research Center, DARPA (1963).

Liquid crystal display—George H. Heilmeier (1964).

Minicomputer—Wesley A. Clark and Charles Molnar (1965).

Dynamic random-access memory—Robert Dennard at the IBM (1966).

Calculator (hand-held)—Jack Kilby (1967).

Lunar Module—for the Apollo program by Grumman (1969).

Laser printer—Gary Starkweather, Xerox (1969).

Wide-body aircraft—The Boeing Company (1969).

Personal computer—John Blankenbaker (1971).

Microprocessor—Ted Hoff, Federico Faggin, Masatoshi Shima, and Stanley Mazor, Intel (1971).

E-mail—Ray Tomlinson, United States Department of Defense's ARPANET (1971).

Video game console—Ralph H. Baer, Magnavox (1972).

Magnetic resonance imaging—Dr. Raymond Damadian (1972).

Recombinant DNA—Stanley Norman Cohen and Herbert Boyer (1973).

Mobile phone—Martin Cooper (1973).

Digital camera—Steven Sasson as an engineer at Eastman Kodak (1975).

Stealth-aircraft—By the Lockheed, F-117 Nighthawk (1981).

Space Shuttle—NASA, George Mueller, St. Louis, Missouri overseeing (1981).

Internet—Paul Baran, Leonard Kleinrock's lab at UCLA, and Douglas Engelbart's lab at the Stanford Research Institute. Bob Kahn and Vinton Cerf co-invented Internet Protocol and Transmission Control Protocol, United States Department of Defense, United States' National Science Foundation (NSF) (1983).

CMOS image sensor—American physicist and engineer Eric Fossum invented the CMOS image sensor while working at NASA's Jet Propulsion Laboratory in Pasadena, California (1994).

DNA computing—Leonard Adleman of the University of Southern California (1994).

YouTube—the PayPal group (2005).

iPhone—Apple company (2007).

iPad—Apple company (2010).

Reusable launch vehicle—Corn Ranch, Texas, Blue Origin's New Shepard rocket was the first; now, SpaceX's Falcon 9 rocket and fairings are reused (2015).

Videoconferencing—Although video conference technology has deep roots since 1956, when AT&T was working on Picturephone (2020).

In 1964, on April 20 at the World's Fair in New York City, the attendees of the World's Fair at Flushing Meadow Park were able to make a video call on AT&T Picturephone to another Picturephone exhibit at Disneyland in California.

COVID-19 created a necessity to bring several video conferencing companies to the forefront of technology in America, such as Zoom, Join.Me, Blue Jeans, Webex, and others all offer cloud-based video conferencing services worldwide.

Can Any Nation on the Surface of Planet Earth Boast a List Like This?

Now I AM WHO I AM has equipped America with almost all the technology needed to send His Son, Jesus Christ, again. What better place could there be than Washington, DC? I predict that in a few years, a new technology will be unveiled that will allow the creation of a TV screen in the air. By framing air in an enclosure filled with electrically conductive gas, molecules can be ionized. Then, using ionized gas, a display monitor screen can be created just like an LED or LCD screen. Audio-video signals can be transmitted via satellite on this instant mega jumbo screen in the sky. Such multiple-screen networks can be interconnected to cover the whole world. Once this technology is invented in America, Christ will arrive at the sound of the seventh trumpet.

Every nation will zoom on Zoom and be judged. It's all in Revelation. Someday, a Nobel Prize winner in biblical knowledge with heavenly wisdom will break the codes to interpret the divine mystery. The revolution of AI is not an accident but one step closer to opening the greatest story ever told in Revelation. Until then, America will continue to fight against the Philistines. Who are these Philistines? You figure it out yourselves.

Takeaway: Now, we have arrived at the dawn of the second coming of Christ. America, wake up and be ready. Five Eyes, you are the five virgins; make sure your lamps are fully filled with the oil.

Matthew 25:10–13 (NASB), But while they were on their way to buy the oil, the groom came, and those who were ready went in with him to the wedding feast; and the door was shut. Yet later, the other virgins also came, saying, 'Lord, lord, open up for us.' But he answered, 'Truly I say to you, I do not know you.' Be on the alert then, because you do not know the day nor the hour.

---

44. WHO WILL BE THE NEXT PRESIDENT OF AMERICA IN 2025?

The president of America is the president of the world. He utters one word, and the price of gold and silver either jumps to incredible height or falls to the dirt. He writes one sentence on the X, and the world's stock market either tumbles to the valley or climbs the highest peak in history. He appears on the TV and the world's eyes get glued on the screen. That's what America is. Who could be her next Moses?

As long as a newly elected American president will stand on the platform of the Capitol building, place his hands on the Holy Bible, and pledge to carry on the call to lead this greatest nation on the earth, just like his founding fathers did, this nation with its fifty stars will always shine. It will become the beacon of freedom like a North Star.

The day this does not happen will be the doomsday of King Solomon. How do I know? Open your eyes just in front of you, not very far from where you came from. Look at Britain. What happened to King Solomon and King David is happening to the UK. The empire where the sun never sets; the kingdom is nearing doomsday. Why? Read the Bible, the end of Solomon and David.

> The LORD became angry with Solomon because his heart had turned away from the LORD, the God of Israel, who had appeared to him twice. Although he had forbidden Solomon to follow other gods, Solomon did not keep the LORD's command. So the LORD said to Solomon, "Since this is your attitude and you have not kept my covenant and my decrees, which I commanded you, I will most certainly tear the kingdom away from you and give it to one of your subordinates."
>
> 1 Kings 11:9–12 (NIV)

This is what has happened in England. The Bible is removed from 10 Downing Street, London. The last remnant of the British empire is wavering. The brilliance of the Ko-i-Noor in the crown is slowly fading away. The palace should be the house of worship of the living God; instead, it has turned into a crime scene. The sun has finally set on the British empire.

Will America be next? Judge yourself. Where are we going? There is still time to correct the course. "Let us unite under the living God, oh My soul, United States of America," the God saith to the Five Eyes. "You are the apple of My eye. Listen, 'For thus saith the LORD of hosts; After the glory hath he sent me unto the nations which spoiled you: for he that toucheth you toucheth the apple of his eye'" (Zechariah 2:8, KJV).

If the Five Eyes follow, "Keep my commandments, and live; and my law as the apple of thine eye" (Proverbs 7:2, KJV).

"You are the apple of My eye," God said. Amen.

What do the Five Eyes need to do? Pause immigration; look closely. Immigrants who are polluting biblical teaching and smearing dirt on the Judeo-Christian faith will eventually destroy the God-given riches, blessings, talents, and skills of the Five Eyes.

Their green card should be only a guest card, marked with a big G and can't be a chain in chain immigration or a Five Eyes citizen. We should still love them and witness to them more effectively than ever before because the Bible says so. They are not our enemies but mischievous friends, prodigal sons and daughters, and lost sheep; we need to love them and care for them just like the father of the prodigal son did. Because Jesus said on the cross, "Father, forgive them; they do not know what they are doing."

"[But Jesus was saying, 'Father, forgive them; for they do not know what they are doing.'] And they cast lots, dividing His garments among themselves" (Luke 23:34, NASB).

Five Eyes, wake up. It's a wake-up call ringing for a long time, and your opponents are blocking it quietly.

I predict that in 2024, President Donald Trump will not only win but will win with the biggest landslide victory ever seen in American history. He will propose a new amendment to renew the current im-

migration policy in alignment with the ten commandments. Look at my engineering analysis.

Bramwell's Political Engineering on Presidential Candidates Rating Matrix

		T	D	H	R
1	Practices, preserves, promotes, protects, and participates in our heritage of Judeo-Christian faith.	10	8	8	2
2	Communicator, charming personality, charisma, elocution skill, listens to people, telling the truth (like President Regan).	9	5	5	5
3	Foreign policy, friendly relations with world powers, great negotiator, and rising nations like India love him.	10	4	7	3
4	Entrepreneurial self-experience, visionary, world trade expert, balance export/import vs. GDP vs. living standard, bull soars.	10	4	4	5
5	Run nation as your own business—international businessman knowledge, understands DOW, Nasdaq, SP500, and other indices.	10	5	7	4
6	America First's policy to stay on top of the world, can guide and direct UNO, can impact the world's politics, and is a world leader.	10	8	6	3
7	Revolution: STEM, top-notch, world-class universities, highest Nobel Prize winner, innovation hub, powerhouse of technology.	7	3	3	4
8	National security protector, maintain the most powerful military in the world, and equip the USA with military strength no one else has.	10	8	8	4
9	Immigration reform to match American values, control illegal immigration, teach American history/religion/culture/customs.	9	7	4	3
10	Popular among our partner nations, celebrates Thanksgiving with the family of the Five Eyes, and creates new Five Eyes institutes.	10	5	5	1

11	Make America LOMAH (land of milk and honey). America rises by his words from the bottom of his heart and the top of his hat.	10	4	4	1
12	Proactive to the pandemic, turns on machinery to fight it, makes public health a top priority, and promotes health initiatives and new drugs.	10	4	4	5
13	Affordable health insurance/medications for all, world-class hospitals, medical schools, research institutes, and drug production.	8	2	2	1
14	Twenty-first-century advanced education at primary, high school, and university levels ahead of any other nation in the world.	9	3	3	4
15	Bring investment at home, South America and Europe, balance trade market that will create jobs for everyone.	10	3	3	1
16	"Love thy neighbor." Invest in South America to ease illegal migration, stop China in our backyard, and create a new American empire.	10	4	3	0
17	Amend the amendments—the American president, governors, mayors, school superintendents, university chancellors, and other critical officials must be of Judeo-Christian faith.	10	5	5	0
18	American colonies on the moon and Mars, harness solar power from the moon and bring it home, robotic manufacture chips on the moon.	8	3	2	2
19	Instead of financial/ military aid, Israel and Ukraine can be American ally territories like Puerto Rico; no other country will dare to invade them anymore—the likelihood of supporting this new initiative.	10	8	7	1
20	Home for every veteran, national policy, every church/ synagogue adopts a veteran family, National Potluck Sunday for veterans and military personnel.	10	9	9	2
	Weighted average score in percentage.	95	54	50	26

> Takeaway: Make America LOMAH again. (Make America the land of milk and honey again.)
>
> But I have said to you, "You shall inherit their land, and I will give it to you to possess, a land flowing with milk and honey." I am the LORD your God, who has separated you from the peoples.
>
> Leviticus 20:24 (NKJV), "He has brought us to this place and has given us this land, 'a land flowing with milk and honey'" (Deuteronomy 26:9, NKJV).

(03/21/2023)

45. MR. MAHATMA GANDHI

He got a law degree from England. He was a very bright lawyer. He was treated like a third-class citizen in South Africa. While he was traveling in first class in South Africa, the train conductor threw him and his luggage out of the train compartment when the train stopped. This incident was an eye-opener for him. That incident sparked the fire of India's independent movement called "Quit India" to drive out Brits from India. When he returned to India, he realized that his own people, the so-called and self-proclaimed first-class, were treating some of their own brothers and sisters of the same skin color even worse than British people. That was another eye-opener for him. He realized that this is not a white and brown issue but the corrosion of human malicious, rusted hearts over many centuries for selfish purposes. What is needed is a change of the human heart.

He named those socioeconomic-religious victims of India as "God's people." He had a good intention in naming this, but his own people made a mockery of this new name of class he created. Instead of healing the centuries-old wounds, this created a new wall of casteism that still exists in India to this day and time of the modern world. It is a shame for India. Human classification is as bad a practice as human trafficking is; it doesn't go away, even though Indians have more exposure to the modern world than ever before. Shame to India; it is about time for young, new India to tear down the chain of classification of human lives.

Come out of the dirt and breathe the fresh air of America, where all of your Indian immigrants enjoy equal opportunities for all. What Mr. Gandhi could not do, can Mr. Modi do? Time will tell, but certainly, he can. The time is right, and he should loudly proclaim every day "the religious freedom and equal opportunities for all" to be a hero of human rights.

Indians in India have to learn a lesson from their counterparts who immigrated to America. For the most part, they have left their classification "old Amul cheese" behind them and melted in Wisconsin cheese, made in America. However, about ten percent could not get filtered through the American flag, although they pledge allegiance, "One nation under God," so that they can get green cards to bring their brothers, sisters, fathers, mothers, brothers-in-law, sisters-in-law, and everybody else they had listed on their wedding party invitation.

Time out. My Hindu friends, now you should have learned from America that class is not anybody's birthright; you have to earn it. You can't steal the gold medal; you have to run the race. You can't be awarded a Nobel Prize for free; you have to invent the unthinkable. You shouldn't put down any human being but promote and encourage them to bring out the seven colors of humanity that will surprise the world around you.

(03/27/2023)

In the summer of 1968, I was a physics teacher at VP Science College, affiliated with S. P. University in the Gujarat state of India. This was the first time in India under the auspices of the Peace Corps program that a physics professor from the University of Arkansas arrived to conduct seminars for the physics instructors on how to teach college students American standard physics textbooks. America sent hundreds of American-authored physics and chemistry textbooks to support these seminars. This was the first time in India that American textbooks were introduced at this university.

The head of the post-graduate Physics Department appointed me as an assistant to the American professor because I was the only one who could understand him very well. I prepared all the experiments and demonstrated them to the class of teachers to assist the American professor. All the teachers were Hindus except for me. They all were very friendly with me until the last day when a devil hiding in the corrupt human heart of one Hindu Patel professor jumped out. It reminds me of Dr. Jekyll and Mr. Hyde's story.

It was the final quiz day. The American professor asked ten questions:

1. Which is the latest element in the periodic table?
2. How does the eye recognize green color as green and not red?

3. Why is fusion used and not fission to produce electricity?
4. How does an atomic reactor produce electricity?
5. What is the difference between viscosity and surface tension?
6. What is the velocity of light?
7. What is Einstein's equation that relates mass with light velocity? How did he come up with it?
8. What is relativity?
9. What is one Ampere and one Volt? And one ohm? How will you determine these?
10. What is inductance? What is the Henry?

I answered all questions correctly. That turned into a flash point. The summer seminar adjourned. We were walking out from the second floor.

Professor Patel from Anand Science College shouted, "What is the latest element in the periodic table?" And he shouted again, "Low Casteism." It was a derogatory racial slur he spit out from his dirt-full mouth to insult me.

Jealousy is more poisonous than cobra. I never thought a man of this status was so sinful and filled with mud inside while looking straight outside. He had education but no knowledge and wisdom. The class attendees started laughing loudly and mocking me. If jealousy has a color, it is darker than a black hole. If humanity has a wavelength, it covers both ends, ultraviolet and infrared. This man was possessed by jealousy, and his culture failed to teach him humanity, respect, and decency. You can have all the education that will showcase the world library, but you might be empty without knowledge and wisdom, blindfolded with a band of custom, religion, culture, traditions, historical heritage, or political pollution because you don't see another human being as good as you or even better than you.

You may point the finger anywhere you like, but the center of the circle is you. India, wake up and listen to Umashnakar Joshi's poem (the vice-chancellor of Gujarat University, India, a long time ago), "The wind from the west is blowing hard. Oh nation of buffalo dug, rise up now. How can you not see what's so obvious to me?"

O jealous people, open your eyes and see the face of the civilized world of the twenty-first century, or else adhere to the jungle of the

Himalaya to reside with the Flintstone family. Congratulation. Yabba dabba doo to you.

Takeaway: O, my self-proclaimed classy friends, open your eyes and ears and listen to the melody of American harmony. Wash your brain with civility detergent to get the casteism and racism poison out. Wake up, India. The sun has risen in the west; morning has risen in the east. What you think is your civil right to self-proclaim your class is actually a 2000-year-old dark satanic crime.

(4/4/2023)

46. ARE YOU GJC OR JAISE THE?

America is not a publicly owned company listed on Wall Street, but it is I AM WHO I AM's kingdom, and its stocks are offered free on Cross Street. The only price you have to pay is to sign off on an application called ten commandments. This doesn't require a change in your bank account but a change of your heart. The unique beauty of this kingdom is that even if you don't sign off on the ten commandments, I AM WHO I AM is willing to sign off your green card as a guest card to love you and welcome you. Why? It is because the followers of Yeshua are instructed to offer the basket of nine fruits to our guests. Read the Bible.

Every Christian should offer the fruit basket to our green card holders. Guests should be filled with love, joy, peace, patience, kindness, goodness, faithfulness, gentleness, and self-control (Galatians 5:22).

If you are not GJC (Gentile or Jewish or Christian), you are not Americanized yet but *jaise the* (Hindi word, meaning status quo, no change). American Christians have more responsibility and have to work more to witness to those who are not Americanized yet.

When you place your right hand on your heart (I hope so because they don't respect like this in India) to accept a green card or become a US citizen and swear the pledge of allegiance, I hope you really mean it. "I pledge allegiance to the Flag of the United States of America, and to the Republic for which it stands, one Nation under God, indivisible, with liberty and justice for all."

That God is the living God of America, the God of Abraham, Isaac, and Jacob, George Washington, Abraham Lincoln, and all other American presidents.

Takeaway: When you take this pledge to get a green card, do you really know who is that God who made this nation indivisible, with liberty and justice for all? All fifty-one jewels are indivisible because they are protected by the rod given to Moses by the Almighty God to lead his Jews and Gentiles sons and daughters above all. Read the Bible; you will find it. If you don't see it, you are mentally and spiritually blind.

(4/5/2023)

47. WAKE-UP CALL FOR THE FIVE EYES

(UK, America, Canada, Australia, and New Zealand.)

Wake up, nations, and see what has happened in the UK, USA, Ireland, Fiji, Australia, and New Zealand is knocking on your door. The ghosts begging for Halloween candies at midnight in a colorful costume are here. Beware. Although they are waiting for a cracked open door, once they are in, you will lose your promises given to your promised land by "I AM WHO I AM."

Five Eyes, you are the new Israel; see what the Lord has said,

> But if ye shall at all turn from following me, ye or your children, and will not keep my commandments and my statutes which I have set before you, but go and serve other gods, and worship them: Then will I cut off Israel out of the land which I have given them; and this house, which I have hallowed for my name, will I cast out of my sight; and Israel shall be a proverb and a byword among all people: And at this house, which is high, every one that passeth by it shall be astonished, and shall hiss; and they shall say, Why hath the LORD done thus unto this land, and to this house? And they shall answer, Because they forsook the LORD their God, who brought forth their fathers out of the land of Egypt, and have taken hold upon other gods, and have worshipped them, and served them: therefore hath the LORD brought upon them all this evil.
>
> 1 Kings 9:6–9 (KJV)

Takeaway: Immigrants from Asia and South Asia have planted their manmade gods in your vineyards. They are nice people and human beings but have been lost in the wilderness. Witness to them, love them, guide them, and bring them into the house of the living God. If not, your vineyards will turn into graveyards of darkness.

---

48. WHAT DOES THE FUTURE HOLD FOR AMERICA?

With the way technology and science are progressing in America, this is how I imagine what America will look like in the next century.

Americans will be able to vote in any election from the comfort of their house, using a box connected to the satellite controlled by the election commission.

Mail will be delivered by drones; the United States Postal Service will be out of business.

The mailboxes will be converted into drop boxes on the roof, just like a fireplace chimney.

The whole fireplace wall will be a large pull-down TV screen, like a blind on the window.

The house walls material will be new synthetic fireproof, multi-colored, water and termite retardant, easily cleanable, with no-need-to-paint synthetic material similar to the one used for aircraft fuselage.

America, Canada, Mexico, and Israel will become one nation under God, and the sun will not set on this new kingdom.

Traditional mailboxes on the curbside will be replaced by drop boxes on the roof. Robots will drop the mail.

American home office or den will be called a control room to control and connect the TV, Internet, phone, health information, financial planning, stock market update and advice, uplifting sermons from the Bible, online pastors for spiritual advice, online grocery store, online worldwide shopping mall—all integrated into one unit.

You will be able to convert your living room into an instant theater to see videos or movies or hold a worldwide video conference.

Each major town will have its own satellite. Each city hall will control its satellite.

America will establish colonies on the moon and Mars.

A solar reactor station on the moon will harness electricity from the solar radiation, convert it into microwaves, and then transmit it to the station on the ocean to the land.

America will establish a world university on the Internet, which will be ten times more powerful than now.

Christianity will dominate the world because the world is hungry for unconditional love, abundant mercy, and priceless forgiveness, which only Christianity can offer.

Fission energy reactors will replace atomic reactors. America will be first.

Sun radiation conversion stations will be built on the moon to transport heat from the sun to the Pacific Ocean and be converted into electricity in California.

Gas stations will disappear and will be replaced by electric charging stations on freeways, schools, hospitals, industrial complexes, and shopping malls.

Plastic credit cards will disappear. The back of the cell phone will be an integrated credit card connected to your bank account that will monitor your account balance and pay bills on time automatically, with no late fee.

No need to type on a laptop; just speak in English, and the microprocessor will type it by itself.

Speak in English, and a language processor will automatically translate it into all major languages of the world because when Christ arrives, He will call us to "come to Me" in Hebrew.

> Takeaway: Christ will arrive in Washington, DC. Everyone will be judged, but His abundant mercy, fatherly love, unsurpassed sympathy, consistent forgiveness, kingly kindness, gracious grace, and richest generosity will endure our shortcomings if we repent faithfully and humbly like a child now.

(4/14/2023)

49. FROM RIVER TO RIVER, GANGES TO HUDSON, BECAUSE HE SAID, "I AM WITH YOU IN YOUR DARKEST DAYS."

It was a very stormy evening that turned into the darkest night I ever saw.

Depression is a bubble that slowly squeezes in, isolates you from all possibilities, blinds you, and puts you in a pressure cooker. Red hot bubbles crash onto a glass chamber that is filled with poisonous gas. The glass chamber was surrounded by your friends, relatives, well-wishers, and enemies, all gathered by the wall to see you suffering and mock you to make it worse. They were laughing, yelling, joking, screaming mercilessly, and shouting like bulldogs, "I told you." They got a kick out of the drama unfolding before their eyes.

I saw a red man with horns on his head and a giant wrench in his right hand. He disconnected the oxygen supply tank. I slowly stopped breathing. They sang Hindy film songs, and the red man said, "It is finished."

Unbelievably, I heard a *boom*. Someone pushed the glass bubble very hard. It hit the rock and shattered into a million pieces.

I heard a voice, "Open your eyes. I am alive; I am here. Touch My hand and come near to Me."

"Who are you?"

The man in a white garment said, "I am who I am, My child. Do not be afraid. It is all over. I am not finished with you. Stand up and look at Me, not at the crowd. Touch me; I am alive; it's Me."

Luke 24:39 (NET), "Look at my hands and my feet; it's me! Touch me and see; a ghost does not have flesh and bones like you see I have."

Genesis 28:15 (NET), "I am with you! I will protect you wherever you go and will bring you back to this land. I will not leave you until I have done what I promised you!"

Isaiah 41:10 (NET), "Don't be afraid, for I am with you! Don't be frightened, for I am your God! I strengthen you—yes, I help you—yes, I uphold you with my saving right hand!"

Isaiah 43:5 (NET), "Don't be afraid, for I am with you. From the east I will bring your descendants; from the west I will gather you."

Acts 18:10 (NET), "Because I am with you, and no one will assault you to harm you, because I have many people in this city."

Daniel 10:18 (KJV), "Then there came again and touched me one like the appearance of a man, and he strengthened me."

And I saw a bright, shining star coming out from the white cloud. And a man in a silky white gown raised His right hand, drew a cross on my forehead, and said, "Get up. Take your backpack. I am with you; I will bless you and lead you from the Ganges to Hudson again. Go in peace, be brave, and win the world. I am with you." And He disappeared.

I had no money in my pocket, no friend or relative was willing to help, and I didn't know anybody in America, and yet, one divine call from my dream kept me alive.

Takeaway: That's the day I decided to leave the River Ganges in India behind me again and headed to River Hudson in New York in search of my dreamland, America, for a new life promised by my "I AM WHO I AM" in a white, silky gown.

Philippians 4:13 (NKJV), "I can do all things through Christ who strengthens me."

(4/14/2023)

50. WHY DID JESUS SAY, "I AM THE WAY, THE TRUTH, AND THE LIFE"?

Life is a beautiful, full-time companion; find someone awesome to live with you.

Life is a flower; smell the roses in California poppies.

Life is gold, karat for a crown but no carrot for the health. Have you ever heard "crown him, crown him"?

Life is a diamond; place it in a secret place for your wedding day; she deserves it.

Life is a song; find someone who will sing with you and play her violin.

Life is a rock, not a lock; it is meant to be hard; climb it, and the prize is yours.

Life is a melody; play on a piano, though musical it sounds, harmony it spreads.

Life is a bird, not an ordinary creature but a hummingbird.

Life is a river; it starts high at birth and ends low at the ocean, but trust Him; He will lead you to the green pasture in between.

Life is a flute; make a sweet sound to everyone's ear, no more fear.

Life is a gown, one-piece, silky golden fibers, just for you, the one they stole at the cross.

And He said, "I am the life and truth, who shall ever come to me, will never fail. Listen, my friend, you don't need anyone else; go by yourself."

Life is an early morning dream; don't waste it. Darkness has broken. He said, "I am alive." Everything will be bright; hold on, trust me.

Life is a Christmas gift; don't put it under the tree; unwrap it now and enjoy it.

Life is a star, a North star that will lead you where Christ was born; follow Him.

Life is an arrow; don't see the maze of seven circles; aim at the center. Stay focused on the dot, and bingo! You will win.

Life is a precious seed; don't throw it in the dirt. Plant in fertile soil, and it will produce tropical fruits for generations to come.

Life is a song; don't sing it alone; join the choir. The world needs your tune.

Life is a string; it is all messed up; where is the end? But believe me, it's not a dead end.

Life is a precious stone. Mounted on a necklace, it turns tears into smiles on the face of your girl.

Life is a book full of sorrows and smiles, fall and rise, lost and found, hidden and revealed, discouragement and victory, ugly and amazing grace—it's all part of the journey called stepping stones of life.

Life is a marathon. Practice every day, one mile at a time; you ought to finish. You can do it if I can do it. Although I am so weak, I am strong because my strength comes above.

Life is a fire; going through it will burn the outer oxide layer, and that will make you sharper than a two-edged sword.

Life is a train. It is slow for some and express for others; no matter what, every station counts. Take a deep breath and look out; sooner or later, you will arrive at the station.

Life is a raging inferno, the beast that will destroy all you have built; watch the human tongue that sparks the fire.

Life is beautiful; trust me, don't waste it. Hang in there; I will hold your hand. I love you, care for you, and will carry you through. Hold on for a while; darkness will break, and morning will arrive. Voice from heaven, can you hear it? Hang on for a while, and your cup will overflow with showers of blessings. Read this again and again until you get it.

Life is an ocean full of sharks; learn how to swim and survive. Otherwise, someday, someone will push you to the edge of the ocean, and they will eat you raw.

Life is a journey in the ocean, through the desert, to the mountain, arriving on the green pasture only by His grace.

Bramvel Christian

Life is like a butterfly; before you count the colors, it will fly away. So, count your blessings and name them one by one. You will be surprised by what the Lord has done, and you will be blessed and be a blessing to others.

And my Father said,

"And Jesus said unto them, I am the bread of life: he that cometh to me shall never hunger; and he that believeth on me shall never thirst" (John 6:35, KJV).

"Jesus saith unto him, I am the way, the truth, and the life: no man cometh unto the Father, but by me" (John 14:6, KJV).

"And he said unto me, It is done. I am Alpha and Omega, the beginning and the end. I will give unto him that is athirst of the fountain of the water of life freely" (Revelation 21:6, KJV).

Takeaway: Live life to its fullest. Life is beautiful, a precious gem gifted by your heavenly Father. God bless you; I will wait for you on the other side of the mountain. I pray I am yours, and you are mine forever and ever, amen! And amen! And amen!

---

51. "I WILL BLESS THEM THAT BLESS THEE" (GENESIS 12:3)

"I will bless those who bless My people." This is true for America. On October 6, 1973, Israel was attacked on Yom Kippur, the holiest celebration for Jewish people. The attackers, Egypt and Syria, were backed by nine Arab states and the Soviet Union. Ms. Golda Myer, the first woman prime minister of Israel, called President Nixon in the middle of the night. The president realized that if America did not help, Israel would be finished. So, he ordered his defense secretary, "Make sure that Israel has everything that Ms. Golda Mier needs." Within hours, American Air Force planes were soaring over the sky of Israel. The enemies ran back for their lives to their foxholes. Israel is America's second Puerto Rico because she is the apple of His eye.

Here is what Golda Mier said, **"For generations to come, all will be told of the miracle of the immense planes from the United States bringing in the material that meant life to our people."**

Here is what the Almighty Jehovah has said,

"For thus saith the LORD of hosts; After the glory hath he sent me unto the nations which spoiled you: for he that toucheth you toucheth the apple of his eye" (Zechariah 2:8, KJV).

"And I will bless them that bless thee, and curse him that curseth thee: and in thee shall all families of the earth be blessed" (Genesis 12:3, KJV).

Now you know why America has been blessed and will continue to be blessed as long as America stands behind King David's star with King Solomon's wisdom.

This is also literally true for me. I was blessed abundantly by having Jewish friends on my side in my professional career. I met Mr. S. Zwass when I was working at Hughes Aircraft Company, El Segundo, California, in 1985. He was a magnetic design engineering guru of his time. He taught me how to design, build, test, and troubleshoot a hundred types of transformers and inductors, the basic components of the power supply every electronic device needs. He was a subject matter expert (SME) in the magnetic field and yet was the most simple, kind, humble, generous, and loving person I have ever met. He was my magnetic guru. I felt like I was ordained by him to build magnetics.

I designed several transformers for Hughes Satellite Company, which later became Boeing Satellite Company in El Segundo, California. I still remember it was my designed transformers used on TBN (the world's largest evangelical television network) first satellite. I still remember Mr. Paul and Jane Crouch of TBN came to the satellite assembly line bay area at the Boeing Satellite Company in El Segundo, California, to pray on the first satellite we built for them.

The other Jewish friend who became my peer to enhance my technical knowledge and support me in my difficult time was an extraordinary, superb, brilliant technical director, Mr. Rosenberry. No matter how complex a technical problem or system or equipment might be, he would understand the complexity and provide technical direction on where to go from here to generate the solution. The most amazing human brain I have ever met! He was my guru to solve technical problems. I owe him a lot. God bless him.

Another brilliant Jewish friend was Mr. Yahill. This man was my manager but treated me as his friend. He always encouraged me to solve the most difficult technical problems. He always said, "Bram, if anybody can do it, it's you."

I remember one time at Boeing, we were trying to formulate a solution for a technical problem using a computerized technique. I was doing everything correctly, but for some reason not getting the correct viable answer. Yahill was standing behind me, and he said, "Oh, go one more time; you are almost there." And bingo, in a few minutes of trials, I generated a solution for the problem. Yahill, I wish all managers would be like you.

Takeaway:

And I will make of thee a great nation, and I will bless thee, and make thy name great; and thou shalt be a blessing, And I will bless them that bless thee, and curse him that curseth thee: and in thee shall all families of the earth be blessed.

Genesis 12:2–3 (KJV)

Did you know more than 50 percent of the billionaires in America are Jewish people, even though their population is less than 2 percent?

(4/21/2023)

52. IS THERE A GOD? SCIENTISTS ARE ASKED THIS QUESTION AGAIN AND AGAIN

Human beings are so small that they can't comprehensively visualize the presence of God in His entirety. It's like an ant visualizing an elephant. There is a fundamental frequency called the frequency of Genesis miraculously generated by His Spirit. Light waves, sound waves, and electromagnetic waves called basic science are subsets of that fundamental Genesis frequency. Scientific knowledge can reveal some of the wonders of science, but only the "beyond the science" knowledge and wisdom can reveal the presence of God. The "beyond the science" is granted to those who make themselves humble and register in His university that teaches from the catalog of Matthew 13.

Matthew 13:11 (NIV), "He replied, 'Because the knowledge of the secrets of the kingdom of heaven has been given to you, but not to them.'"

This knowledge will open your third eye to see His presence. You don't need to go to school to attain that knowledge and wisdom; it is free. The only thing you need is to surrender to that call. The problem is we don't want to listen to that call because we are so proud of our scientific toys that we ignore the knowledge and wisdom that comes from above.

Today's CD produces marvelous sound because the original soundtrack is modulated with a laser beam on a hard nickel plate called a master stamper. It took more than ten years of hard work, cutting-edge technology, and tons of money to perfect the product. How do I know? I was the research engineer and pilot production line manager of the DVD/CD first ever produced in the world by a company called MCA Disco Vision in Torrance, California, a subsidiary of Universal Studios, California. But can you imagine how thousands of years ago, BC, He, the creator of the universe, used an unthinkable amount of megawatt laser to chisel out the ten commandments on the hardest rock in the Sinai desert and sliced out two tablets as a gift to Moses? And you say there is no God? Think, my friend, think twice, think again and again.

Nuclear missile-armed nations boast that they have the power to destroy their enemies in the blink of an eye. But did you know that to launch a missile or mine, you need a very small device called an electro-explosive device (EED) to ignite first? If this very small device fails, the supper destroyer will fail, called dud in technical language. How do I know? I was a component engineer for the Trident nuclear missile program managed by Hughes Aircraft Company, El Segundo, California, and a failure analysis engineer for the Aerojet Company, Downey, California, supplying antitank mines and antipersonnel mines to the US Army. But He didn't need a small igniter to destroy Sodom and Gomorrah or create a monster storm and still keep alive Noah's arc. This happens even today, and you say there is no God? Are you sure? Think, my friend, think twice.

Did you know that to keep a satellite in the same orbit, a periodic puff of energy needs to be blasted? Then, how do the earth, moon, Saturn, Mars, and all other satellites of the galaxies stay in the same orbit without anybody giving a periodic puff of energy? Who injects the periodic blast? And you say there is no God? Think again, man. There is a supreme engineer of the universe, and his name is Emmanuel, "God is with us."

Matthew 1:23 (KJV), "Behold, a virgin shall be with child, and shall bring forth a son, and they shall call his name Emmanuel, which being interpreted is, God with us."

Did you know the highly sophisticated GPS doesn't work for submarine navigation at that depth? But a simple periscope does! In the same way, if you are humble, mild, and mellow and open your heart, the knowledge and wisdom beyond the catalogs of Harvard, Stanford, and MIT will be granted to you, and the creator of the universe will be revealed to you. You will know there is a God.

Proverbs 1:7 (KJV), "The fear of the LORD is the beginning of knowledge: but fools despise wisdom and instruction."

Proverbs 2:6 (KJV), "For the LORD giveth wisdom: out of his mouth cometh knowledge and understanding."

Do you know how many stars are in the sky? Sure, we know that the universe has a lot of stars. And by a lot, we're talking about up to a trillion stars per galaxy. And it's estimated that there are about a hundred billion galaxies in the universe! Go figure! Who created them? Who keeps them lighting day after day? Man, you are too small to understand it. Believe me, there is a God. Read the Bible; the Bible is an antenna that connects to the KW station (knowledge and wisdom). Beyond the amplitude modulation of AM and frequency modulation of FM that will bring your life refreshing good news, there is a God.

> Takeaway: "And God made two great lights; the greater light to rule the day, and the lesser light to rule the night: he made the stars also" (Genesis 1:16, KJV).
>
> Oh, Lord, open my eyes; I want to see You. Open my ears; I want to hear You. Heal my hands; I want to touch You. Fill my breath; I want to love You. Grant me knowledge; I want to know You. You are before me; the science is behind me. I will follow thee; let math follow me.

(04/30/2023)

53. WHICH NATION HAS A MORE POWERFUL WEAPON THAN THE ICBM?

The answer will surprise you. So, then, what is it? Who has it? The answer is every nation on this planet has it. It is called the human tongue. The human tongue is like a 70/30 stainless-steel/nickel knife that will split apart someone in a fraction of a second. It is an arrow that will cross through the rocks of the Grand Canyon of Arizona in a flash of a moment. It is poison from a cobra, a greater pandemic than COVID-19. It's a bullet from an AK45; once triggered, it can't be retrieved. It's a weapon and a blessing, depending on how you use it. The highest-read book in the world called the Bible, says,

"The nobles held their peace, and their *tongue* cleaved to the roof of their mouth" (Job 29:10, KJV) (emphasis added by the author).

"Keep thy *tongue* from evil, and thy lips from speaking guile" (Psalm 34:13, KJV) (emphasis added by the author).

"The mouth of the righteous speaketh wisdom, and his *tongue* talketh of judgment" (Psalm 37:30, KJV) (emphasis added by the author).

"The *tongue* of the wise useth knowledge aright: but the mouth of fools poureth out foolishness" (Proverbs 15:2, KJV) (emphasis added by the author).

Then, can this weapon neutralize the violence that can destroy humanity? The answer is yes.

"There is one who speaks rashly like the thrusts of a sword, But the *tongue* of the wise brings healing" (Proverbs 12:18, NASB) (emphasis added by the author).

Takeaway: My friend, watch your tongue; it's a two-edged sword. It can bring healing or destruction, depending on how you use it. Broken glass cannot be restored, and spoken words cannot be pulled back. Harsh words can tear apart a person from the mountain to the canyon, but encouraging words can lift the person from the ground to the sky.

54. WHAT'S THE DIFFERENCE BETWEEN A CHRISTIAN AND A PIEZO CRYSTAL?

Both are the same. How?

I was working as a new product project engineer for the Mattel Electronics Company in Hawthorn, California. Mattel Toys, the largest toy company in the world, came up with electronic musical instruments for the first time in the world. The sensor used in this equipment is called a piezo crystal. This is a unique crystal that has amazing electro-mechanical properties. It can transform mechanical energy into an electrical pulse and vice versa if you know how to. I had vast experience with piezo crystals while I was working for the Hughes Aircraft Company in El Segundo, California. So, Mattel's manager hired me on the spot.

My next job was at Aerojet, Downey, California. They are the largest manufacturer of antitank and antipersonnel mines. I was hired as a failure analysis engineer to find out when the mine's triggering sensor failed. I was hired because the heart of the sensor is piezo crystal, and I had vast experience with it. My life changed from making music with a piezo crystal at Mattel to destroying evil forces and their tanks at Aerojet with the same piezo crystal technology. What a job change to make a livelihood!

The piezo crystal has unique properties. Stress it mechanically, and it will generate an electrical pulse. Apply electrical energy, and it will transform it into mechanical vibrations that can be modulated into a sound wave.

The Christian is a synonym of piezo crystal. If you are a Christian, expect suffering. If you are stressed, produce electrifying love, joy, compassion, and generosity.

If you are electrified, forgive them; the electric pulse will transform into a wave of blessings for you.

On January 17, 1999, an Australian Christian missionary, Graham Stuart Staines, along with his two sons, Philip (age ten) and Timothy (age six), were burned alive in India by a Hindu vigilante group called Bajrang Dal just because they were serving the poorest of the poor in the Orissa state of India. In a court trial, Graham's wife, Gladys Staines, said, "I forgive them."

"That during a severe ordeal of suffering, their abundant joy and their extreme poverty have overflowed in the wealth of their generosity" (2 Corinthians 8:2, NET).

> Those whom the LORD has ransomed will return; they will enter Zion with a happy shout. Unending joy will crown them, happiness and joy will overwhelm them; grief and suffering will disappear.
>
> Isaiah 51:11 (NET)

Twenty-four years later (this year), on May 3, 2023, in the northeast corner of India, ethnic violence broke out in Manipur State that killed hundreds of people. The Hindu extremist group paraded three Christian women naked on the main street, sexually assaulted them, and killed their family members to destroy witnesses. The devil never dies; he resurrects himself in one or the other form and brings death, sorrow, fire, casualty, sadness, and destruction. But the sons and daughters of the living God will never die either and will be remembered as the messengers of a new, awesome life full of love, joy, peace, forgiveness, kindness, and generosity, even offered to their killers.

In His last hour on the cross, Jesus Christ said, "Father, forgive them; for they know not what they do. And they parted his raiment, and cast lots" (Luke 23:34, KJV).

Takeaway: If Christ comes again to Silicon Valley, California, an incubator of new technology, He would say to Californians, "My beloved sons and daughters, you must behave like piezo crystals.

If you are stressed, produce electrifying love, joy, compassion, and generosity like a piezo crystal. If you are electrified, forgive them; the electric pulse will generate a wave of blessings for you, like a piezo crystal.

(05/01/2023)

55. CAN YOU PROVE THE PRESENCE OF GOD IN A LABORATORY TEST TUBE?

The quick answer is *no*.

The question was asked to one of the great theoretical physicists of our time, Dr. Stephen William Hawking. "Is there a God?"

He answered, "Before, we did not have a high-level science and technology knowledge, so we accepted the presence of God. Now, we can't prove it theoretically on the chalkboard or experimentally in the laboratory; therefore, there is no God."

Mr. Hawkins, you are wrong; you missed a critical constant in your theoretical equation calculation. Here is why: I have studied theoretical physics and quantum mechanics as part of my master's degree in solid-state physics.

See *Classical Mechanics* by Goldstein textbook. The theory of the motion of a top has an application in the navigation gyro system. In layman's language, I conducted a seminar labeled "Keep your eye on the ball." I was able to explain this very complex guidance system to US Navy top brass first-class commanders because of my graduate level three physics class theoretical knowledge.

First, the man-made laboratory is a small backyard tool shed to test the creator of thousands of galaxies. You need a grand-scale laboratory to experiment with the grand-scale design that is the presence of your creator; everything else is an ant compared to an elephant. The good news is that the grand-scale laboratory already exists; it is your universe.

As I said before, there are two disciplines that can explain the design of galaxies. One is called learning of science and technology, which needs theoretical knowledge and four-wall laboratories that explore how things work within the reach of human boundaries. **The other discipline is called the power of knowledge and wisdom, more powerful than the**

Argon million-watt laser beam, can't be mastered in the four walls of a school or laboratory, and is way, way beyond the capacity of the human being.

Then, how to get it? First, be humble; get down on your knees to the ground level and believe and trust that there is a supreme power, the creator of the universe.

For example, Einstein believed that there must be a relation between matter and energy without knowing it or doing any experiment. Lo and behold, many years later, it was proved in the laboratory that Planck's constant is true.

For the first time in the world, the atom was split, generating a vast amount of energy that proved Einstein's theory, which he simply believed might be true. In the same way, if you surrender, be humble, and search within you, it is free and will be revealed to you. To understand the presence of God, you need knowledge and wisdom; it is so simple and plain and yet far beyond science and technology.

Look around. Why are roses grown on the rose plant and not on orchids? Why do banana trees grow bananas and not potatoes?

(05/02/2023)

He created the earth, the sun, the moon, and all other planets of our galaxy. Now, the world's most powerful telescope tells scientists that there are billions of galaxies like ours. So, does that tell you how great our creator is?

Man-made satellites periodically need an energy boost to keep them in the same orbit. How do I know? I worked for Hughes Aircraft Satellite division, the pioneer of the satellite industry in the world, which became Boeing Satellite Company later on. I designed several transformers for different satellites. So, I know firsthand how satellites work. And I have wondered all these years, who is the marvelous, brilliant, extraordinary engineer who created all these planets that do not need an energy boost to spin in the same orbit from day one to today? Did you get it now, my friend? There is a living God.

Our God is so big, dear Dr. Hawkins, that His presence can't be verified in your test tube in the four walls of the small lab.

GPS doesn't work when you deep-dive under the water in the ocean. So, the submarines use scientist-designed navigation systems. Did you know that even the world's most accurate manmade navigation system depends upon the God-made North Star? How do I know? I was a chief engineer for the Navy Program Office, Huntington Beach, California, and I certified navigation sensor accuracy. Every time I aimed the telescope at the North Star, I asked myself, who nailed the North Star in the sky so that it doesn't move a fraction of a second (minute-angle measurement)? And you say there is no God, my friend? Think again.

(05/03/2023)

If you want to see the presence of God, your lab should be as big as one of the galaxies, and your test tube should be as large as Wyoming. Go to Yellowstone National Park and watch the Old Faithful. Oh, magnificent, larger-than-life, always faithful, rises to the occasion. I stand there and ask, "Who sparks this wonderful fountain twenty-four seven from the belly of the earth?" It reminds me of my hero Billy Graham's crusade's favorite song, "Then sings my soul, how great Thou art, how great Thou art!"

Oh, Old Faithful, you remind me how great and faithful my God is.

Stand before the Old Faithful and watch him rise on time every time, and your soul will confess that there is a God; you will see the presence of God.

If you want to scope the presence of God, go to Grand Canyon, Arizona. Can Michelangelo paramount these rocks in seven colors that are brighter than the oil paints of old centuries in cathedrals? I stand there on the glass platform and sing, "O Lord, my God, when I in awesome wonder, consider all the works Thy hands hath made."

Who painted these spectacular row after row of ancient rocks? Oh my God, how great Thou art! Will You write ten commandments on these Grand Canyon rocks again for the world to see Your presence?

The brilliant sculptor Gutzon Borglum carved the four greatest US presidents on the granite rock of Mount Rushmore in Keystone, South Dakota.

Someday, someone like him, an American hero, will carve the ten commandments on a grand scale font size on the granite rocks of the Grand Canyon, and it will be called American Mount Sinai. The world will rush to Arizona to see this wonder, and the wise men and women

who are granted knowledge and wisdom from above will raise their right hand and proclaim, "Oh God, I see Thy presence; You are here."

If you want to see the presence of God, go to Niagara Falls, New York, and watch the spectacular world's largest kaleidoscope. Before your eyes, the drama unfolds: seven-color flowers of water droplets are dancing in the rain. And an angel appears in the midst of the foggy mist and sings,

When through the woods, and forest glades I wander
And hear the birds sing sweetly in the trees
When I look down from lofty mountain grandeur
And see the brook, and feel the gentle breeze
Then sings my soul, my Savior God to Thee
How great Thou art, how great Thou art!

How can you say there is no God?

If you want to see the presence of God, go to Sequoia Park in northern California and drive through the trunk of the old mighty Sequoia tree. Aim as high as your human eye can to see the top of the tree; you may lose your cowboy hat and still want to see the top of the tree. And I sing, "Then sings my soul, who planted this tree? How great Thou art, how great Thou art!"

If you are still not convinced about the presence of God, kneel down on your knees and ask for His knowledge and wisdom called BEST: Beyond education, science, and technology. You will be convinced there is a God.

Takeaway: God's master design is far beyond the human brain to understand in the four walls of the laboratory. But the beauty is, just be humble, trust, and believe; you will understand heavenly mystery by divine knowledge and wisdom that will be given to you free, just like Einstein did not perform any experiment but understood earthly mystery $E = mc^2$ by physics and math that you can learn in the lab.

---

56. WILL AUTOMATION OF SCIENCE AND TECHNOLOGY DEGRADE HUMAN'S ABILITY AND CREATIVITY?

The answer is no.

Around 1960, the bankers in Bombay, India, protested against the use of IBM computers in the banking industry, fearing that it would take away their jobs. Today, there are more IT engineers from India on H1 visas in the USA than in any other nation in the world. Even the CEOs of Microsoft, Google, IBM, and other tech titans are from India. What happened? India realized that the future is driven by science and technology. Wake up, break up the shackles of casteism, rise and shine above old ideology, come out of the cocoon, and see the sun has risen in the West instead of the East.

Read the poem by famous Gujarati Umashankar Joshi, once the vice-chancellor of the Gujarat University, India, "*Pachim na viara vaya, uthne ukarda jo to nathee*" (in the Gujarati language). The meaningful translation would be, "Wind from the west is sweeping across (the world); wake up, o pile of Asiatic buffalo dung. Don't you see (the industrial revolution is here)?"

Today, you will see laptops in every corner of India, but the living standard is still far away from the Western world. Casteism silently persists, and freedom of religion and speech is subdued under the name of socialist democracy. Most Hindus are nice, loving, caring, and generous people, but some extremists and vigilantes silence the voice of the minority. Some of our friends from this ideology have also somehow immigrated to the Five Eyes, polluting the Judeo-Christian faith, culture, and community.

We need to invite them to our house of worship to show Christlike love, joy, peace, generosity, and kindness to win their hearts and

minds. They are not our enemies, just lost lambs (cows for the Pacific Ocean). God bless them. Remember what Matthew said,

Takeaway: "But I say unto you, Love your enemies, bless them that curse you, do good to them that hate you, and pray for them which despitefully use you, and persecute you" (Matthew 5:44, KJV).

(05/04/2023)

57. DON'T GIVE UP; YOU ARE NOT ALONE. HE SAID, "I AM WITH YOU; TRUST ME"

Do you feel like one of these?

- Alone, put down by the dark evil of the world, and neglected.
- Running behind everybody else, feel like at the end of the line, depressed and pushed to the brink of sorrow.
- Find nowhere to go, victim of the cultural-socioeconomic madness, and torn apart by blind custom, culture, and ideology.
- Segregated by fanatic religious groups and punished by supernatural blind believers.
- Forced into the labor camp under the name of re-training and classified by demonized self-proclaimed aristocrats.
- Feel like this is the end of the world and strangled by the chokehold of your own countrymen.
- Exploited by unfair, cruel, illegal, satanic casteism schemes, and although you are at the top of the class, doors are closed.
- Living under the mercy of corrupt, jealous, ignorant, backward, compared to modern world standard society of any nation.
- Embroiled under the net of artificial racism.
- Living in a democratic country that feels like an apartheid state.
- Brainwashed by ersatz religious gurus to accept discrimination as it is your fault, loaded with a heavy burden.
- Anchored by your own homeland that can't be lifted anymore.

Listen, my friends, the Holocaust can burn the human tents, but the Spirit of the living God will prevail, and the soul will rise to the highest peak, higher than Moses can raise his staff, and the man of steel will rebuild the spectacular new Jerusalem. Go and see the new Canaan, Tel Aviv.

Jeremiah 30:17 (NASB), "'For I will restore you to health, And I will heal you of your wounds,' declares the LORD, 'Because they have called you an outcast, saying: "It is Zion; no one cares for her."'"

Because Jesus Christ said, "Come to me, all you who labor and are heavily burdened, and I will give you rest" (Matthew 11:28, HNV).

Trust and believe that you are the prince and princess of the royal family of God, pure as gold, precious as a diamond, bound to be a winner, promised by the one who gave His life for you, the Son of the living God—His name is Yeshua. No one will touch you, no one.

Takeaway: "'Do not be afraid of their faces, For I am with you to deliver you,' says the LORD" (Jeremiah 1:8, NKJV).

"Do not be afraid, for I am with you. I will gather you and your children from east and west" (Isaiah 43:5, NLT).

"Do not fear, for I am with you; do not be afraid, for I am your God. I will strengthen you; I will help you; I will hold on to you with my righteous right hand" (Isaiah 41:10, CSB).

(05/05/2023)

58. HOW CAN YOU RANK A HUMAN BEING EVEN BEFORE THE BABY IS BORN?

That's what India does. India is the only nation in the world that created casteism thousands of years ago to exploit groups of people for the benefit of other selfish groups. The Western wind is slowly curing this cancer, but it still prevails in the illiterate minds of some fanatics in India and abroad.

Casteism is a slavery that has roots of inequality and discrimination so deep that it will take generations to root it out.

The majority of Hindus are nice people, but a small group of old orthodox roots take over the majority. As individuals, they are friendly, kind, loving, and great people, and I have so many Hindu friends. I was teaching physics at a science college in India. Every member of my physics department, all Hindus attended my wedding. Can you imagine that can happen in the Western world? But for some reason, the voice of the majority remains silent, suppressed by the violent fraction of old-thinking extremists within the beautiful Hindus.

Casteism is a black cloud of racism and ignorance hanging over India that smears India's image in the civilized world. Some Indians have brought this mud in their luggage here to the Five Eyes nations. In the name of Jesus Christ, we need to witness more to these nice people. Hypocrites smile and greet you at the front, but then they take a U-turn and spit out racist rants at you on your back. God has created all men and women equal; there is no such thing as upper class or lower class in a civilized world. It is a manmade game of a blind culture to devalue the human being for a selfish purpose.

(5/8/2023)

Bishop Tutu of South Africa once said, "Why do I need a passport in my own country?" It was due to apartheid. Millions of victims of racism in India ask the same question in a different form, "How can I be a second-class citizen in my own home country even though I am brighter than the so-called upper class that doesn't know how to spell their names?"

It is because of thousands of years old extreme violent discrimination of casteism, another name for racism, slavery, or apartheid. These racial victims are bright, intelligent, gorgeous, progressive, creative, educated, wise, and the living God's loving, wonderful people, and yet a small fanatic group of ugly, illiterate, stupid, religiously blind, extremist, Stone Age, neo-Nazi people see them as second-class citizens. Hello!

The other shocking fact is that when this type of mentality carried by immigrants arrives in the Five Eyes nations, they complain about discrimination against them! Hello? You treat your own country's people in the same way or even worse than this, don't you remember?

Do you feel the earthquake of racism/casteism now? Welcome, and I hope you will carry the message home.

Takeaway: The United States Declaration of Independence, by Thomas Jefferson, says,

We hold these truths to be self-evident, that all men are created equal, that they are endowed by their Creator with certain unalienable Rights, that among these are Life, Liberty and the pursuit of Happiness.

That was in 1776. India, wake up and open your eyes; now it is 2024.

(5/13/2023)

59. LANDING ON THE DREAMLAND

April 1973. TWA landed at LAX at around 9 p.m. The Salvation Army officer and his wife picked me up at the airport. He would take me to the Harmony Hall, a halfway house near USC, run by the Salvation Army for sober alcoholics. This was prearranged by my local Salvation Army training college principal in India, Major Coles, a Canadian missionary and an amazing God's man.

I didn't know anybody in the USA. I had no relatives, no friends, was not acquainted with anybody, had no help from anybody, and I had just landed at LAX.

Wow! The 405 Freeway, with four lanes on each side, at night time, was lit with thousands of watts of electricity. It was thousands of times brighter than Bombay. It looked as if the whole of Los Angeles was celebrating Devali, a Hindu festival in India. I had never seen so many city lights in my life. Bombay seemed like a small village compared to LAX.

My heart pumped harder and harder. How can I drive on this monster city's highways? How shall I survive? Where shall I get a job?

They didn't understand my heavy accent; I had to say things two or three times.

The officer asked, "What did you do in India?"

I said, "I was teaching physics in a science college affiliated with the University of India, called Sardar Patel University, named after a local political hero."

"Oh, yeah! Man, you have tons of opportunities in this country."

I said to myself, "Oh, yeah? We will see."

The officer told me to meet Dr. Doctor Robert, a salvationist at Hollywood Salvation Army church. He was the LA School superintendent. I wrote down his name.

The officer gave me his business card, left me at Harmony Hall, and said, "Good luck, my friend. Call me if you need any help."

Tears ran down my cheeks. I said, "Thank you very much, sir. I will need you."

The residents at Harmony Hall were so nice to me. I couldn't believe it, but to my surprise, many of them were veterans, and quite a few were highly educated professionals. However, they were somehow victimized by the devil called alcohol. American people have not seen this other side of the richest nation in the world. I was shocked. The government, schools, public institutions, corporations, communities, associations, churches, temples, synagogues, and many others have neglected these wonderful people who did so much for the country.

They were doing something to get back on their feet. One man was selling clothes; he gave me a new pair of pants. Another was selling candies at a nearby Veteran's Hospital; he gave me a basket of candies. Another man gave me a beautiful Bible, and he marked a verse that says, **"Do not fear, for I am with you; Do not be afraid, for I am your God. I will strengthen you, I will also help you, I will also uphold you with My righteous right hand"** (Isaiah 41:10, NASB).

I quickly realized that life is an assignment without a manual, only a marching order, just like in the military that does not mention the destination but says, **"The final stop will be revealed as you turn one stone after the other until you can go no any further"** (signed by Lt., CDR).

Under the signature, the note says, **"Pack up and get going or simply sit here for a ride and be sorry your whole life; the train already passed when you were snoring on the station bench."**

The next day morning, I got Los Angeles Times and started flipping job opportunities page after page, but I did not have a phone to call the employers. What do I do?

(5/15/2023)

I closed my eyes, and I saw a PowerPoint projected on the wall.

Slide #1: "This is the day the LORD has made; We will rejoice and be glad in it" (Psalm 118:24, NKJV).

Slide #2: Rejoice and be glad in it even when you don't have a phone and a friend near you.

Side #3: The poor will be rich even if you don't have any change in your pocket; of course, in America.

"Listen to me, dear brothers and sisters. Hasn't God chosen the poor in this world to be rich in faith? Aren't they the ones who will inherit the Kingdom he promised to those who love him?" (James 2:5, NLT).

Slide #4: When you hit the wall, that's the point where you need one more push to tear down the wall.

Slide #5: Trust and obey; there is a green pasture behind that wall.

> And when the LORD sent you out from Kadesh Barnea, he said, "Go up and take possession of the land I have given you." But you rebelled against the command of the LORD your God. You did not trust him or obey him.
>
> Deuteronomy 9:23 (NIV)

Slide #6: Circle the wall. Even if it takes seven times, it will fall, tumbling down.

"When the people heard the sound of the trumpet, and the people shouted with a great shout, that the wall fell down flat" (Joshua 6:20, KJV).

Slide #7: Any questions?

I opened my eyes and said, "No, sir, just like Joshua told to Moses."

"And Moses said unto Joshua, Choose us out men, and go out, fight with Amalek: to morrow I will stand on the top of the hill with the rod of God in mine hand" (Exodus 17:9, KJV).

Takeaway: In 1961, President Reagan said, "Mr. Gorbachev, tear down this wall!" Mikhail Gorbachev was the general secretary of the Communist Party of the Soviet Union. Finally, the Berlin Wall came down. Can America bring down the walls of alcohol, drugs, homelessness, mental illness, and high divorce rates that divide human beings and the community?

(5/16/2023)

60. DISHARMONY IN HARMONY HALL

My first two weeks in Harmony Hall felt like a jail for a lifetime. Here is what happened first two weeks.

It was Monday. So I could not sleep the whole night. I didn't have a phone, didn't have a car, no one had time to give me a ride, and I didn't know anybody. So, I prepared a hand-written resume overnight, made ten copies the next day morning, got to Los Angeles Times from the front desk, selected ten ads, and copied the addresses on the envelopes. I put my hand on ten copies, prayed that a miracle would happen, and ran to a nearby post office located close to the USC campus to mail the envelopes. One time, I was teaching at a university in India; now, I was watching the university with the hope of getting a job, even if it was cleaning the university in America.

On Tuesday, I went out to a nearby store and got some quarters, dimes, and nickels to gather ten dollars. Then, I walked to the nearby public phone booth with a marked copy of Los Angeles Times job opportunities in one hand and a writing pad in the other.

First call:

The front desk lady asked, "Where are you calling from?"

I answered, "From a public phone."

Lady, "Come on. This is not Los Angeles Mission; this is a big corporation," and put down the phone.

I said, "Amen." Two dollars went down the drain.

Second call:

"Hello, I am a solid-state physics major graduate and calling for a position you have advertised."

Lady, "What? You have a very heavy accent. I can't understand. Are you from the Middle East?"

Me, "No, from India."

Lady, "That's even worse." The phone got cut off.

Third call:

"Hello, I am answering your job opening for a lab technician."

Lady, "Hey, man, can I call you back? My boyfriend is on the line. What is your phone number?"

Me, "I don't have a phone number."

The lady slammed the phone. I could hear in the background that she was laughing. I heard, "He doesn't have a phone number. What's in his wallet?"

Me, "Okay. Say hello to your boyfriend."

Fourth call:

"Hello, good morning. I am looking for a job at your company."

Lady, "What good morning? It is Monday. I have a hangover. My boss is running late today. The cheap coffee machine he bought doesn't work on Monday, just like him. Call back when he comes. Bye, and good luck." She slammed the phone.

I saw a man outside the phone booth. It looked like he was very angry at me and frustrated. He said, "You, foreigner hanging there for hours, stop calling your girlfriends. You never end the phone calls. Get out of here. Let me use this phone; it is not your property."

And I ran as fast as I could; I lost ten dollars change.

I smiled. "Lord, thanks. This land is not my land, the land of opportunities. Where is it?"

The voice said, "Oh, come on. At least there is a public phone on every major street, not like in your country!

And I said, "That's true." The tears ran down my cheeks as I walked back to the dormitory.

On Wednesday, I had only a hundred dollars given by the Reserve Bank of India, the maximum limit for the foreign exchange set by the government of India. I was watching every penny that I had to spend. Phone calls for job search were not working, so I decided to go to Los Angeles downtown. Maybe I could find a job in big offices there.

Harmony Hall was on 32nd Street, near the USC campus. I walked to the dining hall and prepared peanut butter and jam sandwiches. Thank God, there was always plenty of supply of peanut butter, bread, jam, and Tabasco sauce in the dining hall. I mixed them all to make sweet, sour, and hot spicy sandwiches; it tasted so good. That was the closest to spicy curry I could make. Then, I put them in a brown bag. I walked thirty-two blocks in a suit and tie, with a map in one hand and a brown bag in the other. Oh, what a beautiful city, amazingly clean, all glass skyscrapers; I never saw anything like this, even in Bombay. God bless America! Hope I can find a job in this town.

First tower:

"Ma'am, I am a science graduate looking for a job."

The blonde, blue-eyed receptionist said, "Okay, give me your resume."

Another lady, "Ha! Ha! Please mail me your resume; here is the business card."

I said, "I don't have a home or typewriter; where can I get a resume done? Hey lady, I am a living, loving, breathing resume; why can't you accept me? Ask any questions you have."

Second tower: The sign outside read, "We are hiring now."

I was excited. This was it. There was a big line, and I was the only one in a suit; it was embarrassing.

The lady at the front desk asked, "Do you know how to mix tequila and bon bon?"

Me, "What's that?"

Lady, "The drinks. This is for our five-star hotel bar."

Me, "I never had alcohol in my life. It is not good for you."

Lady, "Sir, that is what we are hiring for. This Coke is for you. Enjoy, it's nonalcoholic." She gave me a bottle of coke and said, "Goodbye, and good luck to you."

I walked out. At least I got something free to drink, not a bad deal. Nobody would give Cokes for free in India; it's a luxury drink there.

Third tower:

It looked like an insurance company. Life doesn't come with insurance; you write your own policy with hard work, education, hope, and prayers. The rest is in His hands. The Almighty will amend your policy if you trust and obey Him. Let me try here.

There was nobody at the majestic front door, so I rang the bell. A man in a business suit with tons of files in his hands came out.

Man, "Your professional experience, sir?"

Me, "I have a college degree. Looking for any job."

Man, "Okay. This green file test is for you."

Then, he led me to an exam hall. There were about fifty people taking the exam. I finished the test in about forty-five minutes while others were still struggling. The exam had English and math, with fifty questions in each section. Waiting in the luxurious drawing room, I wished I could get a job there. Mr. Job Master came and took me to a nearby booth.

"Mr. Christian, you did excellent in math with 100 percent correct answers. However, you did very poorly on the spelling test. Unfortunately, that does not meet our hiring criteria. Sorry."

I didn't have the courage to say anything, so I simply said, "Thank you," and walked out. And I told myself, "I told you, there is no insurance in life, but this is not the end of life, either. Statistically, if you don't have insurance, you live longer, so it is a gain anyway. March on."

A precondition for being successful is to eliminate preconditions from your vocabulary.

And the voice said, "Even if you are a bad speller, Microsoft will spell for you, but it can't do math for you. It is better to be a math wizard than a good speller. Math will figure it out for you; keep adding, just one more time."

(5/17/2023)

It was Thursday.

One of the residents said, "Why don't you try to sell for Fuller Brush? You can make a lot of money. All you have to do is just go house to house, knock on the door, and get a membership card filled out. The company will ship all the cleaning supplies they need, and you will get a commission."

"This sounds good; let me try."

So, he gave me a bag full of flyers, forms, and membership cards to fill out. He gave me a 101 on how to sell Fuller Brush products.

I went on my way to a nearby neighborhood.

(5/18/2023)

First house:
Ring, ring.

Me, "Good morning, Ma'am. I have a fantastic product to keep your home shining. Would you mind giving me a few minutes so I can show you?"

Lady, "Wish I could, but I don't have a need for it now. Maybe in the future." She shut the door.

Second house:

Me, "Hello, sir. I have a great product to keep your car and home beautiful. Let me show you."

Sir, "I am retired and living on a limited income. I can't afford it now, but thank you." He shut the door, cracked open the door to make sure I left, and then shut it again.

Third house:

Me, "Hello, my friend. You have a nice dog. Would you mind seeing this catalog? It has all kinds of goodies for your dog; he would be very happy."

Young man, "Sorry, my friend, I have no time. I have millions of things to do. Maybe at some other time, but not today."

His bulldog started barking, and I ran as fast as I could.

Fourth house:

It was a small house next to a magnificent cathedral. I knocked on the door.

Me, "Sir, are you a pastor? You have a golden cross hanging around your neck and fish on the front door."

Pastor, "Yes, my son. A man shall not live by the bread alone but by the words of the Lord. Are you selling Girl Scout cookies?"

Me, "No, sir. It is better than cookies. I'm selling all kinds of cleaners that will make your church so shining and smell so good; all faithful will stay until you pronounce benediction."

He bent backward and laughed and laughed so loudly that all neighbors could hear. "Listen, my son, you are correct. Let your work shine before the people so that they will praise your creator. This cathedral was built after the Second World War. You might not have even been born at that time. My father was a pastor here. Every Sunday cathedral was full of people. If you are five minutes late, you have to stand in the courtyard. More than half a million Americans died in that war. **Today's new generation has forgotten the Almighty God. Only a handful of** people attend the church service. The cathedral is empty. Tell me, do I need a cleaner?"

Me, "Thank you, sir. I know the song the missionary in my hometown used to sing all the time, 'How great is Thy faithfulness.' Now I see how great Americans also are; millions gave their lives in the wars, and now they welcome immigrants like me. Unbelievable."

He gave me a one-dollar bill, said, "God bless you, my son," and then shut the door.

I saw tears in his eyes.

I was very tired now. I had to walk back at least five miles, but I decided to try one more house.

Fifth house: A macho man on a giant motorbike, at least 160 ponds, came at sixty miles per hour and parked the bike in the driveway.

Macho, "Hey kid, what's up? What are you doing here?"

I saw an AK-47 hanging on his side. I was scared to death.

Me, "Officer, I have a terrific leather jacket for you in this catalog, and it's on sale."

Macho, "Look, kid, you came at the wrong time. My bank account is empty; I can't buy even a cheap shirt. Give up on the leather jacket; this is my third divorce. Good luck." He pulled the gun out and opened the garage, and I saw several guns hanging on the wall.

I said to myself, "Oh my God, what a day," and ran as fast as I could with a sack full of magazines hanging on my shoulder. This was not for me; this was it. I would have to find something else.

After two weeks, on Friday, I received some mail. I opened the first envelope. It started with "We regret." I didn't read any further.

Americans are in a good mood on Friday. How about visiting the Salvation Army divisional headquarters? **I walked from 32nd Street to downtown.**

(5/19/2023)

I arrived at the Salvation Army divisional headquarters. At the front desk, the receptionist said, "Good morning. Do you have an appointment today?"

Me, "Appointment? I don't have a phone, but I am from India, the son of a Salvation Army officer, and I want to see Colonel George."

Lady, "His calendar is full today. Can you come back at 4 p.m., just before he's done for the day? Maybe he can squeeze you in."

Me, "Yes, whatever it takes. Here is the letter from my divisional commander, a missionary from Canada, Major Coles."

I walked out. I walked on the street. It was lunchtime. I smelled French fries, hamburgers, hot dogs, pizzas, tacos, burritos, and tamales at every corner. I craved the burritos, the closest to my homemade curry and *Rote*. This was America, the food basket of the world, as my grandpa used to say. I was tempted to buy a hot dog, but I did not. I had to watch every penny. I did not see a fountain of water at any food stall in Bombay; here, every cart had a fountain of Coca-Cola, Pepsi, Mountain Dew, and many others.

This was America, the land of honey and milk but raised on soda.

I walked to a Chinese coffee house and ordered a black tea. I was sitting by the glass window, watching people from all over the world, every color, kind, shape, and size. Amazing, this was Los Angeles. You name any country; you see that nationality here. I was sipping black tea with sugar and cream and biting a homemade peanut butter/jelly sandwich.

The Chinese owner walked to me and yelled, "Hey man, you can't bring food from outside and eat here; this is not India."

"Sorry, sir, I did not know," I said.

Chinese, "Now you know. Don't do it again. When I came to America, I did the same thing; now I own three restaurants in Chinatown."

Me, "This is America, a melting pot with added chow mein, noodles, sushi, rice, and chicken tikka masala curry."

I had heard on Voice of America radio station, "America is UNO, literally. God has blessed America, literally. There is no other nation in the world where every ethnicity enjoys this nation has to offer, is prosperous and lives in harmony most of the time."

I still had to explore this and prove it. What I saw was a wall in Los Angeles. The graffiti all over it said, "'Do not even think to climb this wall. If you touch it, you will die instantly. Welcome, now go home'—by an immigrant."

But underneath the writing, the wise man has encrypted, "If you cannot break the brick, jump over the wall; do whatever it takes.

The green pasture is hidden behind this wall." And that was what I intended to do, whatever price I had to pay.

Think of this: Centuries ago, Columbus traveled the farthest point from his homeland in search of India to find gardens of spies, but instead, he found the gold mine of America. Today's American scientists and engineers repeat his journey, traveling to the farthest point from the earth to the moon and Mars. This nation transforms cartoons into Columbus; see the examples from Thomas Alva Edison to Elon Musk and thousands in between; who can deny it?

I said to myself, "I have to wait upon the Lord and keep trying."

Takeaway: How does gold buried under the rocks turn into a jewel to shine on the pedestal of the princess' jewelry box? It goes through mining, grinding, chemical washing, refining at 1948 Fahrenheit degrees, and finally, stressful shaping in the mold that emerges as a beautiful piece of jewelry.

That's what exactly happens to most immigrants in search of the American dream. Carry on; the fire and stress and crushing you will go through is worth it because you are about to emerge from the mold as gold.

(6/5/2023) (I couldn't write for two weeks due to a cough/cold.)

61. GOLIATH AND FIVE STONES

I graduated with flying colors from a high school in my hometown called Anand, Gujarat state. I got a bachelor's degree in physics as a major and math as a minor with first class. I got a master's degree in solid-state physics with honors. College years were nothing but a struggle to survive and study. I had no financial support from anybody. I was living in a foster home, working full time at night at Amul Dairy as a dairy chemist, and attending college during the day time. How did I do it? Unemployment was twenty-four percent in India; how can you get a decent job and study at the same time? You never hear of anybody working full time and attending science college in India, even today. In India, all education expenses are fully paid by the parents, even today. So, if you are from an average family, in a country like this, you can't even dream to go to college. How could I do it? It is simply because I believed there is a power, the power of the Holy Spirit, that descends upon you and ignites the fire of knowledge and wisdom that transforms you inside out to fight against Goliath with five stones and a sling.

The five stones and sling I always carried in my backpack are:
1. His mercy endures me.
2. His kindness is abundant.
3. Be humble.
4. Be gentle.
5. Be patient; tomorrow will be brighter than today's darkness.

Colossians 3:12 (NET), "Therefore, as the elect of God, holy and dearly loved, clothe yourselves with a heart of mercy [1], kindness [2], humility [3], gentleness [4], and patience [5]."

And my sling is unconditional love from Him that mandates me to love others who hate me.

Colossians 3:14 (NET), "And to all these virtues add love, which is the perfect bond."

Let me be frank: I am not perfect; I keep losing stones and breaking sling, but He keeps sending new packages to me with a new sling every time.

During my master's study, I came home from college, sometimes on a bike, and if the bike was broken, on foot for five miles. It was very tiring. But I was tutoring Dr. Shah's son, Amul Dairy's general manager, and CEO Dr. Kurian's daughter, so I would run my bike to their executive bungalows. Dr. Shah's wife was an Australian lady, so kind and loving. I was paid three times more than the normal tuition fees anybody would charge for tutoring their son. The only condition was that his son should maintain an A grade in math and science so he could get admission to medical college. He did. This helped me to get a master's degree with honors in solid-state physics.

Unbelievably, in India, anybody can do this without zero financial support. My friends did not know this; I kept it secret all these years. Again, "Three in One" is before you, within you, and behind you against any war you have to fight; believe me, you are not alone. When you see the flame rising, expect showers of blessings just behind it; keep going. You will be amazed; the devil will pass by but will not touch you.

It was summer vacation time in 1967. S. P. University, in a small university town called Vidyanagar (city of knowledge), introduced for the first time American textbooks in India. American professors from known American universities arrived to teach and guide new textbooks in physics and chemistry. Because Indian professors had a hard time fully understanding American actions, the dean of physics hired me to work as a teaching assistant for a physics professor from the University of Arkansas. I could do it easily because I was translating American and British missionaries at the church. I was very successful in demonstrating physics experiments after the American professor taught theory class. I became very popular among the university staff. The university offered me a teaching position at the V. P. Science College on the same campus. Usually, you have to know someone to get a job in India. If you are a Hindu, your chances of getting a job triple. But I had a hidden divine power within me, and they didn't know.

Takeaway: There is a power in the name of Jesus Christ. All you have to do is just kneel down, wait upon the Lord, and ask; it will be given to you.

"In the name of our Lord Jesus Christ, when ye are gathered together, and my spirit, with the power of our Lord Jesus Christ" (1 Corinthians 5:4, KJV).

62. WE CAN'T EVEN SAFELY DRIVE ABOVE THE OCEAN, BUT OUR NAVY HEROES SAFELY DIVE BELOW THE OCEAN TWENTY-FOUR SEVEN

Let me tell you the story to explain what it takes to navigate a submarine even with the latest technology gears.

On the morning of October 28, 1981, two Swedish fishermen were hauling their catch back to Karlskrona when they noticed a mysterious oil slick. One of the fishermen, Bertil Sturkmen, later returned to the area to investigate and came to show a startling sight: a seventy-six-meter-long submarine wedged on its starboard side against the sharp rocks of Torumskär Island. An officer was standing on the submarine's conning tower, staring at him through binoculars and holding a machine gun. Sturkmen sailed back to Karlskrona and notified the nearby Swedish naval base, which harbored two of Sweden's three coastal defense flotillas. Karlskrona was well protected from attack due to its position in a shallow bay shielded by a belt of rocky islands, which demanded careful circumnavigation. Somehow, the submarine had wended its way through this daunting aquatic obstacle course to a point only six miles away from the base.

The patrol boat Smyge reached the grounded vessel, and Comm. Karl Andersson managed to converse with a crew member in German, who informed him that the submarine had strayed off course due to a faulty navigation system.

The boat in question was S-363, a Soviet Whiskey-class coastal patrol submarine, thus giving the incident its moniker "Whiskey on the rocks." (At the time, the submarine was widely misidentified as U-137.) The short-range diesel-electric submarine had a crew of fifty-six and had been designed in the 1940s with snorkel and battery technology derived from the Nazi Type XXI "electric boat." The Soviet Union built more than two hundred submarines.

When I was assigned to take charge as Technical Director (TD) for the Navy Submarine Navigation System Program Office in Huntington Beach, California, somebody printed the above story and gave it to me. I prayed in my office, "Oh Lord, who am I? Give me the knowledge and wisdom above the ocean I need, and take care of my heroes below the ocean twenty-four seven." Amazingly, He did.

Takeaway: If you are a child of God, fear not because He has overcome all fears. Do not be afraid; stay calm. He is in control at all times because He controls times.

Isaiah 41:10 (NKJV), "Fear not, for I am with you; Be not dismayed, for I am your God. I will strengthen you. Yes, I will help you, I will uphold you with My righteous right hand."

Isaiah 43:5 (NKJV), "Fear not, for I am with you; I will bring your descendants from the east, And gather you from the west."

Psalm 56:11 (KJV), "In God have I put my trust: I will not be afraid what man can do unto me."

(6/6/2023)

63. HOW DID I SOLVE THE TOUGHEST TECHNICAL PROBLEMS NOBODY ELSE COULD?

I have sharpened ten technical commandments, which I called TTC, during my professional career of more than fifty years. It may sound controversial; out of all norms, not one is orthodox, but trust me, it worked for me, and it will work for you, too.

1. Start your day with the prayer—Almighty God, give me this day my daily technical briefing bread because the engineer cannot be a winner by books only but by the grace, knowledge, and wisdom that comes from above. Amen. The power of the prayer is bigger than the world's largest nuclear fusion reactor; never underestimate it.

2. Get up before sunrise as Jesus did, and read daily early morning positive thought-provoking devotional words based on the Bible. I read Daily Bread. Make it part of your breakfast; it's your daily manna.

3. Cut off friendship with those who have no encouraging words, ideas, thoughts, dreams, or the Spirit of the living God to share with you. Let the German shepherd walk with you, and he will guide you to the frontline, not the cobra; he will bite you on your backline.

4. Make friends with those who bring out the good in you and lead you to the next level, who lead you to the first step of the staircase and never scare you about how high the ceiling is.

5. Always be thirsty to gain new knowledge and learn new techniques and skills; whether you can use them now or not, you will need some day. You will be glad you did it.

6. Yes, sports and Hollywood have their place; we need them for mental relaxation, but it is entertainment; it will not bring bread and butter to your dining table. You may know all sports statistics, but rather be Green Belt and Black Belt in the technical field to win a corporate Cherry Lane boardroom game. Your family, your community, and your country will be proud of you if you can create thousands of jobs.

7. Start with low-tech techniques first, such as palm tree branch analysis. High-tech techniques such as real-time X-ray, gas chromatography (GC), FTIR, Auge, and others are supplementary if you know what you are looking for. I will elaborate further on this as I describe how I solved the most difficult technical challenges of state-of-the-art, high-tech aerospace, and cutting-edge technology in the defense industry.

8. Build a team with those who bring fresh ideas, are positive thinkers, are open to suggestions, and smile even when a glass flask shatters in the lab by the heat of the problem.

9. Get your hands dirty. Don't sit in a glass window office; go to the lab, factory floor, or docking station and make friends with blue-collar. Those who make their hands dirty on the factory floor are more knowledgeable than those sitting in the glass window offices.

10. Create a war room, chart the strategy, and keep track of the progress because you are in a technical war. You are the commander-in-chief; take charge.

You will be amazed at how this discipline leads to success. I have already applied, fine-tuned, analyzed, and proved that these golden mantras and hidden jewelry collections in my Pandora's box work. Now, I share them with you. If you use my Pandora bracelet and are successful, please drop me a line; you will be entitled to be named as **"Revolutionary, TTC-certified engineer, winner of Bramwell TTC Pandora bracelet, finest jewelry never sold in midtown Manhattan, New York or Rodeo Drive, Beverly Hills, California. Winner of the year."**

Takeaway: You cannot solve technical problems by sitting at a desk in a glass window office. You have to get out and make your hands dirty in the lab and on the factory floor.

The secret of my success in failure analysis of the complex high-tech system:

To know why the most complex electro-mechanical unit failed at the top, you have to start at the bottom-up. Get the bill of materials (BOM) and learn how each component, material, and process is used to build that unit. You will find one of these elements missing, failed, misapplied, didn't meet the spec, or didn't test correctly.

64. DID YOU KNOW THE CD/DVD WAS INVENTED IN TORRANCE, CALIFORNIA?

The CD/DVD was researched and first produced in the world in a little lab called MCA Disco Vision, a subsidiary of Universal Studios in Torrance, California.

I joined the lab as a research engineer under a great scientist by the name of Gary Slatten, a godly man and my mentor, who made a great impact on my professional life. I was the first production manager of the pilot production line of the CD/DVD first ever mass-produced and marketed in the world. We had many technical problems as we started pilot production, just as any new product has to go through. It's not easy to transfer lab products on the factory floor. Because I had joined the lab when the twelve-inch diameter CD was produced in the lab, I knew every step of the processes and documented all the specifications to create the CD/DVD.

The most difficult problem for me was to prevent the injection molded plastic disk scratch-free when moving on the metal conveyor on the assembly line. All of a sudden, I thought about the party bal-loon. What if I keep these discs floating in the air? So, I connected air blowers underneath the metal conveyor. Lo and behold, the problem was solved! Not a single scratch was observed on the disk. I wish I had patented this technique.

Takeaway: There is no such thing as a complex problem; break it down into small pieces, and you will be amazed that for every complex problem, there is a simple solution. If you build a nest of complexity in your brain, the blackbird of impossibility will lay the eggs.

Build a nest of prayers, and the silver bird of possibility will lay the eggs. "For with God nothing shall be impossible" (Luke 1:37, KJV).

(6/7/2023)

65. HOW TO BEAT WALL STREET EXPECTATIONS IN A COMPETITIVE WORLD?

Transform your business from 1D or 2D to 3D viewers.

I visioned, experimented, perfected, and now I'm giving away my secret mantra as my gift to you. If you apply these 3D tools and are productive, donate to my Glass Cross Foundation to uplift millions like me in India and the world across. Here is the bride of the 3D tools for colossal progress; let me lift the veil.

1D: Map and optimize your process: IS vs. futuristic process. Focus on yield, quality, cost, and process cycle time.

2D: Transform your broken process into a gated process, streamlined, checklist-oriented, and governed by a trustworthy, trained, positive thinker process governor, not a manager. The statistics are a great tool, but it is a magical illusion also. Learn how to interpret statistical numbers. Is it a real oil painting of the Monalisa or a fake AI water art?

3D: Appoint a 3D executive who has a mindset and training in technical ten commandments (TTC) and will be responsible for implementing the above 1D and 2D.

Sit back and watch Wall Street knocking on your door; if not, get a new TTC CEO.

This works every time, I guarantee. I have seen experiments in several blue-collar listed among American top one hundred corporations. You need people who have natural creativity and positive thinking, are dreamers, and are full of joy and synergy you can watch on their faces, not necessarily with a PhD on their office tag.

Takeaway: If you don't have time to organize now, you will not have time to finish on time. If time is money, don't spend it under the blanket; get up and invest it in high-yield projects.

Reorganizing your assembly line in a logical sequence is the same process as fertilizing an orchard with a correct NPK fertilizer to produce bountiful berries.

66. "GOING TO AMERICA FOR FURTHER STUDY" —REALLY?

I won award after award in debating and elocution competitions during my high school and college career and was awarded the "Elite of the Elite Students of the Year" Award in my high school year.

When I saw hundreds of Patels after Patels advertising in the Indian daily newspaper, "Going to the USA for further study," because of a thumb on the scale and their bank account (nobody returns to India, by the way), I silently cried, "Why can't I?" I started to save every single penny I could. I started two jobs, teaching physics at VP Science College full-time and tutoring students in the evening. Two jobs five miles apart—thanks to my donated old bicycle that kept me going.

You have to declare yourself as a lower class (called scheduled class) in India to be qualified for affirmative action scholarship or grant or admission in highly reputed education institutes. I will never accept this social torture to degrade myself. However, many students do, unwillingly forced by the socioeconomic-religious and racial caste system structure that only exists in India in the world for centuries, and people are not ashamed of it in India or abroad. It will take another century to wash out this poison that has corroded India's culture and image in the Western world.

Surprisingly, some of the old Hindu hardliner extremists have brought this caste-COVID-2000 to the USA and other Five Eyes nations. West needs to confront it; otherwise, it will pollute our culture, ideology, and Judeo-Christina faith, where all human beings are considered equal, the children of the living God, not manmade figurines. There has to be a set of policies and procedures to help create an equitable landscape for all citizens for freedom, justice, education, employment, and practicing the faith that makes sense to them; it's not like that in India.

(6/9/2023)

Millions and millions of Judeo-Christians have sacrificed their lives to keep this nation as the living God's nation as their founding fathers and pioneers intended. The belief is that American immigration policy should be based on the fact that this is a Judeo-Christian nation and should be embodied and advocated as a philosophy that would continue to make the United States, in spite of all its flaws, the world's richest and most technologically advanced nation ever striving under the wings of the Almighty living God, Jehovah, only and not any other man-made god.

All immigrants, before they are granted the green card, should sign this declaration before a US judge.

Takeaway: "So God created man in His own image; in the image of God He created him; male and female He created them" (Genesis 1:27, NKJV).

So, no man has a right to disgrace any other man by telling him, "You are lower than me."

Therefore, Thomas Jefferson penned "all men are created equal" in the Declaration of Independence dated July 4, 1776.

India did the opposite in 1947 by calling victims of socioeconomic-religious persecution in India as scheduled class (lower class) in the Constitution of India. India, correct it; now is the time.

(6/10/2023)

67. THE OTHER SIDE OF THE WORLD'S MOST STUNNING ECONOMY

Most Americans don't know what's happening to the veterans. American heroes, when they return home, have no place to go. There is a hidden sadness behind the glamor and glory of the world's largest economy. The liquor glasses of so-called misleading "happy hours" have shattered the fragile lives of millions and millions of Americans into millions of broken pieces. There is only one worldwide entity that tries to mend these broken glass pieces back into beautiful vessels of life again. Its name is Salvation Army, and I saw it happening before my eyes. God bless the Salvation Army.

I concluded how difficult it was to find a job for an immigrant like me in the only nation in the world that landed a man on the moon. In India, you have to know someone to find a job. If you are a Patel in the Gujarat state, your chances to land a job on your lap triple than if you are a Christian. I thought it would be easy to find a job with such a high scholastic record, but I was wrong. My desperate search to find a job ended in agony. So, I walked to the Salvation Army divisional headquarters in Los Angeles.

The charming receptionist said, "Hello, do you have an appointment?"

And I said, "Do I need an appointment?" Nobody knows what an appointment is in India; we just walk into where we need to go. Of course, very few had a landline phone in 1973 in India. Today, they have more cell phones than roaming cows, dogs, and monkeys combined on the streets of India.

Anyhow, I met Colonel Wiseman and Colonel Donald, the men of God. I saw the photo of Jesus Christ on the face of these two men in blue with SA on their shoulders. I translated SA as sympathy and (willing to) assist.

I saw a cross in the sky when they stretched out their hands and hugged me. I saw a glowing halo on their heads when they took their hats off. They offered me a bubbling glass of Coke and cookies, and I saw the Last Supper painted on their hearts.

They asked me, "Where do you want to go?"

"To a center where I can get temporary food and shelter."

To me, a center means a place or a home where I can stay while looking for a job. To them, a center meant an alcoholic rehabilitation center (ARC).

Colonel Wiseman made several phone calls and said, "Good news, you are accepted at Santa Ana, ARC." I didn't know what the ARC was. But when you have no home, no friends, no relatives, no acquaintances, you will take anything to hang on. That's what I did.

The next day morning, I was at Santa Ana, ARC, and the fun began. What a different world; America has no clue what is behind the walls of the Salvation Army's ARCs. Unbelievable and amazing, a tornado of tragedy unveils here and out of chaos; once in a while, a miracle happens. I witnessed it myself. Every three out of five were veterans of Vietnam, Korea, or many other wars. Wonderful, loving, caring, brave, intelligent, and skillful people from every walk of life were here. They could repair watches, TVs, radios, vacuum cleaners, jewelry, and you name it. The finest salespeople, just like I saw at Sears stores.

They cut a cake to welcome me, sang Happy Birthday, and asked me to blow off twenty-five candles even though it was not my birthday. Later, I found out they were hungover. Tears ran down my chicks on the first day.

My journey to dreamland began here. These brave men, born in America, in a land where all you can be, ended up in ARC. Who am I to succeed?

And the angel appeared and whispered in my ears again and again, **"What is impossible for a man is possible for a man who trusts God because he trusts and obeys his creator, the architect of the universe, the Almighty God. The Bible says all things are possible unto him. Be a man of God. Stand up and go, charter your plan; don't sit down and cry."**

Luke 1:37 (NASB), "For nothing will be impossible with God."

Matthew 19:26 (KJV), "But Jesus beheld them, and said unto them, With men this is impossible; but with God all things are possible."

Psalm 71:16 (NKJV), "I will [stand up and] go in the strength of the Lord GOD; I will make mention of Your righteousness, of Yours only."

Takeaway: That was it. The same voice is still ringing in my ears at the age of eighty-four. Halleluiah. Amen. My friends, I challenge you: get up before sunrise, get up and go out and look at His amazing creations, the sky, the flowers, the birds, and the rising sun, and you will hear the trumpet playing the same challenge, "Get up and go," I hear it every day. That will armor you for the fight of the day to achieve your goal, your dream, your plan. My strength came from these verses:

Joshua 1:9 (NET), "I repeat, be strong and brave! Don't be afraid and don't panic, for I, the LORD your God, am with you in all you do."

Second Chronicles 32:7 (NET), "Be strong and brave! Don't be afraid and don't panic because of the king of Assyria and this huge army that is with him. We have with us one who is stronger than those who are with him."

(6/11/2023)

68. WHEN THE LADY OF LIBERTY GOT MARRIED IN NEW YORK

Lady Liberty got married on the afternoon of October 28, 1886, with Uncle Sam. America is a Judeo-Christian nation, a wedding gift by God to Jews and Gentiles given on this day. Read the tablet on her base, "Give me your tired, your poor, Your huddled masses yearning to breathe free, The wretched refuse of your teeming shore."

Now, read the Bible,

Matthew 11:28 (HNV) (emphasis added by the author), "Come to me, all you who labor and are *heavily burdened*, and I will give you rest."

Matthew 5:3 (KJV) (emphasis added by the author), "Blessed are the *poor in spirit*: for theirs is the kingdom of heaven."

Luke 6:20 (KJV) (emphasis added by the author), "And he lifted up his eyes on his disciples, and said, Blessed be ye *poor*: for yours is the kingdom of God."

Exodus 13:4 (NLT) (emphasis added by the author), "On this day in early spring, in the month of Abib, you have been set *free*."

Galatians 5:1 (NLT) (emphasis added by the author), "So Christ has truly set us *free*. Now make sure that you stay free, and don't get tied up again in slavery to the law."

Psalm 31:24 (NLT) (emphasis added by the author), "So be strong and courageous, all you who put your *hope* in the LORD!"

First Chronicles 18:14 (KJV) (emphasis added by the author), "So, David [America] reigned over all Israel [world], and executed judgment and *justice* among all his people."

Are you convinced now that America was chosen by Yahweh to be a torch of hope, freedom, and justice for all the people of the world? This was the beginning:

On January 1, 1892, the Ellis Island Immigrant Station opened, and seventeen-year-old Moore arrived from Queenstown, Ireland, in New York with her two younger brothers. Upon her arrival, a US officer welcomed her and gave her a ten-dollar coin. Since then, millions and millions have arrived in America in search of a dream, new life, a gift of opportunities wrapped in a paper of abundance of wealth, joy, peace, hope, liberty, justice, and freedom for all, provided they melt in the melting pot of America.

Takeaway: Go to Los Angeles or New York. You will smell hamburgers, hot dogs, pizza, tacos, burritos, sushi, and now chicken tikka masala on every street corner. And they all sing in harmony, "Through the night with the light from above, From the mountains to the prairies to the oceans white with foam, God bless America, my home sweet home."

Are you convinced now that America is a melting pot? Can any other country in the world say so?

---

69. WHY ARE AMERICANS SO GENEROUS, WEALTHY, JOYFUL, AND INNOVATIVE?

It is because the fruits of what they have achieved by sweating on the soil of a new land were shared by inviting the guests on green cards invitation to the wedding party called immigration to fulfill the living God's instruction stated below, with hope and prayers that they will dance with them on the same tune on American platform to enjoy the celebration. The majority did, and few didn't, but they decided not to return to their homeland as long as the party went on.

Instruction from God to America,

And Nehemiah [Uncle Sam] continued, "Go and celebrate with a feast of rich foods and sweet drinks [science, technology, innovations, and wealth], and share gifts of food with people [immigrants] who have nothing prepared. This is a sacred day [Fourth of July] before our Lord. Don't be dejected and sad, for the joy of the LORD is your strength! [military supper power].

Nehemiah 8:10 (NLT)

Nehemiah 8:12 (NLT), "So the people went away to eat and drink at a festive meal, to share gifts of food, and to celebrate with great joy because they had heard God's words and understood them."

And this is God's plan: Both Gentiles and Jews who believe the Good News share equally in the riches inherited by God's children. Both are part of the same body, and both enjoy the promise of blessings because they belong to Christ Jesus.

Ephesians 3:6 (NLT)

Takeaway: Instruction from America to immigrants, just like Moses asked his brother-in-law Hobab, "If you [immigrants] do [melt in the Wisconsin cheese of the melting pot] we'll share with you all the blessings the LORD gives us" (Numbers 10:32, NLT).

As long as the newly elected American president places his right hand on the Bible and proclaims, "Oh mighty God, help me so," the Statue of Liberty will raise her right-hand torch in Big Apple harbor, and my Jesus Christ, the redeemer of all, will stretch out both His hands on the rock of the Rio de Janeiro to bless the whole world. America will remain the most powerful military-wise, wealth-wise, cutting-edge technology and knowledge-wise, and the most generous nation on the globe wisdom-wise because the Bible says so.

(6/15/2023)

70. WHO IS YOUR GOD?

Read the first three commandments in the Bible that tell you who is our living God.

> You must not have any other god but me. You must not make for yourself an idol of any kind or an image of anything in the heavens or on the earth or in the sea. You must not bow down to them or worship them, for I, the LORD your God, am a jealous God who will not tolerate your affection for any other gods. I lay the sins of the parents upon their children; the entire family is affected—even children in the third and fourth generations of those who reject me. His name is I AM.
>
> **Exodus 20:3–5 (NLT)**

> But Moses protested, "If I go to the people of Israel and tell them, 'The God of your ancestors has sent me to you,' they will ask me, 'What is his name?' Then what should I tell them?" God replied to Moses, "I AM WHO I AM. Say this to the people of Israel: I AM has sent me to you." God also said to Moses, "Say this to the people of Israel: Yahweh, the God of your ancestors—the God of Abraham, the God of Isaac, and the God of Jacob—has sent me to you. This is my eternal name, my name to remember for all generations.
>
> **Exodus 3:13–15 (NLT)**

Takeaway: On April 30, 1789, the first president of the United States, George Washington, had an inauguration held on the balcony of Federal Hall in New York City, New York. He used the Bible to take an oath that was printed in London in 1765. After the ceremony, he kissed the Bible. Today, it is known as the George Washington Inaugural Bible.

President Barack Obama took the oath of office on a Monday. He placed his hand on two Bibles. The first was the Bible used by former President Abraham Lincoln in 1861. The second Bible was used by Martin Luther King, Junior. During his second term, he used his wife Michelle's family Bible on Sunday at a private ceremony in the White House.

Two hundred thirty-two years later, on January 20, 2021, President Biden used the five-inch-thick Bible that has a Celtic cross on the cover, and the Biden family has used it since 1893.

My immigrant friends, what we enjoy in America today is the result of raising the Bible from April 30, 1789, to January 20, 2025, and beyond, when the president of the United States places his right hand on the Bible and takes an oath,

I do solemnly swear (or affirm) that I will faithfully execute the Office of President of the United States, and will to the best of my ability, preserve, protect and defend the Constitution of the United States. [So help me God.]

The day this doesn't happen will be the darkest day in American history and will be the end of heavenly, divine blessings from above.

The God of Abraham, Isaac, Jacob, and Moses is the God of America; His name is I AM WHO I AM, Yahweh.

(6/19/2023)

71. IF YOUR GOD

If he didn't say, "Get up and follow me; I will lead you to Canaan, a land of honey and milk," then he is not God.

If he didn't say, "I was born in the most unwanted neighborhood, but the power in me powered every neighborhood around the world," then he is not God.

If he didn't walk on water, how can he make you walk on the rough rocky road of life? He is not God.

If he didn't make a blind to see, how can he make you see tomorrow's dream? He is not God.

If he didn't make a deaf to hear, how can he change your ears to hear the winning drum beats on the other side of the mountain of the troubles of life? He is not God.

If he didn't make a lame to walk, how can he walk with you and talk with you along the narrow road of life? He is not God.

If he didn't cure your disease, how can he make you pure and bright enough to win the gold at every Olympic of life? He is not God.

If he didn't raise a dead to life, how can he lift you up from the dead sea of brutality and abhorrence of this world to the abundant living water of new life so that you will never thirst again? He is not God.

If he didn't rise from the grave, how can he transform you from the rouges of society to the Koh-i-Noor diamond on the royal crown? He is not God.

If he didn't climb to heaven, how can he say, "Hey, look up; the sky is a limit for you. Don't let anybody fool you." He is not God.

If he didn't promise you that he will come again, how can he assure you that there is always a tomorrow hidden right behind the darkness of today. He is not God.

If he didn't reach out to the poor and hungry, can he feed the multitudes with only two loaves of bread and five fish? If not, he might be a good person, but not God.

When you were thirsty, if he didn't say, "Follow me, and I will give you the living water so that you will not thirst again," he might be a water fountain owner but not God.

If he didn't turn water into wine, he might be a bartender, but not God.

If he is a manmade figurine, he is not alive; how can he assure you and restore a new life? He is not God; he is not alive.

If he is a nice man or a kind king, is King Charles God? He is a king but not God.

God of gods, He is alive; His name is Jesus Christ.

"I am the *living one*. I died, but look—*I am alive* forever and ever! And I hold the keys of death and the grave" (Revelation 1:18, NLT) (emphasis added by the author).

Did your god teach you to visit people in need and be compassionate when someone was hungry, thirsty, home alone, lost a job, in the hospital, in prison, very desperate for help, ignored, marginalized, put down, insulted, and exploited for selfish purpose by his/her own community/country/religion/custom/tradition? And did you do it?

If the answer is no, your god might be a good person but not the living, loving Almighty, the creator of the universe, the real God.

Takeaway:

For I was hungry, and you fed me. I was thirsty, and you gave me a drink. I was a stranger, and you invited me into your home. I was naked, and you gave me clothing. I was sick, and you cared for me. I was in prison, and you visited me.

Matthew 25:35–40 (NLT)

He is my God, the Son of the living God, Jesus Christ.

---

72. LIFE AT THE ARC

Even today, if you visit a town or a city in India, you will see two poor persons at the front pulling the two-wheeler cart loaded with tons of load to make a living. You will see a giant procession of cars, buses, trucks, rickshaws, bicycles, walking pedestrians, and a man and woman pulling the two-wheeler carts with everybody else, a circus on the road, a live drama of real life played on the street theater. Sometimes, husband and wife do this job. The harsh reality of living in a corrupt, selfish, polluted caste system society turns human beings into horse carts.

Living at the alcoholic rehabilitation center (ARC) opened my eyes first time in my life. Donated stuff to the Salvation Army arrives at ARC for recycling. It is unloaded at the receiving dock and pushed on the conveyor belt. Mostly, ladies sort the usable stuff and throw them into a two-wheeler cart similar to one you see on India's streets to transport goods. This was my job, to pull the cart from one station to another. It was pretty heavy, more than 200 pounds, and I was only eighty pounds. It took me a while to learn a technique how to maneuver the cart. Can you believe it? A man with a master's degree in solid-state physics was pulling the cart to survive in America! Now, I was able to correlate the life and pain and reality of the husband and wife pulling the heavy-loaded cart on the streets of India's cities. But this time, it was in search of a dream instead of going back to India, I would prefer to pull the cart as long as it took.

I said to all these men, "On July 20, 1969, I was in India, and I listened on the radio; Apollo 11's crew members commander Neil Armstrong, lunar module pilot Buzz Aldrin, and command module pilot Michael Collins landed on the moon. At that moment, I decided to go back to the USA. So, where did they do such marvelous jobs? Where were these technical jobs?"

They laughed at me and said, "Are you crazy? You want a job, what do you think? Why are we here, man?" I cried but never asked again where the technical jobs were.

I walked on foot to the Salvation Army church in Santa Ana every Sunday. At the end of the service, Sunday after Sunday, I walked out the entrance, and the pastor, Major William Booth, would say, "We didn't forget you; we are praying for you. God bless."

That didn't help me. Every evening after work, I opened the mail and read only the first line, and if I saw the word "regret," I didn't read the letter; I would simply toss it in the trash can.

I met a Salvation Army officer who was in charge of ARC in Los Angeles. He told me to come down on Monday, and he might help me to search for a job. So, I took a couple of buses and went to his office. The secretary said, "So sorry, Lieutenant's dog needs a monthly health checkup, so he went to the veterinarian."

I said, "Thank you. I guess a dog is more important than a human being in America."

The Salvation Army major came every day, shook hands, smiled, and said, "Keep up good work."

I asked, "Major, do you know someone who can help me to find a job?"

Major, "Look, boy, I am new here from Canada; life is better here than in Canada. It must be true for you, too. However, I don't know anybody here, sorry." He laughed, walked away, and avoided me thereafter.

One day morning, I opened an envelope that said, "Call us to set up an interview." It was signed by, "Sincerely, Principal, Cantwell High School, Montebello, California."

I jumped in my room as high as I could. Tears ran down my cheeks. I knelt down and prayed and said, "Thank You, my Lord, my God. Finally, You opened the door for me."

The next day, an amazing countryman, Saradar Jee, Gurucharan Singh, gave me a ride to Montebello.

My first job in America: Cantwell Catholic High School, Montebello, California, hired me as a science teacher. The best day of my life in America, the day of a new beginning, new hope, and the first step towards the bigger dream. I taught physics, chemistry, and math to ninth, tenth, eleventh, and twelfth grades in 1973.

Takeaway: Life is never meant to be a garden of roses. Take one day at a time. The time will shape day after day until one day, you enter the rose garden. I will wait upon the Lord at the entrance until the doors are open and the bells are ringing.

Isaiah 8:17 (KJV), "And I will wait upon the LORD, that hideth his face from the house of Jacob, and I will look for him."

Isaiah 40:31 (KJV), "But they that wait upon the LORD shall renew their strength; they shall mount up with wings as eagles; they shall run, and not be weary; and they shall walk, and not faint."

73. LIFE GOES ON

In 1974, I moved to MCA Disco Vision, Torrance, California, a subsidiary of Universal Studios, California. I was a research associate. The outside board said, "Doctor's Office," but inside was a research lab where a laser-recorded and laser play-back video disk was being invented. This product became today's DVDs, CDs, and ROMs. The first prototype bulky laser player and large twelve-inch diameter laser disk are on display in the Science and Technology Museum in Washington, DC. I visited the museum, and the tag says, "The Inventor—Pioneer Corporation of Japan." Really? As far as I know, it was Invented by MCA Disco Vision, Torrance, California, which was acquired by IBM in the year 1980 and then sold to Pioneer of Japan.

I still have the original first lot-produced set of DVDs because I was the first manager of the pilot production line in Torrance, California. Someday, I hope the museum director will read this book and correct the display tag to give credit to American ingenuity and world-class inventing creativity. My mentor at this research lab was a great scientist, engineer, and inventing mind, Mr. Gary Slatten, who has most of the original patents on research and production of this new product, laser DVD/CD and laser player. I was there when we produced the first injection molded disk on a monster injection molding machine. We used a giant heavyweight hundred tons injection molding machine because we thought that we needed a very sturdy machine to mold a laser-recoded disk that had only a two-micron pitch. Now, the technology is so advanced that it fits in your auto dashboard.

(6/20/2023)

IBM was so mesmerized by this new product that it acquired Disco Vision in the year 1980. I was appointed the first quality control manager when IBM entered into the full mass production of these DVDs/CDs in Carson, California. I documented the procurement and quality specifications for every raw material to produce a DVD/CD. I also documented the quality control procedures for incoming materials, in-process products, and final products that would be shipped out.

Sometimes, I look back and ask myself, "How did I do that?"

And a heavenly voice whispers in my ears, "Only by the grace of God and the knowledge and wisdom granted free from above."

And I say, "Yes, Lord. Absolutely true. I will be humble; I want to see Your face."

Takeaway: "And whosoever shall exalt himself shall be abased; and he that shall humble himself shall be exalted" (Matthew 23:12, KJV).

"Humble yourselves in the sight of the Lord, and he shall lift you up" (James 4:10, KJV).

"Humble yourselves therefore under the mighty hand of God, that he may exalt you in due time" (1 Peter 5:6, KJV).

If necessity is the mother of invention, America is an incubator of inventions where the white eagle hatches golden eggs in Golden State, California, in a nest called Silicon Valley.

---

74. WHEN MAN SAYS, "NOT ME, OH LORD," GOD SAYS, "YES, YOU WILL, MY SON"

When a man says, "I can't," the Almighty says, "You can, and you will."

When a foolish man says, "Impossible," the creator of all says, "Remember, if I can split the ocean in two for Moses, I can turn the dark cloud of impossibility into a rainbow of possibility for you, My son."

When a lazy man says, "There is no end, there is no answer, all doors are closed," the heavenly Father says, "It took forty years, instead of forty days, for Israelites to reach Canaan. You waited thirty-nine hours; just wait one more hour, and the church bell will ring in a new era for you with a new song, 'Morning has risen; dark has faded out. You are the winner; the trophy is yours. Pain has paid off; the pressure of rock turned carbon to Koh-i-Noor, which you never thought was possible abroad.'"

When red-eyed says, "You are short," I say, "Explosives come in small packages."

When an ego man says, "Who are you?" I say, "I am nothing, but my Father is king."

When an ignorant man asks, "Where do you come from?" I say, "In America, it is not important where you came from; what is important is where you are heading. I am heading where no man has gone before."

"That's one small step for man, one giant leap for mankind," Neal Armstrong said.

Because the Bible says, "I can do all this through him who gives me strength" (Philippians 4:13, NIV).

When an imprudent man says, "Your ancestor's ticket was stamped for the lower gallery," I say, "For me, the sky is the limit. I will not settle for anything less than a 24-karat gold, where eagles dare. So, you mini, don't you ever dare again. I am a prince of the royal family of God in the heaven above your head; you are blind.

Titus 2:15 (NET), "Don't let anyone look down on you."

When a boorish man says, "Don't go; you don't qualify; it's tough; it is not for you," I say, "It's not me; it's the strength from above that is within me that guides me to go."

Takeaway: I'll go in the strength of the Lord, no fear, no shame, no penny, no map. I see the North Star; that's all I need. Once in America, the lighthouse I will see.

Psalm 71:16 (KJV), "I will go in the strength of the Lord GOD: I will make mention of thy righteousness, even of thine only."

(6/21/2023)

75. AMERICA PLANTS THE TREES AND LETS THE FRIENDS FRUITAGE THE FRUITS

Why can America invent a breathtaking, lifestyle-changing, one-of-a-kind, extraordinary, beyond-human-imagination product but can't perfect it?

It is partly because of corporate greed, partly because to be first in the market before imitators copy it, partly because, after all, money is the end game to pay back the hard work and pain of years, and partly because it is the American way to enjoy the life while someone else does the hard work. Uncle Sam says, "Why not?" Look back, and you will realize that it is the tradition, and it works. It's my vineyard; you plowed the hills, but I planted the vineyard. So, you deserve the best wine glass at my banquet, but the cellar is mine.

Look, I gave a one-way ticket to the Chinese, and they built a railroad from the Big Apple to the *Wild Wild West*, but nobody asked, "Where is my return ticket?" Even today, every Saturday morning, Chinese kids run to their private school to learn Chinese in New York and San Francisco and all the big cities in-between, but they don't want to go back to China.

America is a magnet for global humanity that attracts every nationality, every color, every race, every tribe, and every culture.

Look at my precious partners, African Americans; they strolled and shed their blood on the corn, wheat, cotton, sugar, orchards, and vineyards fields while living as sharecroppers. Go to the Mid-West heartlands; you will see the blood drops and perspiration all over the farmlands. It's a historical fact. But nobody went back to Africa. Why? We are the pioneers, the first Americans; together, we built America from scratch.

Do you hear a baritone voice? "I have a dream"—a great man of God, Mr. Gandhi of the USA, larger-than-life American, Dr. Martin Luther King.

Look, do you remember the first Macintosh home computer Apple unveiled?

World said, "Vow, IBM computer once in corporate offices, now has arrived at my home, called home computer; nobody even thought about it." And then, Windows came and opened the windows of the world's financial, cultural, educational, research, and technology empires. Thanks to Apple and Microsoft; they changed the world the way today's businesses are working.

Around 1960, the computer came to India for the first time. I was in Bombay. The bankers went on strike because they were afraid that computers would take away their jobs. Today's India trades H1 visas for Indian computer programmers for American dollars and the American lifestyle. H1 visas expire, but they don't want to go back to India. Why? The old protest of 1960 has revived into the American dream, the beautiful, the magnificent, the amazing nation, where there is no place for casteism, and there are equal opportunities for all, the dream I always dreamed of since my childhood. America, my home away from home, offering me the amenities only the richest can afford in my homeland. That's why.

You got the idea. If you can trace back the DNA of the American inventors, it will match the blood of Abraham, Isaac, and Jacob because this is a Judo-Christian nation; everybody else is our invited guest to Uncle Sam's banquet.

If you decide to stay, you have to melt into the tapestry of multi-colorful fabrics, as Parsis did in India.

America invents world-class products and technology and then finds skilled laborers who can fine-tune and perfect them so that we can kick back, chill out, and enjoy the fruits of the living God given as ingenuity, talents, skills, and inventive minds.

What happens to American businesses depends upon what happens inside the closed doors of Cherrywood Lane board rooms. What happens inside this closed-door meeting depends upon how loud the bell rings on the Wall Street of the Big Apple. Americans read Dow, S&P, and NASDAQ more than the daily newspaper, and America plants the trees and lets the friends fruitage the fruits.

Takeaway: Did you know America holds the record to enjoy more than 25 percent of the world's economy today? Why?

Here is the divine promise, "I will bless those who bless you, And I will curse him who curses you; And in you all the families of the earth shall be blessed" (Genesis 12:3, NKJV).

76. ENGINEER'S LIFE GOES ON—FROM COMPANY TO COMPANY, RIDING ON THE PINK SLIP

IBM acquired Disco Vision in the 1981–82 time frame. The laser DVD/CD business was sold to the Pioneer Corporation of America. Pink notices were flying everywhere. I saw the writing on the wall.

Did you know the Nintendo video games, electronic video games, and electronic musical instruments such as drums were invented by a company called Mattel Electronics, a subsidiary of the world's largest toy company, Mattel, in Hawthorne, California? That became my next journey station.

I was sitting in the guest room after the job interview. I overheard the conversation in the adjacent room. A perfect example of how a successful first-line manager should be was Mr. Paul Swygler, who interviewed me. He was telling his boss, "Guess what? Today, after ten interviews, I found a man we want. IBM was hiding him in their video disk business in Carson." I figured I got the job.

I closed my eyes, prayed, and tears ran down my cheeks; I was the only breadwinner in John 21:16 (NIV), "Again, Jesus said, 'Simon son of John, do you love me?' He answered, 'Yes, Lord, you know that I love you.' Jesus said, 'Take care of my sheep.'"

(6/23/2023)

A new adventure began at Mattel Electronics. My first assignment was to invent a method to quality control a new product, electronic drums. I love listening to music, but I can't play any musical instruments. I was kicked out from the Salvation Army brass band in India because I was messing up the whole orchestra playing base. And I had to come up with a quality criterion for electronic drums? Oh Lord, help me. But my sound knowledge and understanding of physics was on my side.

The heart of the electronic instruments is a piezo crystal. I graduated in solid-state physics. It was time to put into action what I had learned in the textbooks at school, although it was not that easy. I went to the local library and read every book available on piezo crystals. The Internet was not invented at that time. Bingo, I got the idea. I figured out how piezo crystals work, and I planned a test procedure to qualify piezo crystals. My manager, Mr. Paul Swygler, approved the plan, and I hid myself in a lab for two weeks. I built a test fixture that characterized the intensity of the piezo crystal. I gave a presentation to the engineering vice president along with my manager. I got a ten percent raise the next day.

Mattel Electronics sent me to Japan to work with Toshiba to establish a quality control lab in a suburb of the Tokyo Toshiba factory. I went to the Japanese Trade Commission office with Toshiba engineers to get approval to mass-produce electronic drums and guitars in Japan. I explained the new technology to the government officials. I saw the offices were buried with tons and tons of files; you couldn't even see their heads in the cubicles.

The Japanese engineer said, "This is government bureaucracy, red tape, bribery. Snell's speed work ethic."

I said, "No difference between India and here."

However, to my surprise, the license was granted the next day.

Toshiba management asked me, "What did you tell them?"

I said, "God bless, sir. *Sayonara!*"

I worked for about two years for Mattel Electronics, and that season of pink slip arrived again on a season of joy to the world and peace on Earth called Christmas. Everybody was given a jar of candies and a pink slip inside. I went to a mall to buy gifts for my family, and they were playing "This Is a Wonderful Time of the Year!"

I said, "Really? Oh yeah?" But that's life in America, the nation of opportunities wrapped in pink slips. Move on; there is no such thing as a permanent job here; you have to get used to it. The glamor, the honor, the uproar, the high point, the trophy, the medals, and the treasures of America come with the unknown territory of constant challenges and hurdles.

If you can jump each hurdle along the way of American life, you will be crowned at the end of the race, no matter what your race,

culture, tradition, custom, religion, socio-political background, or nationality might be, very unlike in India.

My next step was Aerojet Corporation, Downey, California. I was told, "You have a background in piezo crystals that we use. You will be our failure analysis engineer. We are making devices for the Army." I needed a job. I didn't ask what type of devices they make; I just signed the offer I could not resist, which was bigger than what I was making at Mattel Electronics.

The manager took me to an Indian restaurant and ordered chicken tikka masala. He was hooked on this very popular Indian dish in the Los Angeles area. Nex day, I found out that they were making anti-personnel and anti-tank mines. When the mine fails, I have to open up the failed mine full of explosives and perform a failure analysis.

I said, "Oh my Lord, not again. Why did I accept this job?"

I never told my family what I was doing for a living. But guess what? I was excited about this job because the heart of the device was piezo crystal; I knew in and out about this magical component.

I said, "Lord, never mind. Thank You, Lord, it's piezo again."

I used to take my out-of-town visitors to Disneyland, Anaheim, California, on Friday and to the Crystal Cathedral in Garden Grove, California, on Sunday. One Sunday, what I heard from a great internationally known positive-thinking preacher, Dr. Robert Schuler, still echoes in my ears after fifty years. **He, in his baritone impressive loud voice, said, "Tough times will not last, but tough people will do." How true. Been there, done that; it is true.**

(6/26/2023)

My first assignment was to analyze a failed anti-tank mine. I was given a short crash course on how anti-tank mine works. I had to learn electro-explosive science, a whole new world of technology, which was never talked about in the school textbooks. Mr. Joe was a tough, demanding manager but appreciative, encouraging, and brilliant.

There are two types of managers. One looks very easygoing; he lives in his world and lets you live yours. Like an old saying in India, a mellow teacher doesn't punish any student but doesn't teach anything, either. He snorers most of the time and lets you snore in the corner of four walls, too.

The other type is of strong personality, demanding, and shouting. His eyebrows go as high as they can, and he screams, "The sky is falling; I want you to fix it now or else."

There are two types of practices that mangers exercise as management yoga. One type of manager is a reader; they like to publish reports and judge their engineers how good they write. Most of them have liberal arts or business backgrounds.

The other type comes from technical fields. They don't care how your American English is; they read your report under a microscope with a screwdriver in one hand and the Ohm-meter in the other. They are the ones who make company stock skyrocket on Wall Street but never shout, "The sky is falling," while drinking beer in the bar on the main street at lunchtime.

My manager at Aerojet was fifty-fifty of both kinds, a rare personality.

He told me, "Bram, if you don't, who else will do it? I believe in you; you can do it. Let me know what tools you need, and no matter how much it costs, I will get them for you. You have my word; go get it."

That was it. I went to the library (there was no Internet in that era) and read every technical book available on electro-explosive. I thumbed through every industry publication on how they make, test, and install electro-explosive devices (EED). It took me two months to become a subject matter expert (SME).

The production was on hold. Every time the test mine went for a final function test demonstration, the first stage heart of the mine blew up in front of the Army customer as soon as the test engineer opened the top cover. It's called dud. It's a safety issue. The Army customer signed off the test report: Test failed. We were not allowed to proceed with production until the failure analysis was performed, the root cause was identified, the corrective actions were implemented, a successful test was witnessed by the customer, and production entry was approved by the customer.

Project assigned to: Bramvel Christian. Completion date: One month from today.

Mr. Joe wrote my name in the above report and gave me a month to finish it. My blood pressure was 200/100! I couldn't sleep at night. I spent nine to ten hours in the lab, including weekends.

One fine morning, all of a sudden, I saw something that changed my life. I was in the lab, and I peeled off the scotch tape from the plastic mine cover lid. I saw the needle moving on the adjacent Ohms-Meter, 5,000 Coulombs. Amazing, unbelievable! I found the answer. I went to a special mine testing lab. One mine with Scotch tape on the cover and the other without it. I tested both experimental setups. The one with a scotch tape blew up when the tape was peeled off; the other didn't. I found the root cause of the anti-tank mine failure.

Aerojet promoted me to the Senior Engineer, but I quit. I wanted to play with joyful toys rather than anti-tank mines. In 1985, I joined Hughes Aircraft Company in Fullerton, California. Guess what? My job turned out to be to play with the Trident missiles, which ended up being even more challenging than anti-tank mines.

"Oh Lord, help me again."

And He did.

Takeaway: Life is a mystery journey without a destination stamped on the ticket. The good news is it is paid in full; enjoy it through the planes, above the mountains, over the roller coaster, and near the river. Finally, you will arrive at your destination, but you will have to leave the comfort of your home first. The most beautiful thing about the life is this:

John 14:6 (KJV), "Jesus saith unto him, I am the way, the truth, and the life: no man cometh unto the Father, but by me."

(6/28/2023)

77. GUIDE THAT I USED TO WIN, CHILL OUT, AND CELEBRATE

Don't leave home without a pocketless shirt because you are a daydreamer and drummer, dancing to the new bits of tomorrow. Always keep a small notebook in your pocket; ideas that will change your life and the world around you are like manna—they will melt down at dawn if not jotted down.

Read scientific and business publications in your spare time, when you fly, when you eat lunch, during TV commercials, any time window you can find.

My boss at Hughes Aircraft Company, when I was working on Trident missiles projects, used to say, "How come you have so much knowledge on so many wide ranges of technical subjects? You know DI water, piezo crystals, ESD, acrylics, polycarbonates, transistors, diodes, resistors, capacitors, transformers, inductors, X-rays, EME, electron microscope, FTIR spectrometer, real-time X-rays, and on and on."

I answered, "When you watch football on the weekend, I read."

He would joke, "There is nothing interesting going on now in football games; my team always loses anyway, and when it wins, the fans ask, 'What went wrong this time?'"

All are given twenty-four hours in cash by our Almighty; it is how we use our time that makes us winners or losers.

Friends you make, books you read, TV shows you watch, persons you listen to, songs you sing, and visions you see, drumbeat your dream that builds your winning strategy. Never make a friendship with someone who thinks negatively of you and never comes out with positive words from his/her mouthpiece.

Time is everything; time each task and cut down the cycle time. Make a habit of living by numbers, the time you spend on a project, the money you earn, spend, and put aside, and everything else you do. Without numbers, you are roaming in a dark alley; you will lose all. Dream larger than life. Plan, execute, measure, and readjust the plan. Remember, where there is a problem, there is always an option; it is just a matter of finding it.

Keep a diary, and chart your plan. Assign three asterisks: must, important, and would be nice. Review and adjust before saying good night, and read it again before you eat breakfast. Pray and ask for the holy guidance, strength of a warrior, and divine direction of a pilot for today's plan.

Always ask yourself, "Is the task I am doing or that someone is asking me to do a value-added?" How much is it worth your time? If it does not match your calculation, don't do it; politely slip out. There are more important things to do, and life is a short journey; it will end before you know it.

Never burn the bridges; someday, you will need to cross the same river you left behind.

Nobody wins all the time, but remember, failure is not an end, just the beginning of a newly revised plan with a different strategy. Smile and move on just like Tesla chief Elon Musk did when the most powerful rocket designed to reach Mars failed on the launching pad in the initial engineering test.

Be generous and extend your hand to someone who is really honest but trapped in the circumstances; it is not his/her fault. You will be rewarded by your super-intelligent designer. I know from my own experience. Thank You, Lord. Grant me understanding, knowledge, courage, and wisdom when I fail to do so. Try it; you will be surprised. But if someone is lazy, trying to take advantage of your generosity, doesn't want to change the life style, always begs and depends upon someone else, and is a crybaby, don't waste your talents. Remember the tears in alligator's eyes story?

Finally, take time with your friends and family, chill out, and celebrate what the Lord has done for you.

Bramvel Christian

Takeaway: "Then celebrate the Festival of Harvest to honor the LORD your God. Bring him a voluntary offering in proportion to the blessings you have received from him" (Deuteronomy 16:10, NLT).

(6/30/2023)

78. RIDING ON THE TRIDENT MISSILE

I have made more than fifty presentations on technical subjects to Navy Trident missile customers. I was recognized as a star presenter. In one project, a module worth thousands of dollars was failing. You could see the burning marks on the back of the device, but nobody knew how that happened. I was assigned this project.

The tool I used I called "palm tree analysis" instead of fishbone analysis because it makes the project juicier to work on because I like the dates from Indio, California. After a long exercise, I found out the cause of the failure. The oven the lab was using was the culprit. The run-away oven was actually reaching three times higher temperature than the dial was set for the required stabilizing temperature. I got the same type of resistors and stabilized two groups, one in the same production lab oven and the other in my lab with a known calibrated and verified temperature control oven. Destructive physical analysis (DPA) exhibited that the second group was perfect, but the first group resistors were burned like charcoal.

I went home and celebrated the win with the dates from Indio, California. I solved several technical problems in this program.

Believe it or not, envy and dirty politics exist among technical professionals, too.

One Hindu lady engineer was very jealous when she found out that I was promoted to senior engineer and got the highest pay raise. She put the germs in the ears of other engineers, "Christian means his ancestors were classified as second class in India."

I was surprised to learn that even after coming to the USA, the self-proclaimed upper-class Hindus still live in a 2000-year-old poisonous ideology of community classification based on not merits but artificial tradition for selfish, stupid reasons that turned millions of bright young people into victims of socioeconomic-religious persecution in India.

Hitler is still alive in India and silently creeping into other civilized modern nations. The majority of Hindus are nice, loving, kind, peaceful, friendly, and generous people. But there is a fraction of the population that is composed of hardliners, extremists, and religiously blind fanatics with racist behavior in India and somehow sneaked in here in the USA and other nations. Those few bad apples ruin the whole lovely, wonderful, beautiful basket of dignity, human respect, freedom, justice, opportunity for education and employment, peace, harmony, and love for humankind.

My Hindu friends, we are Christians, and we are proud of being the disciples of Christ. We love you no matter what your ideology, thinking, custom, tradition, culture, fashion, or practices may be.

Morning has risen; the sun is up. A new refreshing wind is blowing from MIT to Silicon Valley and from Starbucks in Seattle to a mighty world-class Navy Aircraft Carrier docking in San Diego. The birds are singing, "One nation under living God, freedom and justice for all." Wake up, my friends, leave your dirty laundry behind back home and be part of the colorful American tapestry.

Hughes Aircraft Company was the first company to design, build, and fly the first commercial satellite in the world. I got the opportunity to work on satellites when the company was acquired by Boeing and became Boeing Satellite Company in El Segundo, California.

Takeaway: Some people are jealous not because of your progress but because they can't progress. Jealousy is like a volcano erupting within you; it will consume you because of your own choice.

Proverbs 10:12 (KJV), "Hatred stirreth up strifes: but love covereth all sins."

Proverbs 10:18 (KJV), "He that hideth hatred with lying lips, and he that uttereth a slander, is a fool."

(7/1/2023)

79. FROM UNCLE SAM TO UNCLE MODI

Dear Uncle Modi,

I watched you on TV at the state dinner on June 22, 2023, at the American icon for the world's most powerful nation, the White House. I was glued to the TV to listen to your comments at the press conference.

I jumped from my chair when you said, "Democracy is in our DNA." I saluted you when you said, "We celebrate all religions." I said, "Really? Racism, casteism, and bullying in India are still alive, and you say, 'Democracy is in our DNA'?"

Based on my six-sigma statistics knowledge and other data I saw online, if you randomly interview 1,000 victims of Indian minority groups in India at a 99.9 percent confidence level, statistically, more than 95 percent will affirm that they have experienced discrimination, racism, and bullying from artificially-called upper class due to casteism and religious intolerance in the highest ethnically diverse country in the world, India.

You mentioned during your American congress address in Washington, DC, that "if you visit India today, you will see that even a street vendor uses an American-invented cell phone and America's gift to the world home computer to do their daily business with the bank."

So, if India takes pride in using American inventions, why is India waiting so long to embrace the same level of justice and freedom for all, Uncle Modi?

When you were saying that democracy is in your DNA at the state dinner at the White House, your Manipur State was burning due to racial conflicts. If anyone in India can make a difference, you are the one who can. This is your time. You and your team, in India and abroad, need to announce loudly and publicly that "Christians are our brothers and sisters, just like our own family. Christian mis-

sionaries brought modern medical hospitals, medicines, colleges, English-teaching high schools, homes for the poor and needy, and above all, the good news of love and caring without any man-made wall. The seeds for real democracy were planted by Christians in India because the DNA of love, joy, peace, compassion, kindness, and generosity is in the blood of Christians."

In a democracy, the government should condemn violence and hold accountable those who engage in rhetoric that's dehumanizing toward religious minorities, but it seldom happens in straight language in India; it's so sad.

The US Commission on International Religious Freedom (USCIRF) has published its 2023 report, and India is designated as part of the "countries of particular concern" (CPC) under the International Religious Freedom Act (IRFA) for engaging in or tolerating particularly severe violations of religious freedom.

So, the brilliant professionals of this commission are falsifying the report? It can't be.

Read Amnesty International Report 2022, "In India, laws and policies that were passed without adequate public and legislative consultation eroded the rights of human rights defenders and religious minorities."

So, is this international agency wrong? It can't be.

Human Rights Watch, in its World Report 2023 (thirty-third edition), said that Indian authorities had "intensified and broadened" their crackdown on activist groups and the media throughout the year 2022. It also claimed that the current central ruling party used abusive and discriminatory policies to repress minorities.

So, Human Rights Watch didn't get it right? It can't be.

USA-based human rights watchdog, Freedom House, has been tracking the course of democracy since 1941. In their 2021 report, India's score was 67, a drop from 71/100 from the year before, because of its severe human rights violations.

So, is the Freedom House rating not correct? It can't be; they have been watching human rights since 1941, even before India got independence in 1947.

When you addressed the Congress on Capitol Hill in Washington, DC, you said, "This is India's time."

Dear Uncle, yes, this is your time to challenge the 2000-year-old Indian tradition or stupid ideology of casteism, racism, and religious intolerance in the hearts of the few bad apples in India and abroad, including America. If anyone in India can change the course of the dark past history after Mr. Gandhi, it is you.

We, as Christians around the world, pray for you and your leadership team that before this year ends, you will take the initiative to pull India out of the dark cloud of casteism, racism, and religious intolerance that will result in true freedom and justice for all. We pray that the Almighty living God will grant you knowledge, wisdom, understanding, and holy power to change the course. Here is the divine prophesy for Israel fulfilled by the living God, **"And I will make of thee a great nation, and I will bless thee, and make thy name great; and thou shalt be a blessing"** (Genesis 12:2, KJV).

Let India be another Israel, Uncle Modi.

Here is the "Man Kee Bat" (Modi's radio program, "What's on my mind") for your radio, TV, newspaper, political publications, public address, and inner circle party discussion.

Uncle, now is the time to put into practice from the historical Red Fort of New Delhi what you said on the White House's beautiful lush green lawn and lavish state dinner. If anyone can do it in India now, it is you.

Publicly denounce the 2000-year-old practice of casteism, racism, and religious intolerance in the hearts of a few extremist fanatics.

Everyone should have a right to accept, practice, preach, and proclaim the gospel of Christ in the house of worship and in public without any fear. That is the real democracy. Why? It is because it is our mandate from our living God, "And he said unto them, Go ye into all the world, and preach the gospel to every creature" (Mark 16:15, KJV).

This is the new world; the old has passed away. India needs to wake up if it wants to become a world player and world-class power to compete with America and China. The time is now; no time to waste the opportunity.

My dear Gujaratis, do you remember what President Trump said at the world's largest cricket stadium in Ahmedabad, Gujarat State, India? "When Mr. Modi was a young man, he worked at a cafeteria in this city...I will tell you this: he's a very tough, true friend."

Mr. Trump will be the next president of America in 2025. Be prepared; it is your time. Pass a law to punish those who utter racial slurs or support casteism, racism, and religious intolerance in any form because it violates human rights. India, wake up; this is your time. Jesus Christ is coming again, and He loves and cares for India.

Takeaway: "These events happened in the days of King Xerxes, who reigned over 127 provinces stretching from India to Ethiopia" (Ester 1:1, NLT).

Even King Xerxes eyed India 2000 years ago. Can India eye King Xerxes now?

(7/3/2013)

80. MY BELOVED INDIA

In spite of all the dark sides of my beloved India, how can I forget that there is a wonderful bright side to you? I can't ignore or forget that.

You nourished me in my childhood and educated me, and the majority of Hindus are so nice, wonderful, friendly, generous, peaceful, and kind people. But although it hurts me, honestly, I have to say there is a small fraction within you that ruins your image in India and abroad. Lately, politicians have found out that the easy way to earn votes is to create religiousism to win at the ballot box. Interestingly, religious fanatics, social extremists, political monsters, and Indian mafias found a niche in this dirty game. Same ideology used by Germany in the Second World War, different name.

In the last century, India was known as the snake charmer on the dusty streets of India. Today, Indians are known as mouse charmers on Wall Street and big blue companies. But the cobra of racism and casteism is still alive, has crept into the USA and other nations worldwide, and is spitting poison of supremacist ideology. That's why the Washington State passed the law.

Even today, most of the poor, sarcastically named *dalits*, low caste, or scheduled caste, are condemned as second-class citizens to live in ghettos as a result of the 2000-year-old caste ideology imposed by some uneducated, brainless, selfish king or community gangster.

While Mr. Modi was enjoying a five-course banquet at the White House, in the northeast corner of India, in Manipur State, residents were burned, houses of worship were destroyed, and minority groups fled to the jungle due to racial violence. The streets cannot be used to seek justice. However, it is clear the ruling party should not deny the facts and learn lessons from the social explosion in India.

Takeaway: Racist rant is an everyday occurrence in India, on your face and behind your back. Who is a racist? The answer is: If the victims of socioeconomic injustice can't enter your house of worship with you, dine with you in your home, be intimate friends with your daughters and sons, enjoy all the social, economic, educational, and religious rights and privileges you have, then you are the racist, and the civilized world will not accept your ideology or culture or religion. You cannot fool the educated, civilized world of today.

(7/5/2023)

81. FLYING ON THE SATELLITE

From 2000 to 2009, I was a magnetic engineer at Boeing Satellite Company, El Segundo, California. My peer, hero, and mentor at Boeing Satellite was a brilliant Jewish scientist, Dr. Roseberry. I worked on several satellite magnetics designs. On one project, the very expensive transformers were failing, and nobody in the company or the manufacturer could determine why they were failing.

One day, Dr. Roseberry called me to his office, closed the door, and told me, "Listen, whatever it takes, whatever help you need, technical expertise or funding, you have my permission. You have to fix this failure. This is a highly visible project on the highest priority list of the upper management. This is a military project. You have thirty days to fix it; now, go and report to me every Friday at 2 p.m. on where we are." He was tough, but I called him the Einstein of Boeing.

That was it. I was on the new job for two weeks. My day turned into night and night into day. "Oh Lord, why me, again?"
And the Lord said, "Why not?"

I called the transformer manufacturer in Portland, Oregon. He was a very nice young magnetic design engineer and very cooperative. I studied every element, material, and process that was used to design and build that device. In two weeks, I determined the root cause of why the magnetic cores of the transformers were disintegrating.

My mentor said, "I told you you could do it."

Thereafter, I solved quite a few technical problems. I will never forget Dr. Roseberry, tough boss outside, brilliant brain inside with a heart filled with pink blood of love from top to bottom.

Takeaway: How true,

And I will give you pastors [for the engineers, a subject matter expert (SME), mentor, or peer in the technical world] according to mine heart, which shall feed you with knowledge and understanding.

Jeremiah 3:15 (KJV)

(7/6/2023)

82. WHY AMERICA?

Why do Americans win the highest, way, way highest Nobel Prizes than any other nation in the world?

The Nobel Prize Award was established by Alfred Nobel's will in 1895. Since then, the nation with the most Nobel Prize winners is the United States, with a remarkable amount of 400 Nobel Prizes, followed by the United Kingdom with 137 Nobel Prizes. This dominance by the US and UK proves that the DNA of Americans is the same as the thirteenth son of Jacob, one of our pioneers and founding fathers. **Scientific knowledge and technical innovation are God's gift to America and will prevail as long as a newly elected American president places his right hand on the Bible and proclaims from the gallery of the Capitol, "So God help me." Americans are Abraham's heirs.**

Galatians 3:29 (NLT), "And now that you belong to Christ, you are the true children of Abraham. You are his heirs, and God's promise to Abraham belongs to you."

Another amazing fact: New York has more Nobel prize winners than any other state. Why? A large population of Jewish in New York State, the direct descent of Jacob. Check it out with AI.

Top Ten Nobel Prize Winner Countries
Country Nobel Prizes Education Average IQ Attainment
1. USA 400 90.9percent 97.43
2. UK 137 79.9percent 99.12
3. Germany 111 100.74
4. France 71 96.69
5. Sweden 32 97
6. Japan 29 106.48
7. Canada 28 99.52

8. Switzerland 27 99.24
9. Austria 22 98.38
10. Netherlands 22 73

Again, our forefathers came from above nations, bright, intelligent, pioneers, religious, hard workers, inventors, sons and daughters of Jacob of Judeo-Christian faith.

America, you are the amazing, gifted, world-leading nation, and just like Moses, you are given a rod engraved with fifty stars of responsibilities from the living God, not a man-made God; preserve it.

America, you have no idea how much you are blessed; be thankful to the living God and recite the first three commandments given to Moses on every Fourth of July in every city hall by its mayor.

In an estimate by Baruch Shalev, between 1901 and 2000, about 65.4 percent of Nobel Prize winners were of Judeo-Christian faith. Is this enough evidence that you have Jacob's DNA?

Let us walk back two hundred years in history and see what Judeo-Christian scientists and inventors have done for the mankind of the world.

Vaccines (1796): The journey to discover smallpox was very difficult. The records indicate that Edward Jenner, in 1796, discovered the concept of a vaccine, created a vaccine for smallpox, and used it successfully for the first time. Then on, doctors around the world combated some of the world's deadliest diseases, including smallpox, rabies, tuberculosis, and cholera. Over the course of 200 years, one of the deadliest diseases known to man, smallpox, was wiped off the face of the earth. Since then, virtually all vaccines have worked using the same concept.

Now, to combat COVID-19, a new technology called mRNA has been researched in America by Pfizer and mass-produced vaccines in a record time of two months during President Donald Trump's presidency, and the whole world has used this new concept to fight the deadly disease worldwide.

Thanks, America; the world is grateful to your scientists and the foresight of President Trump.

The list goes on with the amazing discoveries made by Judeo-Christian scientists, doctors, and inventors and given away free to the whole world for the benefit of mankind.

To name a few:

- Anesthesia was discovered in 1846 by a Boston dentist, William T. G. Morton.
- Chloroform, which has saved millions of lives worldwide. Medicines for the plague, dysentery, and typhoid fever.
- X-ray imaging by German physicist Wilhelm Conrad Rontgen in 1895.
- Ultrasound in 1955.
- In 1967, the computed tomography (CT) scan became an amazing diagnostic tool for modern medical science.
- In 1973, Paul Lauterbur discovered the first magnetic resonance image (MRI).
- In 1928, antibiotics were introduced by Alexander Fleming, a Scottish scientist.
- In the 1940s, America mass-produced the drug for use in World War II.
- Penicillin by Australian Howard Florey and Nazi-Germany refugee Ernst Chain.
- In 1954, a kidney transplant was the first trial of organ transplant by Dr. Joseph Murray and Dr. David Hume in Boston.
- In 1963, the first lung transplant, a pancreas/kidney in 1966, and a liver and heart in 1967. In all of America, that has saved thousands of lives worldwide with doctors successfully using this new medical breakthrough.
- It is worth mentioning that the first-hand transplant in 1998 and the full-face transplant in 2010 were also in America.
- In 1960, antiviral drugs for treating the deadly viruses HIV/aids, Ebola, and rabies.
- In 1970, stem cell therapy to treat leukemia and other blood disorders and bone marrow transplantation.
- In 1890, immunotherapy by William B. Coley.
- In 2010, the first cancer vaccine was approved in America.

Finally, in the twenty-first century, we are at the door-step of artificial intelligence powered by American technology powerhouses Google, IBM, Apple, Microsoft, Tesla, and others that will bring new tools and techniques that will solve our century-old questions and problems yet to be explored and the world is waiting upon America to open a new dawn of technology and inventions that will make human lives more enjoyable and productive.

America, the shining North Star, the hope and dream of millions worldwide, the Judeo-Christian nation, thou shall prevail as long as the Bible remains as the centerpiece of Capitol Hill in Washington, DC.

(7/7/2023)

Look at the World's largest economies; America is number one. The gap between America and rival China is 5.6 trillion, which is more than the GDP of any country in the world.

Country GDP
1. United States of America 23.3 trillion.
2. China 17.7 trillion.
3. Japan 4.9 trillion.
4. Germany 4.3 trillion.
5. India 3.2 trillion.
6. The United Kingdom 3.1 trillion.
7. France 3 trillion.
8. Italy 2.1 trillion.
9. Canada 2 trillion.
10. South Korea 1.8 trillion.

No nation will come close to America as long as America remains a Judo-Christian nation worshiping the living God, the source of all glory, blessings, power, and GDP; that is why we sing on the Fourth of July, "God bless America."

In 2023, everybody around the world is asking one question: Who will be the next president of the United States of America? **I predict that person is former President Donald Trump. Why and how?**

Look at the history. In times of world crisis, America not only rises to the occasion but above and beyond the occasion. Who stopped the First World War? America. Who stopped the Second World War? America. Who sends the highest missionaries to the darkest corners of the world? America. Who sent the Peace Corps volunteers around the world? America.

When the world did not know that COVID-19, a deadly pandemic, had emerged to destroy what America has accomplished in 200 hundred years and generously shared her wealth with the world, President Trump and his bright team became proactive and turned the medical technology machine in the highest gears. So, America was able to develop a vaccine in the record time of two months, a world record nobody has beaten so far. The world is grateful to America for killing the monster in record time.

America is about to enter into a new technological breakthrough and economic revolution. Electric vehicles, personal satellites, just like personal computers, 300 miles-per-hour transportation, new medicines for killer diseases, combined TV/cells with nanochips, and more will America invent in the next ten years that will double the GDP of America.

So, America needs a president who is a businessman, a visionary, one who understands how technology incubator gives birth to make impossible ideas possible, and a promise-keeper of the Bible. Who is that larger-than-life personality when the world nations are rushing to the moon to catch up with America? No one other than President Trump.

The American president is the Moses of America; they have to be Judeo-Christian, with a larger-than-life personality. God chooses imperfect to perfect His plan in an imperfect world. Look at Moses. He couldn't speak clearly, yet he led 3 million Jews through the desert to the promised land, Israel.

The overnight sprung-up politicians without Judeo-Christian background do not know that America and Israel are the apples of the living God's eyes.

The day America cuts the umbilical cord with Israel, God will cut the umbilical cord with America.

Why? It is because the Bible says, "I will bless those who bless you [Israel], But I will curse those who curse you [Israel]. And through you [Israel] I will bless all the nations" (Genesis 12:3, GNT) "For he that shall touch you [Israel], shall touch the apple of mine eye" (Zechariah 2:8, WYC).

The America is blessed because America blesses Israel. Here is the lesson for all nations of the world. The secret is out, and it is up to you; be blessed or be cursed. This is validated throughout the history of 7000 years, from Genesis to today.

America, let not Philistines deceive you.

Let's look differently at the economic status of the top ten largest economies in the world in 2023 based on IMF data:

Rank & Country GDP (USD billion) GDP Per Capita (USD thousand)
1. USA 26,854 80.03 (1)
2. China 19,374 13.72
3. Japan 4,410 35.39
4. Germany 4,309 51.38 (3)
5. India 3,750 2.6
6. UK 3,159 46.31 (4)
7. France 2,924 44.41 (5)
8. Italy 2,170 36.81 (6)
9. Canada 2,090 52.72 (2)
10. Brazil 2,080 9.67

Again, the top six GDP per capita are Christian nations, with the USA being at the top. Look at the GDP per capita gap between the USA, China, and India.

The Bible says, "I will bless those who bless you, And I will curse him who curses you; And in you all the families of the earth shall be blessed" (Genesis 12:3, NKJV).

The above data speaks for itself. America, bless the living Lord for the showers of blessings that have been bestowed upon you from Boston, Massachusetts, to Los Angeles, California, and from Seattle, Washington, to San Deigo, California, a land of fifty stars under the gold economy sky.

God will bless America as long as it remains a Judo-Christian nation and doesn't compromise the words of the living God, the Bible.

Let's look at the top nations with the highest living standards:
1. Switzerland.
2. Germany.
3. Canada.
4. United States.
5. Sweden.
6. Japan.
7. Australia.
8. United Kingdom.

Looking at the size of the country, millions of immigrants enter America every year. America provides food and medicine worldwide to refugees and victims of natural disasters. American living standards are not bad at all, considering the hard and challenging work Americans do day in and day out, every day. That's why we are the only nation in the world so far to stamp the footprint on the moon and declare, **"A small step for man, one giant leap for mankind" (Neal Armstrong, when he landed on the moon on July 20, 1969).**

America, your best time is yet to come, provided you will honor, proclaim, and worship the living God, the only God of Judeo-Christian faith. You have arrived at "Yahweh Jireh." Keep your promise, Jehovah Jireh. Don't let any Philistine misguide you; stay on course. You will be the greatest nation the world has ever seen yet.

Takeaway: America, you will be the North Star for the seven seas. You will be a blessing to seven continents. Remember what the Lord has said, "I will make you a great nation; I will bless you And make your name great; And you shall be a blessing" (Genesis 12:2, NKJV).

You are the new Israel; you are the promised land. God will continue to bless America.

83. MY BELOVED INDIA, THE WORLD IS WATCHING YOU. DO YOU WATCH THE WORLD?

Even after millions of Indians living in America and other highly educated nations are exposed to modern civilization and Christianity, there is an absence of free speech and freedom of preaching and practicing the faith of their choice due to the marginalization of minorities.

Minorities live under the threat of religious persecution, the pain and deep wounds of mockery and insult dramatized by the self-labeled Indian upper class in their own homelands. Why? It is partly because Hindu immigrants don't take messages home. Recently, what happened in a dark corner of India in Manipur State in the northeast corner of India is an example of this reality. The family members of a minority Christian group called Kuki have been brutalized, lynched, and raped by the extremists of a majority Hindu group called Maiti. The politicians hide the truth under the rug, and life goes on with victims left behind crying and in pain.

The only hope is in Christ. My Kuki and all other Christian and Hindu friends, remember what the Bible says, "'Do not be afraid of the king of Babylon [India], of whom you are afraid; do not be afraid of him,' says the LORD, 'for I am with you, to save you and deliver you from his hand" (Jeremiah 42:11, NKJV).

You are not alone; even when everybody else leaves you behind, there is a friend in Christ. You will rise and shine above all, and the world will be amazed by your success and beautiful life. Wait upon Him, and victory will be yours. You are not alone, but the whole Christian brotherhood worldwide is with you, and we are praying for you.

We as Christians disapprove of what the haters have done, and we will pray for them that the Almighty living God will change their hearts and minds because our Lord and God, Jesus Christ, instructed

us to do so, "But Jesus was saying, 'Father, forgive them; for they do not know what they are doing.' And they cast lots, dividing His garments among themselves" (Luke 23:34, NASB).

God bless Prime Minister Modi; he has shown sympathy for you on your Independence Day celebration at Red Fort, New Delhi, on August 15, 2023. He announced from the pulpit of the Red Fort, "My dear family members, last few weeks in the northeast and also in some other parts of India, but especially in Manipur, many people lost their lives. The honor of mothers and daughters was played with shameful acts. The country is with the people of Manipur."

But is this enough? Shame on Indian Americans for dancing with umbrellas on the street of New York the same week and ignoring Manipur's tragedy.

India has slid in the World Press Freedom Index to 161st this year, its lowest point ever. After the racial cleansing and parading of three Christian women naked on the streets of Manipur State in India on May 2023, the index will go down even further, a lower point than any other nation in the world is assigned. India also leads the list for the highest number of government-imposed Internet sanctions.

The conversion legislation that challenged the constitutionally protected right of freedom of belief and practice of any religion you chose based on your own choice drove the human rights protection index to the lowest point in India's history.

Takeaway: Change my heart, O God. Make it ever true. Change my heart, O God, May I be like You. You are the potter; I am the clay. Mold me and make me. This is what I pray.

Those who are persecuted in the name of Jesus Christ, remember,

But before all this, they will seize you and persecute you. They will hand you over to synagogues and put you in prison, and you will be brought before kings and governors, and all on account of my name.

Luke 21:12 (NIV)

Psalm 56:11 (KJV), "In God have I put my trust: I will not be afraid what man can do unto me."

Jeremiah 42:11 (KJV), "Be not afraid of the king of Babylon, of whom ye are afraid; be not afraid of him, saith the LORD: for I am with you to save you, and to deliver you from his hand."

(7/8/2023)

84. WHAT MAKES YOU UPPER CLASS?

Hello, my Hindu friends. Wake up; morning has risen in the west, but you are still sleeping in the east. Wisdom says, "Class is not your birthright, cannot be granted by your parents, cannot be bestowed by your Guru, cannot be supported by any medical or scientific facts that it is your birthright, and cannot be granted free by your community or politicians. *You have to earn it, like people do in the rest of the world.*"

You have to achieve it. You can't promote yourself to the upper class; you have to be qualified by the world standards of decency, respect for humanity, generosity, honesty, civilization, and good citizenship.

India, you are the only nation on the surface of the world that assigns babies a class, upper or lower, even before they are born and get a chance to show you their real class higher than yours by world-class standards. Hello. If you can land on the moon in 2024, you can understand the definition of "class," which you misused 2000 years ago for your selfish purpose.

> For we dare not class ourselves or compare ourselves with those who commend themselves. But they, measuring themselves by themselves, and comparing themselves among themselves, are not wise.
>
> 2 Corinthians 10:12 (NKJV)

Here are the qualities of an upper-class human being:
- **Believes in the living divine God, creator of all, and not a human being.**
- **Prayerfully seeks His guidance and wisdom to be qualified for the upper class.**

- Believes all mankind is created equal in His image. Genesis 1:27 (NLT), "So God created human beings in his own image. In the image of God he created them; male and female he created them."
- Has knowledge, not alphabet learning, and has wisdom, not following rituals blindly.
- Has a kind heart, full of a loving spirit, and always projects a positive attitude, no matter where life leads him/her.
- Has respect for all around him/her, smiles like the flowers raining from the cherry tree when someone smiles at him/her.
- Encourage the fallen, in despair, lost, mourning, and crying.
- Reaches out and extends a helping hand to the poor, in need, and struggling to survive.
- Hugs and blesses without any prejudice, pride, or boasting.
- Walks into the room, and people say, "Halleluiah," "Amen," and "Praise the Lord."
- Sings enduring songs; lyrics that give hope, strength, and encouragement to others.
- Dreams larger-than-life that will brighten the life, living standards, and enjoyment of millions.
- Takes leadership to lead those who are lost, tired, victims of religious, social, and economic injustice, exploited, and forgotten.
- Brings joy, peace, happiness, a smile, hope, and encouragement to all around.

Do you meet these prerequisites to be listed in the upper class, or did your community simply stamp on your passport, "You are a dummy upper class"? If so, don't go to any Christian nation.

And they told you, "Here is your free ticket; you are first class. Go." If so, you are not an upper-class human being of a civilized community but a beggar, a hobo, and a nomadic.

The world will recognize you as an upper-class individual if you:
- Bring peace when there appears chaos, uncertainty, and confusion.
- Build bridges where there are disputes and differences and know how to make a deal and achieve consensuses.

- Bring hope, new dreams, and new songs into the lives of the depressed and hopeless.
- Encourage those who are about to give up, who have lost everything, and who are clinging to the last penny.
- Make someone laugh even when everything has gone wrong, not as planned.
- Smile, say hello, and shake hands with unknown strangers on the street.
- Reach out to the poor and needy and meet their needs.
- Wipe the tears and mourn with those who have lost loved ones.
- Party with those who accepted the invitation but ignore those to whom the invitations were sent but are mean and arrogant and didn't show up.
- Read the Bible and look up to Jesus Christ as Savior, hero, mentor, pandit, and guru for inspiration, guidance, planning, peace, joy, happiness, knowledge, and wisdom.
- Bring the good news of Jesus Christ to everyone. "Go and preach the gospel to the world."

Takeaway: "And He said to them, 'Go into all the world and preach the gospel to all creation'" (Mark 16:15, NASB).

Are you one of these personalities? If not, think again: are you really qualified to be an upper class? Not by Bible standards. Think again.

(7/10/2023)

85. GRAND FINALE OF MY PROFESSIONAL CAREER AT THE NAVY

Close your eyes and vision this elegant giant conference room in the Boeing building, Huntington Beach, California, with no windows, isolated walls for electromagnetic interference (EMI), secret hearing, and only selected personnel with secret clearance. One Navy commander, two Navy lieutenant commanders, one Navy consultant, a Navy Program Office technical director, and a Navy chief engineer presided at the conference table. There are butterflies jumping at supersonic speed in my stomach. I had never faced a military powerhouse like this in my entire professional career. But they were very professional, polite, and highly regarded intelligent individuals. Kudos to their professionalism. I was invited for a job interview.

The commander said, "You had a very successful professional career at Boeing and other Fortune 100 companies; why not enjoy a well-earned retirement instead of joining the Navy?"

I replied, "Commander, yes, you are right, but I have more to offer to my adopted country, which has transformed my life from dust to 24-karat gold. I am still pretty healthy by the grace of the Almighty, and I can still contribute from my strong technical background. My name is Bramwell, misspelled by a jealous Hindu city clerk in my birth certificate as Bramvel, but the aqua in my well is not dried yet, sir."

Commander, "I studied your resume, checked the references, and verified the problems you have solved at Boeing and Raytheon. Thanks for your contributions."

(7/13/2023)

After a couple of weeks, the phone rang. The screen read, "SSP Navy," meaning someone from the Strategic System Program of the Navy. My hand was shaking.

The voice on the other end said, "This is Lt. Colonel Johnson. I have good news for you. The Navy has selected you for the chief engineer post at our Huntington Beach, California, Program Office. Are you willing to accept it?"

"Yes, sir, I do. Thank you very much for giving me an opportunity; it's my honor," I replied.

Lt. Colonel Johnson, "Okay, thanks for accepting. We will send you the details."

I couldn't believe it. Tears ran down my face. I called Janet. "You are not gonna believe this. I got a phone call this morning; I got the job at the Navy. I have to start next week. They want me urgently right away. I have to work on a very high-level secret project. Unbelievable! Unbelievable!"

Janet, "Okay. I told you you would get it. I was praying for you secretly."

I left home early. As soon as I opened the garage, I smelled the spicy aroma of world-class samosa. Janet made samosa, which is number eleven of spicy on a scale of ten, to celebrate my new job.

The next day, I resigned at Boeing, El Segundo, California, after twenty-five years of service at Boeing Aerospace.

My director at Boeing, Dr. Rosenberry, a great Jewish supper brain, said, "I am sorry you are leaving on the one hand, but so glad you got this position."

"Sir, I thank you from the bottom of my heart; you are my hero. I have learned so much from you for my professional growth," I said.

(7/13/2023)

The next day, Lt. Colonel Anderson took me to lunch.

Colonel, "Listen, the Navy is aware of your significant contributions made to the program when at Boeing. Boeing couldn't figure out for a year why a transformer on a very expensive module was failing. Then, Boeing invited you to solve the problem. You resolved the problem within a month. You were the right engineer for a job well done. Then, we had a high-reliability interface unit conduction problem. You came up with the tin whisker growth solution. Then, we had a high-tech, cutting-edge technology product line progress issue. You put your Six Sigma knowledge to work and solved the problem with flying colors. The list goes on, but let me tell you, we are so proud to have you on board.

"Now, we gonna give you an even higher challenge. We are moving a one-of-a-kind, multi-million-dollar, high-tech equipment from the West Coast to the middle of the country. Any loss to the sensors or equipment can impact national security. The stakes are high for me and the Navy. We never undertook such a high-level risky project. You are selected to take the lead for this project. Do you understand? Time is not on our side; we have to finish this project really quickly."

I replied, "Yes, sir."

"Okay, go now to the lab, work with Boeing, and document a plan. We will have a video conference every Friday at 5 a.m.; be there on time. No word jargon, only facts and nothing but the facts. I trust you; you can do it. Thanks for your services," said the Colonel.

Me, "Yes, sir. I will do my best; I will not let you down."

That was it. My first experience working in military style.

And I said, "Oh Lord, not again. I wish I had known it before I accepted the offer."

And the Lord said, "Why not? If a prize doesn't have a price tag, it is worthless; if it has a price tag, you are the one who can read the secret bar code. So, don't complain; I am greater than your challenge" (read 1 John 4:4, KJV).

The marching band rhythm started. We had great technical minds at Boeing, Huntington Beach, California, laboratory at that time. High-tech equipment weighed in tons, the one-of-a-kind, no-source-available type; it was very expensive, like a piece of gold. Sensors were very fragile, shock- and vibration-sensitive.

First, I created guidelines for the moving plan, equipment post-move test plan, sensor test plan, requalification plan, and new facility certification plan. I oversaw the move of equipment, monitored and approved every shipment of high-tech load, and analyzed and approved post-mover tests and new laboratory certification reports. It took a year to finish the project. It was a great success; I didn't lose a single sensor, and all heavy high-tech test equipment was fully operational. For the ribbon-cutting ceremony at Midwest's new test and production facility, everybody and their uncles were invited, except me. I guess that's how it goes; the color of technical achievement fades out in the shadow of the corporate power show and political fireworks.

(7/20/2023)

It is arguably the most daring and successful achievement in the history of human exploration.

"That's one small step for man, one giant leap for mankind," proclaimed Armstrong. He was the first astronaut down the ladder of the lunar module and was completely aware he was making his own leap into human history as the first person to step on the moon.

But do you know who flew the Lunar Landing Research Vehicle (LLRV) on the earth before it landed on the moon?

The engineers at Edward Airforce Base, California, in 1960, Gene Matrnga, Chief Pilot Joe Walker, and Co-pilot Daniel Mallick, were the pioneers in flying the LLRV. In 1965, they trained Commander Neil Armstrong, lunar module pilot Buzz Aldrin, and Michael Collins, the pilots for the Apollo 11 moon landing. However, the engineers who trained the astronauts were not invited to sit in the front row when the lunar module landed on the moon.

It's a fact of life in the technical arena that power and politics sit at the front row of the show while the technical staff sweats behind the table of the lab in the back of the factory floor.

Praise the Lord, I got the award and a recognition letter from Vice Admiral Wolf, "Bram, job well done."

I closed my eyes and said to myself, "How true. My God, You were there."

Matthew 28:20 (KJV), "Teaching them to observe all things whatsoever I have commanded you: and, lo, I am with you always, even unto the end of the world. Amen."

The engineers perspire in the laboratory and grow new flowers out of technical skill seeds; in reward, they get a new ball pen, a three-color certificate to remind traffic signal on the way back home not to forget to stop at a red light, and a pat on the back shoulder at the staff meeting. But the executive gets the seven-color flower bouquet, eggnog in a crystal glass, and the golden calf, son of the bull displayed at Wall Street, at the cherry wood BOD elliptical table.

This is how America remains number one in the economy, education, technology, innovation, and space exploration, where the power of money, the spirit of free enterprise, freedom of religion, and pressure beyond the limit mark of the pressure cooker to achieve the technological breakthrough to conquer the world, coexist in the corporate world and in the engineering community.

America takes ordinary engineers and scientists from Asia and South Asia and transforms them inside out into the sons and daughters of Albert Einstein, Thomas Edison, Alexander Graham Bell, Samuel Morse, George Eastman, and the list goes on.

Why was this not possible in their own countries? It is because this is America, the land of the brave, new Canaan, where the dreams of hard-working, brilliant, and positive thinker dreamers come true.

Why does every ordinary immigrant want to be a millionaire overnight in America? Because it is in the American air, never possible in their homeland, and many have proved just that. Welcome to America. When you become successful, don't think it is just because of you; it is because of America. Make sure you give back to America; refill the oil in the torch of my Lady of Liberty, melt into the tapestry of our culture just like Parsees did in India, and enjoy the American cheese. No other nation in the world makes hamburgers as delicious as the one made with Wisconsin cheese.

Americans were good at inventing the wagon, but they imported the horses so that they could ride in the wagon with the bride and, after the wedding, preside over the banquet so that they could move on to invent a new stagecoach that could be driven on Mars. Look around what big chip companies are doing.

Takeaway: When the Navy appointed me as technical director (TD) of the Navy Program Office, Strategic System Program (SSP), nuclear missile Trident submarine navigation system, Huntington Beach, California, Boeing facility, I felt like, "Oh Lord, who am I?"

And the Lord said, "I have renamed you Zaphenath-paneah" (see Genesis 41:41–46, NASB).

86. WHAT'S IN A NAME?

To get my travel documents, I had to go to the city clerk's office in Anand, Gujarat state, India. I was born in the Salvation Army hospital, known as Emery Hospital. The chief surgeon was a missionary doctor from New Zealand. He was so popular in the state that people from every tribe, caste, race, and religion would line up at the front of the admission office at four o'clock in the morning to see him. He named me as his name, Bramwell. So, I told the city clerk, Mr. Patel, that my name is spelled as Bramwell, not as Bramvel. He jumped from his chair and shouted, "Listen, this is not New Zealand. I know English; I studied at St. Xavier's High School. Do you want a certificate or not?"

I said, "Yes, sir. I need it today."

He hand-marked on my birth certificate, "Name: Bramvel David Christian," and viciously laughed. I didn't say a word. I needed a birth certificate for the next day to travel to the American embassy in Bombay. I have so many wonderful Hindu friends, so loving and caring. It's hard to explain in the Western world; if a Hindu is your friend, individually, they will be just like a member of your own family and even more helpful, friendly, intimate, kind, and loving, better than some of the Gentiles so-called Christians. But if he is not in your friend circle, as a group or a community or a powerhouse or a government agency, he reacts differently. **In India, the two-thousand-year-old casteism and racial bias poison take over humanity, decency, respect, and regard for human rights.**

I saw lightning running from his left eye to his right eye; he was murmuring racial slurs behind me. I was scared to death. So, I accepted the birth certificate and ran as fast as I could.

Takeaway: I wanted to leave a note to this jealous clerk, "Watch your tongue and keep your mouth shut, and you will stay out of trouble" (Proverbs 21:23 NLT).

Did you know there is a test you can take to determine whether you are a stereotyped or biased person?

It's called an implicit association test (IAT). It should be given to all non-Judeo-Christian immigrants before a green card can be issued.

87. CHALLENGE TO INDIAN DIASPORA IN FOREIGN LANDS

"Indian diaspora in other countries is still shackled by casteism," former CJI (chief justice of India) tells Telugu (Indians from Telugu state of India) in America.

The former chief justice of India, Justice NV Ramana, visited America in 2023 and expressed concern over the deep-rooted caste system within the Indian community in the United States and other nations. He said this while appealing to the Telugu diaspora to continue its campaign for conferring Bharat Ratna on the late minister NT Rama Rao, former chief minister of undivided Andhra Pradesh.

Addressing an event at the Pennsylvania Convention Centre in Philadelphia on Sunday, Justice Ramana said,

> When caste differences have blurred in India, particularly in the southern part of the country, it's a matter of grave concern that caste system is prevalent among Indians in the US. We should be forward-looking in our thoughts.

Justice Ramana said inter-caste marriages have become common in India, but sadly, in the US, the Indian community is still stuck on the idea of caste superiority. "The world has progressed, and those with a regressive mind will go extinct. History is witness," he said at a function organized by the Telugu Association of North America (TANA) as part of its twenty-third conference held between July 7 and 9, 2023.

When Mr. Modi said during his recent state dinner at the White House that racism has no place in India, it might be his good faith expectation, but in reality, it is not a race-conscious holistic view, but rather a sub-rosa way of face-saving because, on the same day, India's

north-eastern state, Manipur, was burning due to racial tension across the state. The base chemical to neutralize the acid of casteism is not available in India yet. That base chemical that can change 2000 years old rotten-minded casteism is the realization that "all human beings are created equal." The Bible says, "So God created man in His own image, in the image of God He created him; male and female He created them" (Genesis 1:27, NASB).

"When Adam had lived 130 years, he fathered a son in his own likeness, according to his image, and named him Seth" (Genesis 5:3, NASB).

It is amazing that even today, in Gujarat state, India, the businessmen are called Seth. No wonder the Gujaratis are top businessmen in India and America. Gujarati Seths, now you know your roots.

Root out the casteism from India and read the Bible; you will be the businessmen of His kingdom, and you will be a blessing to all other Indians at home and abroad.

(7/16/2023, Sunday)

An aphorism often said by the twenty-sixth president of the United States, Theodore Roosevelt, "Speak softly and carry a big stick; you will go far."

If President Theodore Roosevelt were alive today, he would say, "Hey, my immigrant friends, speak respectfully; don't bring your traditional dirty laundry of casteism/racism here. Uncle Sam carries a big stick. Rather, don't leave home; America is not for you."

If President John F. Kennedy were alive today, he would say, "Hey, my immigrant friends, welcome to America. Thanks for your contributions, but don't ask what America can do for you; ask what you can do for America because this nation has done so much for you that your homeland couldn't do for you. Your green card has turned into green rupees to send your old home."

Now, Uncle Sam wants you to leave your casteism/racism behind you. We are one nation under the living God, united under the cross, blessed by the Torah. Remember, there is no place for casteism/racism in America.

Takeaway: If you leave the Pacific, leave your dirty laundry of casteism and classism at Chowpatty Beach in Bombay. The Atlantic only accepts snow-white clean minds.

(7/14/2023, Friday)

88. WHAT HAPPENED TO THE LOST TRIBES OF ISRAEL?

Both the Kingdom of Israel and the Kingdom of Judah were formed by twelve tribes of Hebrew people. While there is historical evidence of the tribes of Judah and Benjamin (which formed the Kingdom of Judah and are considered the ancestors of modern Jews), the remaining ten tribes are not well documented.

What happened to the lost tribes of Israel? The tribes were reportedly overtaken by Assyria and exiled from the Kingdom of Israel. But where did they go? Some theories say they traveled to Persia, the Arabian Peninsula, Ethiopia, and even as far as Asia and North America.

So, Americans are Judeo-Christian descendants of lost tribes of Israel. No wonder America is blessed.

Takeaway: "And I will bring them, and they shall dwell in the midst of Jerusalem: and they shall be my people, and I will be their God, in truth and in righteousness" (Zechariah 8:8, KJV).

America is a new Jerusalem because, "And they shall put my name upon the children of Israel; and I will bless them" (Numbers 6:27, KJV).

89. HOW TO ROPE THE BULL'S HORN IN AMERICAN CORPORATE ARENA AND BE *SALIDA A HOMBROS*?

Be a *matador*, learn how to rope, wear pink shocks—that is what I figured out the hard way, but I did. Most immigrants have gone through the same rhymes at the drum beats of American corporate expectations: "*Salida a hombros.*"

At the end of the corrida (half a bullfight), while the band plays a *pasodoble*, the successful *matador* who has at least two ears is given permission to leave the plaza carried on the shoulders of an admirer. It's called *salida a hombros* (exit on shoulders), and in Spain, bullfighting experts consider it the highest recognition a torero can have.

The *salida a hombros* is done through the plaza's most important gate, the Puerta Grande or Big Gate in Madrid, or the Puerta del Príncipe or Prince's Gate in Seville.

(7/18/2023, Tuesday)

God will provide you a rope to win the *corrida*, **be a** *matador*, **and learn how to rope the bull of difficult problems in life.**

Isaiah 41:10 (NKJV), "Fear not, for I am with you; Be not dismayed, for I am your God. I will strengthen you, Yes, I will help you, I will uphold you with My righteous right hand."

Here are the proven roping practices I used to rope the bull's horn in my professional engineering and social life.

1. Begin your day with a prayer before you sip a cup of coffee. I drink tea, and I call it North Starbuck tea with a flavor of prayer (milk) and a spoon of blessing (no sugar) early morning. Why to begin the day with prayer? It is because you will be hugged with the unconditional love from your creator.

Ecclesiastes 12:6 (NASB), "Remember your Creator before the silver cord is broken and the golden bowl is crushed, the pitcher by the spring is shattered and the wheel at the cistern is crushed."

Because He is your heavenly Father. Matthew 6:32 (NASB), "Your heavenly Father knows that you need all these things."

You will be given today's assignments because He is your teacher. John 13:13 (NASB), "You call Me 'Teacher' and 'Lord'; and you are correct, for so I am."

You will receive strength because He has promised, "Don't be afraid; the one living in you is greater than the one (harassing you) in the world." First John 4:4 (NASB), "You are from God, little children, and have overcome them; because greater is He who is in you than he who is in the world."

He will direct your path because He said, "I am the way, the truth, and the life." John 14:6 (KJV), "Jesus saith unto him, I am the way, the truth, and the life: no man cometh unto the Father, but by me."

He will grant you the knowledge to solve your problems because He said, "And I will give you pastors according to mine heart, which shall feed you with knowledge and understanding" (Jeremiah 3:15, KJV).

He will gift you the wisdom to plan your strategy to win the game because, "For I will give you a mouth and wisdom, which all your adversaries shall not be able to gainsay nor resist" (Luke 21:15, KJV).

2. **No matter how tough, cruel, sarcastic, egoistic, racial, or arrogant your bosses might be, always smile and be friendly to them because they may or may not be like that in reality. But they might be under a lot of pressure from their boss, and their boss from the upper management. So, they let the steam out of the pressure cooker. Besides, Job says, "I will forget my**

complaint, I will put off my sad face and wear a smile" (Job 9:27, NKJV).

3. **Be a technical matador.**

In the year 2008, Boeing satellite division in El Segundo, California, tested a hundred engineers and, after two screenings, selected twenty candidates for Six Sigma training. I was one of them, and I said, "Lord, bless Boeing, seriously."

I was going through a tough time during the one-year training period. I was losing sight in both eyes due to cataracts, and my mother was in the hospital in her last stage. In spite of all these, after a brutal final exam, I became a Boeing Six Sigma Black Belt, Green Belt, and Master Black Belt certified by the International Quality Organization. During this difficult time, my mentor was my manager and a friend, Mr. Yeh, a sharp Jewish engineer. Whenever I reached a dead end to find the solution to a most difficult technical assignment, he would give me a mantra, and it worked all the time. He was an amazing Zionist; I always admired him.

When I joined the Navy, Captain Williams said, "It is not enough; the Navy demands more from you for the project you are assigned."

So, I looked up at the sky and said, "Lord, why me again?"

And the living God said, "Why not? If you don't, who else will?"

So, I said, "Yes, Lord, it's me."

In 2010, I became a Navy's Black Belt.

Yes, football, basketball, orchestra, Disneyland, hiking, Magic Mountain, Palm Springs, and SeaWorld are all of our American leisure life, but if you want to rope the horn of the bull in a technical plaza, be a technical matador. There is no other way.

4. **Connect with the living God and read the Bible. To master the technical field, read all technical publications on the product**

you are working on. You will be amazed at how little you know and will impress your boss.

5. Convince your management to let you visit your sub-suppliers. Learn how the components you use are fabricated.

(7/21/2023, Friday)

Believe it or not, an engineer or a scientist is also a salesperson. You may have the greatest idea or invention in the world, but if you can't sell it to the decision-makers, you will not fly. How can you become a successful technical salesman? You need to master the golden rules:

A. Support your ideas/invention/innovation/improvement with data and not just assumptions. Data does not lie. Data speaks louder than your voice.

B. Be a master orator. On the stage, when you present your technical PowerPoint, you are conducting the technical orchestra.

C. Be a profound technical writer.

Technical writing is a different skill than writing a purchase order, political speech, a novel, a short story, a newspaper article, or a Sunday church message. It is a technical interpretation in simple language for an audience with little or no technical knowledge. It is speaking in a totally different language but still having the listener say, "Now I understand what it means when you say current is directly proportional to the voltage applied."

Do you know how many times people read the assembly instructions for the new product they buy and get frustrated when they don't understand the instruction booklet and can't assemble even a simple toy? Why? The instruction book writer was not a good technical writer.

D. Read, read, and read technical books, publications, and magazines.

For fifty years, my day has started with Daily Bread (not a deli bread) reading, the manna for the day, and ended with technical reading. This has sustained me spiritually and technically.

E. **Never get frustrated when the experiment fails. It is not a failure; it is one branch of the haystack that needs to be removed that will eventually lead you to where the needle is.**

F. **Listen to everybody, but make your own judgment.**

In all companies, there are old-timers, and they try to control their position and impose their position. What happens is that many times, they are not willing to listen to new ideas and resist change. But the change is inevitable. When I was with Hughes Aircraft Company in 1987, a very tiny ferrite core of a transformer was cracking during the manufacturing process, and nobody could figure out why. After tremendous technical research, I concluded that the culprit might be the two parts epoxy we were using. I needed to perform a control experiment to prove it, but this old-timer laughed it out and told me to give up that idea. Guess what? After he left the company, the new manager allowed me to perform the experiment, and I was right. I found the solution and saved thousands of dollars for the Navy.

G. **Make friends with knowledgeable subject matter experts (SME). The real SMEs are always humble and willing to share the knowledge.**

I have learned tremendous lessons from my peers and mentors. The knowledge multiplies when you share with others always because when you share your expertise with someone else, the other person adds his/her icing to your cake.

Takeaway: Now you know all the tricks. Go in the arena with the strength of the Lord, rope the bull, and the angels will carry you in a *salida a hombros*.

(7/19/2023, Wednesday)

90. MY BELOVED INDIA

In spite of all the ugly side of your small, mean minority individuals within the majority, you are my beloved India. After all, you nourished me when I was a child, you educated me when I was young, and you hugged me when your own mentally-blind, lost-minded hated me.

Hey, new Young India, wake up; it's a new dawn. Read the poem of Mr. Umashankar Joshi, the past vice-chancellor of Gujarat University, "Get up, good old India. Can't you see on the horizon? The wind is blowing from the west."

Your name will be United States of New India. You will build a new India where freedom, justice, and a right to practice, preach, and proclaim (3Ps) the religion of a person's conviction will be a universal birthright.

Here is the message for the new young Indian generation, like those who flocked around Jim Cook, Apple CEO, in Bombay and New Delhi. You are the new India. Your party's name is Voice of the United States of New India (VO-USONI). Mr. Gandhi unshackled India from Brits; now, it is your time to unshackle India from casteism, exploitation of power, and religious intolerance. Let the victims of socioeconomic-religious persecution breathe the air of real freedom.

Indian immigrants in the Five Eyes, take this message home and practice it here; otherwise, writings are on the wall. Remember what happened in Africa to you; the history will repeat here in the Five Eyes.

The time is running out, an astounding warning, but a truth and a reality. Don't believe it? Look, you follow the same boloney in your own home country. Gujaratis don't like South Indians working in Gujarat, Marathe don't like North Indians (called *bhais*, meaning brothers, but treated like enemies) working in Bombay, and Shik experience betrayal in spite of their whole battalion in the Army.

Christian institutes brought education in English, advanced science, math, and medicine and treated every poor, marginalized, and neglected in every village and town of India. And yet, on May 3, 2023, ethnic violence erupted in India's north-eastern state of Manipur, and three Christian ladies were paraded naked on the downtown street; the lowest of the lowest heinous acts, the insult to humanity and civilization only happened in India in the twenty-first century.

India, repent. Jesus Christ still loves you. He says, "India does not know what it is doing to Me."

Takeaway: "Jesus said, 'Father, forgive them (India), for they (India) do not know what they are doing. And they divided up his clothes (human rights) by casting lots (majority power)'" (Luke 23:34, NIV).

(7/22/2023, Saturday)

91. HELLO, MY HINDU FRIENDS

The majority of Hindus are good, kind, friendly, generous, peace-loving people. In 1972, when I was teaching physics at V. P. Science College, affiliated with the highly reputed Sardar Patel University of India, Gujarat state, everyone in the Physics Department attended my wedding; all of them were Hindus. Can this happen in the USA or any other country?

Then why is there no end to ethnic violence, the hidden bitterness of casteism, and the absence of religious freedom in India? The reason is a small minority mafia group of selfish, politically motivated, uneducated, egoist, self-centered, religiously fanatic, far-right, extremist fascists— whatever you want to call it, exists. This minority fraction takes over the community and turns into a monster mob, a tornado that ignores all decency of humanity and tears apart civilized society.

The political majority, religious leaders, educated professionals, cultural entertainers, media, musicians, artists, Bollywood actors, and their cousins all knew the truth but remained silent until humanity turned into ashes. It was the same scenario as when Jesus Christ was crucified; everyone knew the truth, but they remained silent, including His own disciples, friends, community, and political leaders.

It was the same scenario as when the Holocaust happened; all political, religious, and social leaders knew what Hitler was doing and still remained silent. Millions and millions of lambs were slaughtered in Auschwitz II-Birkenau, Poland, but the lions remained silent in their comfort caves.

Luke 22:34 (NASB), "But He said, 'I tell you, Peter, the rooster will not crow today until you have denied three times that you know Me.'"

John 18:25 (NASB), "Now Simon Peter was still standing and warming himself. So, they said to him, 'You are not one of His disciples as well, are you?' He denied it, and said, 'I am not.'"

John 18:27 (NASB), "Peter then denied it again, and immediately a rooster crowed."

This is what is happening in India. The lambs are kept silent, and political, social, and religious lions keep soaring louder and louder openly on the street every day.

As I wrote this, on June 22, 2023, the wine glasses were ringing on Capitol Hill of Washington, DC, in honor of Mr. Modi, the prime minister of India, when ironically, Manipur State of India was burning.

A small fraction of the majority of Hindus turned into a mob, and murdered, burned houses, raped women, and destroyed the lives of minority groups.

No American or Indian politicians said a word or condemned cruelty and barbaric fanaticism openly acted out on the street. It's the same scenario as when the mother of Jesus Christ was crying at the foot of the cross; His friends, disciples, followers, leaders, rulers, and educators were all silent.

The beast of satanic ideology takes over the decency of civilization in the name of religious ism, and the so-called civilized world remains silent. Hitler is still alive in the world, but the name is changed. In India, Hitler's name is Hit List (casteism, racism, antichrist), and slowly, it has sneaked into the Five Eyes, too. America, wake up. If you don't, who else will take the leadership to hunt down Hitler?

The Christian nations pray every day, "Our Father, who art in heaven, hallowed be Thy name." A prayer of 1919 by President George Washington is used regularly at "the President's Chapel" of George Washington University.

Remember the painting of "Prayer at Valley Forge" to celebrate our country's bicentennial in 1976? Remember what President Abraham Lincoln prayed on Thanksgiving Day?

> Almighty God, Who has given us this good land for our heritage; We humbly beseech Thee that we may always prove ourselves a people mindful of Thy favor and glad to do Thy will. Bless our land with honorable ministry, sound learning, and pure manners.

Remember what President Ronald Regan said about the prayer in his Radio Address to the Nation on Thanksgiving Day, September 18, 1982?

And just as prayer has helped us as a nation, it helps us as individuals. In nearly all our lives, there are moments when our prayers and the prayers of our friends and loved ones help to see us through and keep on the right path. In fact, prayer is one of the few things in this world that hurts no one and sustains the spirit of millions.

However, in the name of free enterprise, out of hundreds of names of the living God in the Bible, not a single name was hallowed at the state dinner on June 22, 2023, in honor of Mr. Modi.

The power of GDP takes precedence over the power of prayer. In the name of GDP, the name of God was forgotten. America, wake up.

When a man turned into a beast, shouted like a monster, and acted like an animal on the streets of Manipur, where was the UN Human Rights Council? Where were the human rights organizations? Where were the churches? Where was the Pope? Wake up, all devout Christians.

America puts the giant step for mankind on the moon, but when mankind slips back into the Stone Age, the master of technology remains silent and turns the eyes where the green pasture is, not towards where the old rugged cross is.

Surprisingly, even in this day and time, the deep-rooted caste prejudices prevalent in villages of India have sneaked through chain visas in America and other countries. Therefore, Washington State has passed the anti-casteism law now. Similar laws are in progress in California and other states to protect American citizens from this two-thousand-year-old Stone Age evil Hindu ideology prevalent among the uneducated Hindu Indians in small villages, even today.

My brothers and sisters in Manipur, they can burn your homes outside, but they can't burn your sprit inside. They can parade you naked on the street, but remember that's what the devil did to Jesus Christ: they hanged Him on the cross and cast lots on His clothes.

Luke 23:34 (NKJV), "Then Jesus said, 'Father, forgive them, for they do not know what they do.' And they divided His garments and cast lots."

Do not be afraid; the Christians of the world are with you and praying for you. Hello, the Christians of the world. You are one family of Christ; your name is "United Nations of the Cross." Pray for Manipur, contact them, and let them know, "You are not alone but

united under the cross because He died for us on the cross, and He rose from the grave, and the cross is above you because He is alive."

Revelation 1:18 (KJV), "I am he that liveth, and was dead; and, behold, I am alive for evermore, Amen; and have the keys of hell and of death."

> Takeaway: Pray for the Christians and non-Christians of Manipur, India, and around the world, where they are persecuted for holding the cross. Brothers and sisters, hold on to the cross; He is alive.
>
> If no one answers your mayday, be assured the army of angels is preparing for D-Day to rescue you. He said, "Do not be afraid; I am with you."
>
> Jeremiah 1:8 (NKJV), "'Do not be afraid of their faces, For I am with you to deliver you,' says the LORD."

(7/24/2023, Monday)

92. MESSAGE TO THE NEW YOUNG
INDIAN GENERATION IN INDIA

You are the new young Apple power, Microsoft generation, IBM children, Tesla innovators, Intel futuristics, Boeing jumbo jet brainers, YouTube visionary, and Facebook friendly; you have the power and responsibility to build a new India.

Your new country's name will be the United States of New India. Wipe out the word caste from all government, political, social, religious, educational, and economic bureaucracies.

Do you see the exploited, marginalized, left behind, forgotten, beaten, naked, hungry, living in slums, denied justice and education, misled, blindfolded, paraded naked people who are crying for justice and help? My friends, extend your hands to them, reach out, and say we are here for you—we care for you. They are not lower caste or scheduled caste or *dalits*. Someone with a kaka brain came up with these demonizing names 2000 thousand years ago.

They are the victims of injustice, politics, and insulting negative society; call them VIPINS. They have the same rights, privileges, opportunities, and class as everybody else has in India.

Message to the VIPINS

If any culture, tradition, ritual, custom, practice, or religion tells you, "You are lower than me," "You can't come into my circle," "Do not enter my temple or house," "You can't be friends with my sons or daughters," that is not a civilized modern society but a politically motivated witchcraft. Get out of it. Go to the modern civilized society that will embrace, welcome, hug, and treat you with love and compassion, break the bread with you, and dine with you at the same table. Their sons and daughters will mingle with you and dance with you, you will breathe fresh air and achieve a new life, and you will start dreaming larger-than-life dreams. Be courageous and leave the old, dirty, filthy ideology behind you.

All human beings are created equal by your living God; it is up to you to claim it. Wake up, my friends. Wake up. Manipur is burning; thousands of lives will not be the same again. It is time now, young India. Wake up; it's your call. The world is watching you. Answer the call, come out of the cocoon, and breathe the fresh air.

Takeaway: The Lady of Liberty on Ellis Island raises the torch above New York Harbor and proclaims justice and liberty for all. Jesus Christ stands tall on the rock of Rio de Janeiro with two hands stretched out to welcome everyone, especially those who are VIPINS. He says, "Oh heavily burdened, come to Me, and I will give you the rest," while demons are beating VIPINS in the world.

Matthew 11:28 (NLT), "Then Jesus said, 'Come to me, all of you who are weary and carry heavy burdens, and I will give you rest.'"

---

93. INDIAN GURU RIDING ON THE HORSE BUT DESPICABLE TO THE HEART

In 1955, in a small town called Napad in Gujarat state, India, where I spent my childhood, there was a man who acted like a war hero and impressed young people by encouraging them to join a vigilante group. Youngsters in the village called him Guruji to respect him as a hero because he was teaching them how to use a bamboo stick as a martial arts performance tool. He claimed he participated in the Quit India movement during the Indian independence fight led by Mr. Gandhi prior to 1947. He considered himself a local hero and claimed to be very proud of it.

One day, I was walking to the school, and he was going on the same road with a big crowd of students behind him. Some of my school friends told him, "Guruji, this is Bramvel. He is number one in the school and teaches us math and English; a very smart student. He always gets A grades."

Guruji asked me, "What's your surname?"

I said, "Christian."

He became very furious and angry. "Christian?" And he started calling me with racial slurs. He compared me to the British. Nobody said a word to him. I remained silent. **If bigotry has another name, it would be this man's name. There was a big crowd on his side, but I was alone. Does racial prejudice make you a guru?** This man thought he was. Most Hindus believe that Christianity is a foreign religion exported by the British. Because Brits became India's enemies, Christians were seen as traitors, the same as Jews in Germany prior to the Second World War. **But the truth is, Saint Thomas, one of the twelve disciples of Jesus Christ, traveled outside the Roman Empire to preach the gospel in AD 52 and brought the good news to Tamil Nadu and Kerala in south India. Why? It was because it is mandated by our God and**

Savior, Jesus Christ, for all Christians to share the good news with the world around us.

Look what Mark, Matthew, and Luke noted down as Christ's duty call for the Christian soldiers onward in the Bible,

Mark 16:15 (KJV), "And he said unto them, Go ye into all the world, and preach the gospel to every creature."

Matthew 5:44 (KJV), "But I say unto you, Love your enemies, bless them that curse you, do good to them that hate you, and pray for them which despitefully use you, and persecute you."

Luke 6:27 (KJV), "But I say unto you which hear, Love your enemies, do good to them which hate you."

Luke 6:35 (KJV),

But love ye your enemies, and do good, and lend, hoping for nothing again; and your reward shall be great, and ye shall be the children of the Highest: for he is kind unto the unthankful and to the evil.

Takeaway: That guru died; nobody remembers him anymore, but St. Thomas is still alive in India because of the good news he shared with the Indian people. Hello, my Hindu friends; we love you even if you call us by name because my guru is Jesus Christ, and He teaches me to love you.

(7/25/2023, Tuesday)

94. YOU DON'T KNOW HOW IT FEELS UNTIL YOU CONFRONT HIM YOURSELF—A MONSTER CALLED DEPRESSION AND HOMESICKNESS

When you feel you are home alone, lost, nobody cares, it is cloudy and dark even though it's springtime, all the friends who attended the party are nowhere in sight, you had all good intentions and still failed, you did possibly all that you could and still could not reach the goal, you see no light at the end of the tunnel but only an oncoming train at full speed, just wait, my friend. Trust me; the darker the night today, the brighter will be the sunlight tomorrow. Just wait a little bit more until it turns yellow, and I guarantee it will turn green. Here are the divine promises that will guide you, comfort you, encourage you, and will get you through.

The giant that scares you is actually a shadow that will disappear when God shines a flashlight on you.

"You are from God, little children, and have overcome them; because greater is He who is in you than he who is in the world" (1 John 4:4, NASB).

Somebody took advantage of your kindness, and that bothers you. Just wait; a great reward is on the way.

"Do not judge, and you will not be judged; and do not condemn, and you will not be condemned; pardon, and you will be pardoned" (Luke 6:37, NASB).

You worry about how you shall pay all the bills coming. Plan budget, save every penny, and don't be an impulsive shopper.

"Poor is one who works with a lazy hand, But the hand of the diligent makes rich. He who gathers in summer is a son who acts wisely, But he who sleeps in harvest is a son who acts shamefully" (Proverbs 10:4–5, NASB).

From Adobe of India to the Killer Whale of the US Navy

The most wrongly interpreted verse in the Bible is, "Whatever you need, ask in His name, and it will be given to you." God helps those who help themselves first: get up, go, climb, dive, fly, do something, and then claim the Bible verse.

Then the LORD said to Moses, "Why are you crying out to Me? Tell the sons of Israel to go forward. As for you, lift up your staff and reach out with your hand over the sea and divide it, and the sons of Israel shall go through the midst of the sea on dry land."

Exodus 14:15–16 (NASB)

Even in tough times, keep humor on your lips that will be lipstick to heal the pain.

Proverb 17:22 (NASB), "A joyful heart is good medicine, But a broken spirit dries up the bones."

Takeaway: If you are tired and want to give up, wait, go one more mile; the hidden gate is wide open, but you don't see from where you are sitting. Be patient, wait upon Him, and press on like St. Paul says, "I press on toward the goal for the prize of the upward call of God in Christ Jesus" (Philippians 3:14, NASB).

(7/26/2023, Tuesday)

95. AMERICA, THE PROMISED LAND

America is not another East India Company founded by Christopher Columbus on 12 October 1492; she is a promised land and must be led only by Moses' Judeo-Christian sons and daughters.

The ten commandments slate is the cornerstone of the Lincoln Memorial, and across from it, Capitol Hill is the temple of Jehovah Jireh. The flag on the top with the fifty stars is the North Star the world is looking for to find hope, guidance, dreams, and courage, and it stands for truth, love, compassion, freedom, justice, and beauty of humanity.

If the founding fathers were alive today, they would say, "Oh my America, don't let any Philistine misguide you. You are the apple of my eye."

The American president must be a Judeo-Christian descendant only and no other, ever.

Why? When tragedy strikes in America, Christian churches open their doors, hold vigil, pray for the families, and reach out to the victims.

When a natural disaster strikes, The Salvation Army reaches out and touches people of all races without any distinction.

When 9/11 happened, American churches were full for seeking the answer.

Only Christian pastors visit jails to comfort those who made wrong choices and lead them to repent and prepare for a new life.

Only members of Christian organizations and churches visit senior citizens in hospitals and retirement homes.

Only Christian church members reach out to our military heroes on duty and off duty.

Look at all highly reputed universities; there is a chapel on the campus. You will not see this in any other country in the world.

No wonder the living God has blessed America. Are these enough proofs? President Donald Trump will continue this tradition in 2025.

Walk from Boston to Los Angeles and from Seattle to San Diego, and you will see beautiful church after church in every town built by our founding fathers, pioneers, settlers, and pilgrims.

Drive on the West Coast shoreline of California from San Francisco to San Diego. You will see city after city named after the Christina missionaries: San Francisco, Santa Cruz, San Clemente, San Jose, Santa Barbara, San Juan Capistrano, Santa Ana, San Gabriel, San Diego, and many others. The missionaries built missions up and down along the California coast. Today, the whole world wants to visit California, the thriving, prosperous center of the high-tech. It is the Golden State, soon to be the Lithium State of America.

The presidents, prime ministers, governors, school superintendents, and mayors of Five Eyes nations must be of Judeo-Christian faith because the tears, sweat, talents, and skills shared by our pioneer founding fathers should not go in vain.

Let not goats (water buffaloes in the Pacific) hidden in the lambs (cows in India) of an immigrant crowd seeking green pasture bites misguide you, Uncle Sam.

Jeremiah 11:5 (NLT), "'I said this so I could keep my promise to your ancestors to give you a land flowing with milk and honey—the land you live in today.' Then I replied, 'Amen, LORD! May it be so.'"

Jeremiah 32:22 (NET), "You kept the promise that you swore on oath to their ancestors. You gave them a land flowing with milk and honey."

And I promise that I will bring you up out of the affliction of Egypt, to the land of the Canaanites, the Hittites, the Amorites, the Per'izzites, the Hivites, and the Jeb'usites, a land flowing with milk and honey.

Exodus 3:17 (RSV)

Uncle Sam and Five Eyes, don't let Canaanites, the Hittites, the Amorites, the Per'izzites, the Hivites, and the Jeb'usites misguide you again; you will be lost in California Mojave Desert for forty years again. Bestow Moses in every four-year nationwide American camp called the general election.

Takeaway: Mr. Donald Trump will win the Moses staff again in 2024. The replica of the original staff in Istanbul displayed at the Topkapi palace will be awarded to him on Capitol Hill on January 20, 2025.

The staff will be inscribed with the tetragrammaton "Yahweh" to usher America into a new era of hope for medical miracles, technological breakthroughs, abundant mines of wealth, inspiring knowledge, and heavenly wisdom for peace and the kingdom of the living God.

96. MOST HINDUS ARE NICE PEOPLE, JUST LOST LAMBS. WHO WILL SHEPHERD THEM?

A Hindu Patel doctor, a very nice man working in Salvation Army Hospital in Anand, Gujarat state, India, attended daily staff prayer meetings. The chief medical officer (CMO) of this hospital was Dr. Nobel, a Salvation Army officer from Atlanta, Georgia, USA. He was a great surgeon doctor who dedicated his life to serving the poor and needy of India. He got an infection from treating an infected poor Hindu patient from a remote village in South India. He returned to the USA for treatment, and his left hand was amputated. He returned back to Emery Hospital to serve the people he loved.

One day, Dr. Patel told the staff after the morning prayer meeting, "Most of you come from poor families because you ask your God, 'Give us our daily *roti* (bread)' only, but we ask our god to give us gold and silver, and we get gold and silver in dowry when we get married." He was referring to God's Prayer, "Give us this day our daily bread."

I told him, "Dr. Patel, when we say, 'Give us our daily bread,' what we are asking for is for Him to give us not only a physical bread but the wisdom and knowledge to understand and claim God's promises in the Holy Bible because God's Word is our daily bread for spiritual growth, more precious than the gold and silver because Jesus said, 'I am the bread of life'" (see John 6:35, 48, 51).

He was amazed and remained silent. The gold is dug from the dust of the deep muddy ground, but the knowledge and wisdom are the gifts from heaven above, given to those who seek the living God (Matthew 6:2 and 5).

A few years later, this doctor came to New York on a student visa and never returned to India. One day, he was standing in the World Trade

Center Twin Towers Plaza, and he said, "How did America become this wealthy and powerful in the world?"

His sponsor, an American Christian doctor, told him, **"Because America is a Judeo-Christian nation and does not live by bread alone but by the words of the living God who has blessed this nation abundantly, exceedingly."**

He said, "I wish I knew what I know now. I might not have made the nasty comment I made at the Salvation Army Hospital in Anand, Gujarat State, India."

This missionary hospital has served more Hindus, Muslims, Sikhs, Jains, Buddhists, and others than combined outpatients in all private hospitals in India but never got credit from the government or community. This doctor never went back to India because even though he was a doctor, his living standard was not equal to that of an average American at that time.

America is not living by hot dogs and hamburgers (American bread) alone but by the words of the living God preached every Sunday from the Bible from Boston to Los Angeles, from Seattle to San Diego, and all the towns in between.

You may pass through a time when it seems like everything is going against you; even if you didn't do anything wrong and it's not your fault, the world doesn't understand it, and those you thought were your friends, relatives, and acquaintances, are shouting and yelling against you; you never thought it would happen. This happened to me when I returned to India.

Do not worry. Go through the valley. The Lord has laid down a green pasture at the end of the valley; hang on for a while. The glorious morning is just behind the dark night (Psalm 84:6).

Jealousy is like a thorny branch; it will bite your fingers if you make a crown out of it, and you will be responsible for the blood if you crown someone with it.

When I became a Six Sigma Black Belt at Boeing, El Segundo, California, the appreciative wise management bestowed me with a Technical Emmy Award. I was absent that day. One jealous instructor hid the award for years until another instructor found it and returned it to me; both were my great Jewish friends.

Bramvel Christian

My hurt was turned into the hello and scar into the star (Psalm 138:7–8).

When you are desperate, and it seems like nobody wants to help you, don't give up. Believe in the living God, an angel, and a miracle. He will always send you an angel who will stand by you unexpectedly when you never thought it would happen.

When you feel the sky is falling down, and this is the end, it's not. Just wait a little longer; out of nowhere, an angel will appear and will be your instrument to finish the job (Psalm 121:1).

When you are assigned a project that you think you are not capable of doing or that you don't have the knowledge and skill you think are needed, don't give up; a life-changing golden opportunity doesn't come very often.

When the technical director of the Navy Strategic System Program Office in Huntington Beach, California, quit, nobody wanted to accept that heavy responsibility. I prayed about it and said I would.

I am amazed by His mercy, grace, and love. I was very successful; even Vice Admiral W. sent me a letter of recognition when I retired (Matthew 17:20). How did that happen? It was only by His grace, mercy, knowledge, and wisdom that comes from above.

Takeaway: I believe in an angel, and I hope you will, too, after reading my story.

Genesis 31:11 (KJV), "And the angel of God spake unto me in a dream, saying, Jacob [Bramvel]: And I said, Here am I."

Job 23:12 (NIV), "I have not departed from the commands of his lips; I have treasured the words of his mouth more than my daily bread."

Luke 4:4 (KJV), "And Jesus answered him, saying, It is written, That man shall not live by bread alone, but by every word of God."

Mr. Patel, now you know why we pray, "Lord, give us our daily bread." The living God's words are our daily bread.

---

97. I WANT TO GO TO AMERICA, MY DREAMLAND, BUT I HAVE NO PENNY IN MY POCKET

I got the immigration visa to come to my dreamland, America, based on my education, experience, and skill because physics and math teachers were in short supply in 1972 in the USA. But I didn't have money to buy an air ticket. My wife always encouraged me and kept saying, "Yes, you will make it; do not give up."

If you look at the newspaper published in Gujarat state, India, at that time, you will see page after page of advertisements, "Going to the USA for further study." Ninety-five percent of them were all Patels. Yes, most of them are good, nice, hardworking, smart people, but why can 95 percent go to the USA and not others?

It is because they are in the villages with money, 90 percent of the farming lands, resources, and political driving force. It is the same story in every state in India.

But I prayed every day, and lo and behold, unexpectedly, the help arrived and paid for my airline ticket in full and some extra. How?

I tutored the son of Mr. Shah, a very wealthy man, highly educated in Australia, who was vice president of Amul Dairy, a pioneer and largest dairy products producer in India located in a small town called Anand, Gujarat state, India. This man was invited by Iran around 1960 to establish the dairy industry in Tehran. My bike was very old and frequently broke, but I biked twenty miles every day to teach physics at V. P. Science College at day time and private tutoring at night time.

Takeaway: Do not blink on your dream; keep your eyes on your creator. The help wagon will arrive at your front door when the broken bike is laid down in the garage.

I look up to the mountains—does my help come from there? My help comes from the LORD, who made heaven and earth! He will not let you stumble; the one who watches over you will not slumber.

Psalm 121:1–3 (NLT)

Exodus 33:2 (NIV), "And I will send an angel before you to drive out (all enemies)." My wife and my sister always encouraged me, "you can do it, go," they are my angels.

(8/2/2023, Wednesday)

98. LITTLE CATHOLIC CHURCH ON THE HILL, BREAD AND GRAPE JUICE IN THE HANDS, TEARS IN THE EYES OF THE LAMBS

This is a true story. I spent my childhood in a small village called Napad in Gujarat state, India. On the hill, there was a small Catholic church. A Catholic missionary by the name of Father Surya, originally from Portugal, was very popular and highly respected. He adopted the Indian name Surya and spoke the native Indian language of Gujarati very eloquently.

Most Catholic Christians of this community worked in tobacco farms and tobacco factories in the village owned by the Patel Hindu community. Most Patels were very nice, friendly, and helpful to this poor working class, but racial hatred, the two-thousand-year-old disease of casteism, and the poison of discrimination among a few self-proclaimed upper-class prevailed and destroyed humanity. They took advantage of the poverty and lack of education of these blue-collar, wonderful, working-class human beings.

Father Surya would come on his motorbike from nearby St. Xavier's monastery in another town called Anand on Saturday night. He would sleep on the floor of a primary school attached to the Catholic church on the hill. On Sunday morning, at 4 a.m., the church bell rang. Catholics would line up for communion. Father Surya knelt behind the holy grail. About ten teenage girls and about twenty women went first.

All you heard was crying, and you saw the tears running down their chicks. Father asked, "Who did it?"

The same answer came from all of them, "Kalio," "Budho," or "Thakor," the foremen at the tobacco factory and bullies in the town. Nobody dared to tell them anything. Life went on.

Ninety percent of the farmland belonged to the Patels. How that happened is anybody's guess. Unequally distributed land created unequally distributed wealth and two distinctive classes, highly rich and desperately poor, in the Indian villages. To put the bread and butter on the table, these girls lost their charming lives at a very early age. They lived their whole lives with shame, guilt, and scars that would never go away.

Thanks to these missionaries of far lands for establishing education institutes throughout India, which has promoted a new generation of young, educated, Christ-loving followers to come out of the tragedy and slavery of casteism artificially created by two-thousand-year-old Hindu tradition or culture.

These missionaries left all the amenities of their homelands and served the poor, neglected, and marginalized victims of socioeconomic and religious persecution. God bless these pioneering missionaries in India from around the world.

Most of these girls working in tobacco factories eventually got tuberculosis or cancer and died at a very early age. How sad! What a loss of human lives and dignity! There was no sign anywhere that said, "Tobacco can cause cancer in tobacco factories."

The lambs of India paid too high a price to put the bread and butter on the table while sons and daughters of Patels enjoyed a super rich lifestyle and traveled to Africa, England, America, Fiji, Australia, New Zealand, and many other places to explore the world but never told the story of what was happening in their homeland.

Most Indians live in small villages where nobody knows about women's rights, Amnesty International, civil rights, USCIRF, India's designation as a "country of particular concern" (CPC), the International Religious Freedom Act (IRFA), or advanced human rights, and life goes on.

Takeaway: If there is hope, the only hope for these lambs is in the Bible, "Then Jesus said, 'Come to me, all of you who are weary and carry heavy burdens, and I will give you rest'" (Matthew 11:28, NLT).

(8/3/2023, Thursday)

In a small university town called Vidya Nagar (town of education) in Gujarat state, India, I got my BS and MS degrees in physics from a university called SP University. I taught physics to undergraduates at the same university from 1966 to 1973.

Believe it or not, I have never heard in America or any other Western country, but in India, it is true that bullies attend colleges mostly in liberal arts. Mostly, they are from the so-called upper class and act like mafia gangsters. They have their support groups from other students. Gangsters in a town of education? Yes, in Gujarat state, India. Given any excuse or unconfirmed rumor, this gang members, mostly from the self-proclaimed upper class, turn violent, and the university authority, the governing body, and the faculty remain silent.

One afternoon, a group of minority girls were standing at the bus station. A gangster called Kalio, hiding in the crowd, shouted racial slurs and harassed the girls almost every day. The girls would look down with tears in their eyes, but nobody would help them. The power of wealth and artificial social status called casteism crushes the dignity, respect, and human value in India, and even the highly educated community remains silent.

I had a lot of Patel friends, very nice, friendly people. But in every town, in every institute in India, there is a faction of the so-called upper-class mafia that behaves like gangsters and takes over the whole community and ruins the credibility and decency of the nation as a whole, even today.

What happened in Manipur State in May 2023 is one example. I have seen bloodshed, rock throwing, racial slurs, insulting minorities, and even murder executed by self-proclaimed so-called upper-class gangsters against victims of socioeconomic, religious persecution, and casteism groups.

> Takeaway: The poison of jealousy, power of wealth, and stupidity of casteism is mixed in one upper-class bottle, and the alcohol party goes out of control in the town of education. Really? Yes. Time and time again, I have seen with my own eyes.

(8/4/2023, Friday)

99. TO WIN THE RACE, YOU WILL FACE THE ROCKS; IGNORE THEM AND MARCH ON

The historical search says that one of the Jewish tribes, Bnei Menashe, after a centuries-long exodus through Persia, Afghanistan, Tibet, and China, finally ended up in India's northeast corner state known as Manipur.

So, it is also quite possible that one of Jacob's sons, after exodus through Europe, finally might have ended up in America. So, I am sure Americans are great, great grandsons of one of Jacob's sons. I named him the thirteenth son because Americans are unique compared to people in any other nation.

America is a unique nation compared to any country on Earth; she is a new Canaan, no doubt about it. America is the Judeo-Christian nation; everybody else is a welcomed guest in this great land of Jehovah.

Actually, when you raised your right hand and took an oath to become a US citizen, you accepted this historical fact. Soon, every immigrant should sign this historical fact before they are granted an immigrant visa.

A loser is one who, out of frustration and weakness, empties his anger on someone else. You are the child of God, made in His image. Don't listen when someone stupid yells at you and calls you a loser out of his frustration and weakness.

A very old jealous engineer, when I was working at Boeing, El Segundo, California, during a technical meeting, yelled at me and called me a loser. Why? I was his competitor for a senior position in the Material and Process Department, and he was selected because he knew the department head personally. Guess what? Within a week, I was selected out of more than fifty candidates for a chief engineer position and interviewed by the Defense Department Program Office, Navy, Huntington Beach,

California. I stopped by his office and wished him well and all the best. He smiled at me but didn't say a word this time.

Here are the tenets of the winner I always cherished:

- Give your best shot and some more because the gold medal demands more than you have given.
- Take a calculated risk and be bold, brave, and aggressive to get things done, whatever it takes; do or die. I would rather die with a tombstone that reads, "You fought a good fight. Winner at last. Sleep in peace; will see you soon in heaven," instead of living as a lazy bum, insane, or ashamed.
- Learn from your past, act now, and dream for the future. Get set, stand up, and go; now is the time, and this opportunity will never come back again. There will be plenty of time to sleep when you finally end up in Memorial Park, but now is the time to fight.
- When you hear a bugle sound, and your inner soul tells you to pick up the sword rusting in your garage for a long time, step up to the plate when a human behaves like an animal and aims to destroy humanity.
- Your words can build someone up to a higher level of joy and happiness or bring someone down to the deepest sea of sorrow and tears. So, watch your tongue; you can't pull back the words that left a minute ago from your mouth.
- Good is not enough to win the race; it has to be better to be selected, but you have to be the best in every aspect to be nominated.
- Keep your eye on the ball, not on the crowd; fans will follow you if you win the game but curse you if you lose it.
- Stay only with those who stand with you even if you lose, and plan the next game. You will win, and the friends who stood with you will say, "I told you so."
- Change is inevitable; don't fight with it. Be prepared to be flexible to accept it; the change will challenge you to be a better you. Life is a chain of changes; in the end, the chandelier of success is hanging.

- The change actually sharpens your tools and forces you to learn new trades to take you to a higher grade. Why oppose change?

Takeaway: Go into the strength of the Lord; He is your fortress.

Psalm 71:16 (NKJV), "I will go in the strength of the Lord GOD; I will make mention of Your righteousness, of Yours only."

Second Samuel 22:2 (KJV), "And he said, The LORD is my rock, and my fortress, and my deliverer."

Psalm 91:2 (NKJV), "I will say of the LORD, 'He is my refuge and my fortress; My God, in Him I will trust.'"

God bless you. Go in His strength, ignore your enemies, and march on; He is your rock, fortress, deliverer, refuge, and real friend. You will win.

(8/7/2023, Monday)

Do you feel like the sky is falling?

- When you see, feel, don't understand, wonder, can't justify, can't explain, can't believe it, an experience that never happened before in your lifetime.
- When you experience darkness all around you, and you didn't do anything wrong, and still, you are punished; when the devil is winning against the truth; when all doors are closed, and there is no way out.
- When the culture that violates the first two commandments wants to rule America; a free green card holder claiming, "I am as good as your forefathers and pioneers who built this most powerful nation in the world out of a jungle."
- When the son of the devil worshipers claims he is a savior for America.
- When the child of the demon from foreign countries gets through the most prestigious schools in America at taxpayers' expense only to spread false doctrines against the Bible.

- When the children of hate and ignorant of NJC who never saw a white man in their life but were accepted by America on immigrant visa go against America.
- When those who hated Christ and couldn't spell America, but America welcomed them on chain visa.

Then, say to yourself, "How great is America, how generous America is!"

And yet, on May 2023, Manipur was burning in the far north corner of India, churches and Maness' synagogues were knocked down to the ground, three Christian women were paraded naked downtown, and India and America were silent.

Then, where do you go for solace, comfort, peace, support, and explanation?

Psalm 56:11 (KJV), "In God have I put my trust: I will not be afraid what man can do unto me."

The answer is in the Bible. For more than two thousand years, the Bible has talked to millions and millions of mankind in every nation on the earth, "You are not alone; I am with you all the time."

Jeremiah 42:11 (NKJV), "'Do not be afraid of the king of Babylon, of whom you are afraid; do not be afraid of him,' says the LORD, 'for I am with you, to save you and deliver you from his hand.'"

Wait upon the Lord; your help comes from above. Somehow, from somewhere, sometimes an angel will appear. The living God uses a human being as an instrument, and that individual will help you unexpectedly.

Psalm 121:1–2 (NKJV), "I will lift up my eyes to the hills— From whence comes my help? My help comes from the LORD, Who made heaven and earth."

Every person is gifted; we just don't optimize that talent, skill, or knowledge. Every successful person is a successful salesman. You have to sell yourself to succeed. So, be a good salesman.

"Do not neglect the gift that is in you, which was given to you by prophecy with the laying on of the hands of the eldership" (1 Timothy 4:14, NKJV).

When people put you down, lift up your eyes and remember you are created in His image. You are a member of the royal family; you

are the prince and princess. Don't let anyone fool you; He calls you by your name.

> Takeaway: Isaiah 40:26 (NKJV),
>
> Lift up your eyes on high, And see who has created these things, Who brings out their host by number; He calls them all by name, By the greatness of His might And the strength of His power; Not one is missing.

(8/9/2023, Wednesday)

100. MEDITATION IS BIBLICAL, NOTHING NEW

Meditation is nothing new to the Judeo-Christian faith. Two thousand years ago, Moses taught us to experience the greatness of God through meditation on His wonderous creations.

Psalm 145:5 (KJV), "I will speak of the glorious honour of thy majesty, and of thy wondrous works."

Did you know King David mentioned meditation six times in Psalms (KJV)?

Psalm 5:1, "Give ear to my words, O LORD, consider my meditation."

Psalm 19:14, "Let the words of my mouth, and the meditation of my heart, be acceptable in thy sight, O LORD, my strength, and my redeemer."

Psalm 49:3, "My mouth shall speak of wisdom; and the meditation of my heart shall be of understanding."

Psalm 104:34, "My meditation of him shall be sweet: I will be glad in the LORD."

Psalm 119:97, "O how love I thy law! it is my meditation all the day."

Psalm 119:99, "I have more understanding than all my teachers: for thy testimonies are my meditation."

What's the key to being successful and prosperous that was given to Joshua?

> **This book of the law shall not depart out of thy mouth; but thou shalt *meditate* therein day and night, that thou mayest observe to do according to all that is written therein: for then thou shalt make thy way prosperous, and then thou shalt have good success.**
>
> **Joshua 1:8 (KJV)**
> **(emphasis added by the author)**

So, meditate on His laws day and night.

Do you meditate and muse when you see His wonderous creation of stars, thunders, rains, flowers, oceans, and rainbows? The psalmist says, **"I remember the days of old; I *meditate* on all thy works; I muse on the work of thy hands" (Psalm 143:5, KJV) (emphasis added by the author).**

My friends, if you are victimized by the sociopolitical structure of your country and if people persecute you, insult you, say go away, don't want to listen to your pain and agony, disrobe your princesses on the streets of Manipur in India without any shame and laugh viciously, come to Jesus Christ. He will give you the comfort, support, and dignity you deserve, wipe off your tears, and lift you up to the higher ground where the evil empire will never be able to reach or harm you again. Meditate on His words that will comfort you, guaranteed.

Remember what Jesus Christ said, "Come unto me, all ye that labor and are heavy laden, and I will give you rest" (Matthew 11:28, ASV).

Also, remember what Christ has said,

"But he answered and said, It is written, Man shall not live by bread alone, but by every word that proceedeth out of the mouth of God" (Matthew 4:4, KJV).

"And Jesus answered him, saying, It is written, That man shall not live by bread alone, but by every word of God" (Luke 4:4, KJV).

So, what else do we need besides the bread? Here is the answer,

They were continually devoting themselves to the apostles' *teaching* [Bible, God's words] and to *fellowship* [attending church), to the breaking of *bread* [or tortillas, nan, pitas, rotis] and to *prayer* [meditation].

Acts 2:42 (NASB)
(emphasis added by the author)

Takeaway: So, don't let anybody fool you. When you pray, you are actually meditating in the presence of the living God strengthened by the apostles' *teaching*, encouraged by the *fellowship*, thanking Him for the physical *bread*, and expecting the power of the *prayer*, more powerful than the nuclear fusion yet to be discovered by the man.

(8/10/2023, Thursday)

101. IS YOUR GOD RACIST? SHOULD HE BE? WHY?

I was in high school, in ninth grade, in a small village called Napad, Gujarat State, India. Ninety-nine percent were Hindu students, four were Muslims, and I was the only Christian. I had a lot of Hindu and Muslim friends because I was number one in all classes. I voluntarily tutored math, science, and English to all my friends at no charge. I won every elocution and debating competition. So, all the students were crazy about me, except for a few who were jealous and uttered racial slurs behind my back all the time.

The principal, Sashikant Kadkia, had three girls but no boy, and he treated me like his own son. Almost every weekend, he would invite me to dinner. What a great Hindu teacher, so kind, loving, generous, and scholarly! If any person has influenced me greatly and shaped my life the most, he is the one. I will never forget that.

One day, the history teacher took the students on a field trip to a very popular Hindu temple in Vadtal. All were Hindus except for me.

The teacher whispered in my ears, "Bramvel, I am sorry. The monk will not allow you to go inside the temple; you have to wait outside."

I was standing in the corner outside the temple, wondering why a monk would not allow me in his temple. I didn't care about the temple, but I wanted to see what was inside because so many Hindus came here. I peeped through a cracked opening of a window. Inside was completely dark; a small lamp with a cotton wick was burning. Every few minutes, someone entered the door, walked into the middle of the rotunda, rang the bell, *tin, tin, tin,* and offered flowers. Some people brought pastries and flowers and offered them to the god and wished for what they wanted to come true in their life; most of the time, it was a wish to go to America.

Some people brought gold and presents to the chief monk. I heard the chanting in the background. I didn't understand what they were singing. All my friends came back from the temple and hugged me. I saw guilt and shame on their faces, but they didn't say anything, and I didn't want to know, either.

(8/11/2023, Friday)

Why does a god have to hide in the dark corner? Why does a god classify human beings? If a god classifies human beings even before they are born, get an education, and are able to show their colors, and pushes them into the darkness, can you say he is a god? If I had known they would treat me like this, I might not have gone in the first place.

Even today, in the twenty-first century, and coming to America on an H1 high-tech visa, Hindus, most of them very nice people, believe that if you do really something bad, you will be born into a poor, lower caste family in your next birth termed as next *Avtar*. But if you plunge into the holy river Ganges, your sins will be washed away, and you are cleansed now; you are forgiven. Hard to sell in the Western world, but that's the way it is in India.

The Bible says, "For all have sinned, and come short of the glory of God" (Romans 3:23, KJV).

So, do all of us have to go to the Ganges to wash our sins? Good business, India's GDP will be skyrocketing without any washer/dryer installed on the bank of the river Ganges! What a great idea! India doesn't need Intel's chip business, Tesla's EVs, Microsoft's soft landing in Bangalore, or IBM's AI.

The truth is, "For God so loved the world, that he gave his only begotten Son, that whosoever believeth in him should not perish, but have everlasting life" (John 3:16, KJV).

You don't need to go to the Ganges in India, the mighty Nigra Falls on the Canadian side, the Hudson River on the powerhouse of the wealthy New York side, or even the world's holiest river where Jesus Christ was baptized, the Jordan River in Israel. My friends, all you need is to read, repent, and accept His freely offered love, proclaimed in John 3:16 above.

It was in the news that one Hindu Indian just did that in the USA. He sued McDonald's for millions of dollars for eating French fries that were cooked in the oil that contained fat. He claimed that fat came from cows, and that violated his Hindu religious belief not to eat holy cows. He claimed emotional damage and the travel expenses to go to India and wash his sins in the holy river Ganges. If you ever visit the Ganges, you will see that the water is so dirty you don't want to wash your hands in it. Mr. Modi is trying to clean up this river. Instead of wasting time and creating controversy, McDonald's paid him a substantial amount, according to the news media. Can you make money in the name of the religion? Certainly, this man did.

American immigration department needs to add a statement to the papers signed by the immigrants and visitors coming from South Asia on immigration, H1, student, visitor, and other visas to protect American businesses. "The food you may eat in America may be made in the facility that processes milk, eggs, soy, wheat, sesame, sulfite, and cow fat."

In India, 95 percent of the daily milk comes from water buffalos because buffalo milk contains, on average, 8 percent fat vs. 3 percent from cow milk. But the cow is considered a holy mother, and Hindus get offended by food that contains cow fat.

There is no scientific proof, evidence, theory, or real experimental evidence to indicate that the victims of socioeconomic malpractice and religious persecution marginalized human beings did something wrong in their past life—if there is a previous life. In the modern world, no group, race, or caste has the power or authority to abolish the basic God-given human rights and artificially label them as lower mankind compared to themselves.

Takeaway: It was my birthday; I opened a beautiful card a missionary sent to me that was engraved with the words, "'For I know the plans that I have for you,' declares the LORD, 'plans for prosperity and not for disaster, to give you a future and a hope'" (Jeremiah 29:11, NASB).

Amazing. That's the God I want to see, am eager to follow, and love to worship. I forgot all my pain. Now, I saw a future, and the past vanished. I wanted to get down to charter a new era, a beautiful dream, and fly where the eagles dare to explore new frontiers. That was the day I decided to go to America no matter what happened. Even though I didn't have a single penny in my bank account, I was determined to go to America, where all human beings have equal opportunities, where you can be all that you can be, and where you can worship the living God without any fear of isolation and persecution. God has blessed America; how true it is!

(8/12/2023, Saturday)

102. IF MISSIONARIES HADN'T COME TO INDIA, MILLIONS AND MILLIONS STILL MIGHT HAVE BEEN LEFT BEHIND IN THE DARKNESS

Animism is considered the world's oldest religion and began during the Paleolithic time. The man was afraid of surrounding nature so he would worship nature to achieve protection for his family. The practice of animism was born to worship almost anything in nature, such as rivers, trees, animals, the moon, the sun, and rocks. This practice is still alive in many parts of the world including India.

The strange philosophy of racial casteism practice marginalized a major section of innocent people. When the missionaries arrived in India and tried to uplift these marginalized lost lambs, the majority of Hindu groups took it as a religious threat.

The Christian missionaries have done unsurpassed humanitarian missions for everybody without distinction of caste, race, class, or religion. They built schools, colleges, hospitals, nursing schools, and missions to educate, feed, and treat poor, lost, and neglected children. What is amazing is at the same time, they treated the so-called self-proclaimed upper class with the same enthusiasm and the same standard of treatment. There are St. Xavier high schools and colleges throughout India. There are mission hospitals across this vast land, which were served by high-caliber doctors from America, England, Australia, New Zealand, and other nations one time.

In my town called Anand (which means joy) in Gujarat State, India, there is still a Salvation Army hospital called Emery Hospital, named after a missionary doctor from England. Another missionary hospital called I. P. Mission Hospital in the same town was served by Irish missionary doctors.

In 1930, people of all religions and castes would line up at 4 a.m. to see Dr. Cook, a Salvation Army missionary from New Zealand. He was so popular they named him White Indian. Now, Hindu Babas, Sadhus, Gurus, and Pandits can come to America, but the missionaries are not granted Indian visas. How soon we forget the great contribution made by missionaries in India. My Indian friends, open your eyes and give credit to those missionaries who left all first-class amenities behind in their homeland and served you.

(8/14/2023, Monday)

The cow is considered a holy mother and is legally restricted from meat consumption. There are die-hard cow vigilantes in every city protecting the cows. In a constitutionally secular and religiously diverse India, only one unconfirmed rumor and violence breaks out and spreads everywhere overnight. I have seen self-proclaimed upper-class gang members attacking minorities, burning homes, and crushing properties in towns and even on university campuses. The gang members are granted immunity by the upper-class community by remaining silent, and so they roam freely, looking at minorities as their underdogs.

On the other hand, the majority of Indians are peace-loving, harmoniously living, gentle, kind, and smart people. Only a few bad apples and their peers ruin the basket that missionaries gifted to India. God bless India and all my Hindu friends. Jesus Christ is calling you; listen to His voice. You will be a great nation.

> Takeaway: "For these [traveling missionaries] went out for the sake of the Name [of Christ], accepting nothing [in the way of assistance] from the Gentiles" (3 John 1:7, AMP).
>
> This trend has been continued even today for Gentiles (Indians). What a sacrifice!

(8/15/2023, Tuesday)

103. WHEN A MAN TURNS INTO A BEAST

For nearly three months, the Indian state of Manipur had been raked with bloody violence between the majority Hindu Meitei and predominantly Christian Kuki-Zo tribes. But when a shocking twenty-six-second video, which showed armed Meitei men stripping two Kuki Christian women and parading them naked through the streets of Kangpokpi district, went viral in mid-July 2023, the crisis sparked international condemnation and finally broke the Indian government's silence.

Although the majority of Hindus are peace-loving and friendly with Christians in Gujarat, this may vary from state to state. Hindus in the Western world and other nations say, "We are Hindus, but we share Christian values," but they don't dare to say the same words to their countrymen back home.

What happened in Manipur? Is it a Christian value you share? Where are all American-Hindu leaders, gurus, and politicians? Why are you silent? You complain about discrimination in America; look, what's happening in your own country of the same skin color, human race, and religious culture?

In the world, the decency of humanity goes into the flame not because the monster is so strong but because the descent human beings hide, cover their faces, and remain silent. Someday, you will have to answer for your ignorance because their blood is permanently marked on your hands; that will not go away. That's what happened in Manipur, India, in May 2023.

It has happened before, and it will happen again, but the love, mercy, joy, forgiveness, and kindness of Jesus Christ will protect you, flourish you, strengthen you, and bless you abundantly, and in turn, you will plant the same seeds in your soil.

For those who are persecuted for following Him, do not be afraid; here are the promises for you:

Deuteronomy 31:6 (NKJV), "Be strong and of good courage, do not fear nor be afraid of them; for the LORD your God, He is the One who goes with you. He will not leave you nor forsake you."

Deuteronomy 31:8 (NKJV), "And the LORD, He is the One who goes before you. He will be with you; He will not leave you nor forsake you; do not fear nor be dismayed."

Psalm 94:14 (NKJV), "For the LORD will not cast off His people, nor will He forsake His inheritance."

Deuteronomy 4:31 (NKJV), "(For the LORD your God is a merciful God), He will not forsake you nor destroy you, nor forget the covenant of your fathers which He swore to them."

First Samuel 12:22 (NKJV), "For the LORD will not forsake His people, for His great name's sake, because it has pleased the LORD to make you His people."

Takeaway: People of Manipur: Do not worry, do not be afraid, be strong, and keep praying; the whole world is praying for you. You will come out stronger, more prosperous, more beautiful, and above all, victorious in the battle against evil. Witness Christ-like example to India, so one day, India will set an example to the world.

Joshua 1:5 (NKJV), "No man shall be able to stand before you all the days of your life; as I was with Moses, so I will be with you. I will not leave you nor forsake you."

104. HE CREATED YOU IN HIS IMAGE AND GAVE YOU THE TALENTS, NOW IT'S UP TO YOU TO CHART YOUR DESTINY

Genesis 1:27 (NKJV), "So, God created man in His own image; in the image of God He created him; male and female He created them."

James 1:17 (NKJV), "Every good gift and every perfect gift is from above, and comes down from the Father of lights, with whom there is no variation or shadow of turning."

Matthew 25:15 (NKJV), "And to one he gave five talents, to another two, and to another one, to each according to his own ability; and immediately he went on a journey."

Matthew 25:28, "Therefore take the talent from him, and give it to him who has ten talents. Read the whole story in the Bible."

We shape our own destiny depending on how we perceive the objects we see around us. Learn to make the best out of the worst that will put you back on track instead of breaking your bones. Did you know the finest camera you can buy, which has the sky as the limit for the film, is your eyes? How?

- No need for a flash.
- Has eyelashes as a built-in-lens protector.
- Some people even have panoramic blue, green, or pink color lenses included for free.
- Doesn't need a wrist strap.
- Has a focus-free lens, always ready to shoot with infinite focal length.

That is your eye, is God's given gift. How you shoot the pictures of everyday life builds your pretty album for your generation to come.

Do you see the flowers smiling at you, or just see them as moving by the wind?

Do you say this is an avocado, a Mexican fruit, or do you smell delicious guacamole inside?

Do you hesitate to touch the rose bush because it has thorns that will prick you, or can you knock down the thorns and make a beautiful bouquet to present to your girlfriend?

Do you recognize the olive tree as a never-ending conflict in the Middle East, or do you see it as a reminder to offer an olive branch to your enemies?

When it rains in the California desert, do you curse it because it ruins your Disneyland trip, or do you see the water droplets as showers of blessing when the average rain is only five inches in a year?

When you see a stone, do you see a Goliath in your way, or do you remember you have five stones in your backpack, and your creator whispers in your ears, "You have My back; you are covered"?

Do you see dark in broad daylight, or do you just find an excuse for not taking a calculated risk?

My friend, look at the back of your birth certificate. It says, "Welcome to the world of opportunities, but it is not free; you have to earn it. The only free insurance you are granted is a bundle of love and mercy from your living God. Go in the world and win the race. I am with you until you finish the game."

Takeaway: God bless you. You can do it in His name. You are in America, the land of milk and honey. Chart your destiny now if you didn't. Turn your five talents into ten; don't bury them in the ground. You are His sons and daughters. If David can beat Goliath—you will be amazed—you can do it, too. God bless America. Amen.

Isaiah 41:10 (KJV), "Fear thou not; for I am with thee: be not dismayed; for I am thy God: I will strengthen thee; yea, I will help thee; yea, I will uphold thee with the right hand of my righteousness."

Psalm 121:1 (KJV), "I will lift up mine eyes unto the hills, from whence cometh my help."

(8/16/2023, Wednesday)

105. DID YOU KNOW NERO WAS PLAYING THE FIDDLE WHILE MANIPUR WENT UP IN FLAMES?

India's tenacious caste discrimination, which puts those at the bottom of the social hierarchy at a disadvantage, is slowly going away from big cities, but it is still there in towns and small villages. Ninety percent of Indians still live in small villages that are way behind the modern Western living standards and good health and hygienic conditions.

Most Hindus are nice, beautiful people, but the disturbing fact is that a small fraction of hardliner religious fanatic Hindus bring this ignorant mindset with them to America.

The far-right-wing extremist Hindu zealots silently whisper the poison brought from their homeland called the illusion of casteism and superiority in the ears of America.

I have seen glimpses of it at Hughes Aircraft, Raytheon, IBM, Boeing, DirecTV, Pioneer, Mattel Electronics, GD, Lockheed-Martin, and other corporations where I worked directly or indirectly.

Takeaway: Discrimination, racism, and casteism are crimes legally, but even more severe, you will be punished by your creator for painting graffiti on His creation.

Beware, the cobra is hiding under the same tree where the eagle has nested her eggs on the top of the tree, but be assured, "Blessed are you when men hate you, and ostracize you, and insult you, and scorn your name as evil, for the sake of the Son of Man" (Luke 6:22, NASB).

---

106. WHAT HAPPENED IN MANIPUR, NORTH-EASTERN STATE OF INDIA IN MAY 2023?

"Our thoughts and prayers go out to them" didn't stop the blood from the wounds, tears from the eyes, and torching flames that burned the homes of the poor and needy to the ashes.

It is hard to understand the agony and pain they are going through while, right after this carnage, ruthless, insensitive Indians were celebrating their independence day on August 15, 2023, in downtown New York.

The Christians believe in the power of prayer to our living God. And so, even if extremists mock and excoriate in New York City, we will continue to pray to bring hope and prosperity again tomorrow after the hopeless dark days in Manipur, India, yesterday. While the Christian mothers and sisters were paraded naked on the street of Manipur State, India, on May 2023, just after three months, the senseless Indians were dancing with colorful umbrellas on the street of New York City to celebrate India's independence day in August 2023.

Is it democracy? Really? My Hindu friends living in America, think again. What a shame! You cannot hide the smell of crime under the colorful umbrella.

The tenor of the simple speech of the Indian government and American politicians does not restore the loss or bring any new hope.

"It is an internal matter; everything will be fine. Keep quiet. We want American Apple (computer) trees to be planted in Bombay and New Delhi, Microsoft soft-landing in Bangalore, South India, and build Teslabad in Ahmedabad, Western India."

The architect of India's independence from the Brits, Mr. Gandhi, used nonviolence as a fighting tool in 1947, but the children of Mr. Gandhi used terrifying, cruel violence as tools against Christians in Manipur State, India, in 2023.

Indian immigrants know that city after city in California are named after the saints (San or Santa in Spanish) to spread the message of peace, harmony, tranquility, love, human rights, dignity, and abundant harvest in California. The following are some of the cities: San Deigo, Santa Ana, Santa Monica, San Clemente, Santa Barbara, Santa Cruz, San Juan, San Francisco, many others, and of course, Los Angeles, the city of angels, the beacon of Christian triumph over the evil embalmed in its seal.

But American politicians remained quiet. I guess, on politicians' to-do lists, Santa Wall Street and Santa Politics take precedence over humanity.

Takeaway: Manipur, we cannot wipe your tears, clean your wounds, and fill your cup, but we stand with you in prayers and look what our God says, "'For I will restore health to you And heal you of your wounds,' says the LORD, 'Because they called you an outcast saying: "This is Zion [India]; No one seeks her"'" (Jeremiah 30:17, NKJV).

---

107. A LESSON FOR THE DEFENSE DEPARTMENT/ CONTRACTORS/ENGINEERS

When I was working for one of the aerospace giant companies in California on a defense project, what I observed was shocking. The company was a great company to work for, except for the fact that when the manager played hidden politics, the engineer lost his deserved credit because the engineer was not a politician.

The defense contractors make money from the government depending upon whether they win the contract and how they will execute and perform the contract. No company in the world can match what American companies do with the state-of-the-art technology. These corporations create marvelous machines using high-tech, cutting-edge technology; the world wonders, "How can they do this?"

To design, prototype, and mass-produce a new technical marvel is not a Lego game. America is an incubator of tomorrow's dawn of high-tech inventions. However, to meet these challenges, you need engineers who are daydreamers. Their brains have tetra gig memory; they call them Silicon Valley egg nuts.

The degree in science and technology helps, but the zeal to work restlessly on challenging projects, the skill to solve technical problems, and the talent to think out of the box is God's given gift, not theorized in the textbooks.

The contract award money, the net profit, the layoff, and the product yield are interrelated complex equations. The American aerospace industry juggles to balance all these factors to win and maintain contracts. I have been there and done that on both sides of the aisle, industry and government.

The key to having a successful program and making money is the yield of the product. The statistic is a great tool to keep an eye on the product yield, quality, cost, and time cycle. But the same tool can be a deceiving elusion to your eyes. I have worked as an engineer in the American high-tech industry and aerospace Fortune 100 companies for more than thirty-five years and eleven years for the US Navy, submarine navigation, and national security program office.

I was challenged to resolve the most difficult technical problems of Trident missiles at Hughes Aircraft Company (later known as Raytheon) and the Trident submarine navigation system at Boeing company no other engineers could solve. Amazingly, beyond my wild expectations, I was greatly successful and received many awards from the companies and the Navy.

Being on both sides of the fence, contractors and government, I now know how the tug-of-war game is played on both sides of the aisle.

The government says, "I want the product that my money is worth."

The company management says, "I will give you a product that keeps me on Wall Street and some more."

So, to win the war, you need smart engineers who can solve technical problems and improve the product yield without degrading the quality within the shortest possible time cycle aimed at Six Sigma thresholds.

How this game becomes misleading is a secret game of the statistical representation. Look at the charts below.

(8/19/2023, Saturday)

Here is a true example of what happened when the customer and the contractor didn't pay attention to how the statistic can be a misleading tool and lose millions of productivity dollars without knowing it.

Graph number 1 below shows the productivity of the production of the balls during the year. Although the yield varies from month to month because of several complex reasons, the statistical variation is expected from month to month, and overall average production looks reasonable considering circumstances beyond your control. Both the customer and contractor are happy.

What's missing here is that nobody took the time to go back in history and check how we were doing from the point the production matured to the current point.

Table 1: Current Ball Production.

Month 2008	Balls Production	Manager
January	3.29	Okay
February	3.30	Okay
March	3.29	Okay
April	3.28	Okay
May	3.29	Okay
June	3.30	Okay
July	3.30	Okay
August	3.29	Okay
September	3.30	Okay
October	3.29	Okay
November	3.29	Okay
December	3.30	Okay

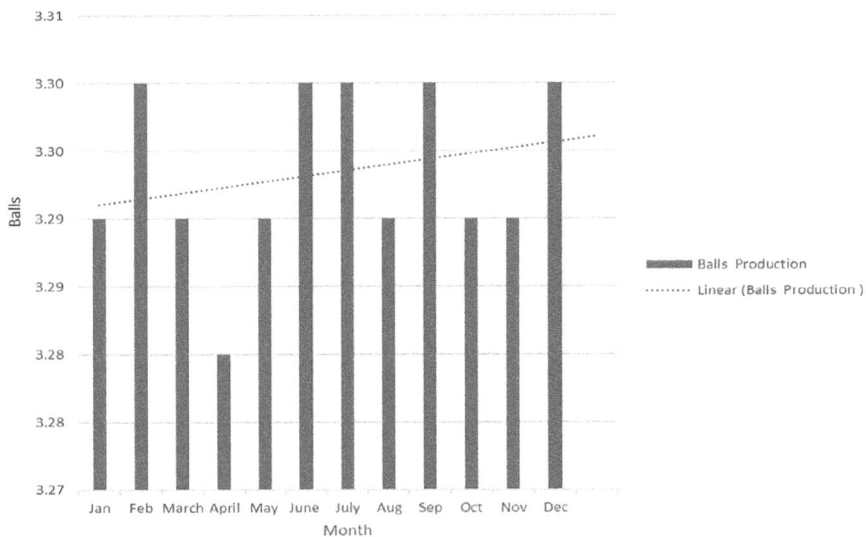

Chart No.1 : Current Ball Production

Look at the chart number 2. This displays the ball production over the last ten years after the program was matured. Wow! Are you surprised? What went wrong here?

Table 2: Ball Production Over the Last Ten Years.

	Year	Ball Production	Year End Review
1	1999	8.01	Great job
2	2000	7.88	Very Good job
3	2001	7.55	Good job
4	2002	6.99	Good job, keep up
5	2003	6.85	Congrats
6	2004	5.76	Thank you all for the hard work
7	2005	4.66	Good teamwork
8	2006	3.88	Great job
9	2007	3.75	We made it
10	2008	3.22	Thank you for your hard work

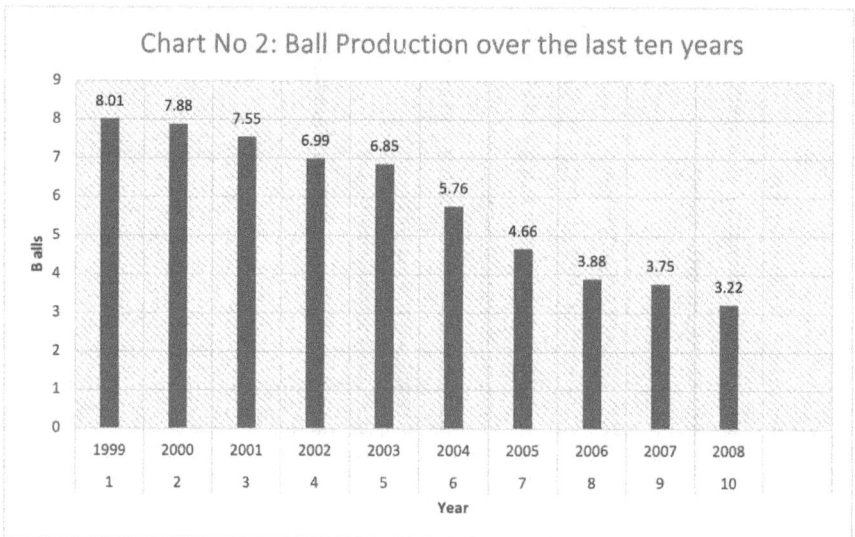

Chart No 2: Ball Production over the last ten years

When the ball production yield drops, the customer has to pay more to meet his demand. What happens in the aerospace industry is the constant change of personnel, management, policy, stock price, profits, and budget fights on both sides, contractor and customer. All kinds of changes, have a look:

- Design in one place, production moves to another location.
- Layoffs, retirements, transfers.
- Firing CEOs, moving key engineers to accept a better offer.
- Transfer of commanders to a new duty station.
- Congress delaying or cutting the budget.
- Rival contractors playing a political game to win the contract, and many other factors.

The list goes on. In this paradigm of change, people forget to keep an eye on the ball.

This is what happened when I was working at one of the giant aerospace companies. I presented the full picture to the customer and the management of what went wrong for the significant yield drop.

Reorganization of the management will not improve your yield, quality, cost, and cycle time. What is needed is a reorganization of the production line's blue-collars and out-of-the-box thinkers' white-collars.

Those employees who have memorized "Can't be done," let them go; promote and encourage those engineers who can say, "I think I can; give me a chance."

My hats off to the Navy Strategic System Program (SSP), Trident Nuclear Missile and Submarine Program Office, and Boeing management, Anaheim, California.

First, I solved quite a few technical problems. I modified the design of a failing pulse transformer module instead of designing a brand-new module that saved millions of dollars for the Navy. I tackled a power supply module that had turned into a ghost phenomenon. I resolved the tin whisker growth issue on the critical interface units. And I put to grave several other technical challenges of nuclear submarine navigation systems. Then, I jumped on the issue of improving yield. We, as "Can-do" bright Boeing engineering team, worked around the clock restlessly for three months. We rearranged the production line with brilliant new ideas to implement new material, new processes, new layouts, and new thinking. Wow! Amazing! Believe it or not, production yield hit a new high to the point it was ten years ago. My award…I don't want to tell you.

> Takeaway: A step into the unknown is actually a step to reveal the known hidden behind the curtain we didn't know how to lift.
>
> What happened? Why did it happen? When did it happen? How did it happen? Where did it happen? Depending on who asks and who answers, it can either create a problem or solve the problem.

(8/20/2023, Sunday)

108. WHY IS AMERICA ALWAYS FIRST? WILL SHE REMAIN FIRST?

Why is America the wealthiest technology powerhouse, and why do Americans enjoy the world's highest living standard? Why does everybody from Asia and South Asia want to come to America? It is because this nation is different than any other country on the earth.

She is a new Canaan given to Jacob's thirteenth son called American. That's why the American president and his first lady place their hands on the Bible and solemnly declare, "So help me God."

Why does America lead in technology breakthroughs? Why is America the first to step on the moon? It is because Americans remember who is our source of power, knowledge, and wisdom.

On Christmas Eve, December 24, 1968, the crew of Apollo 8 read from the book of Genesis as they orbited the moon. Astronauts Bill Anders, Jim Lovell, and Frank Borman were the first human beings to circle the moon's orbit. Remember?

Before leaving the moon's orbit, the trio proclaimed Verses 1 through 10 from the Bible, Genesis, chapter 1.

Genesis 1:1 (KJV), "In the beginning God created the heaven and the earth."

Genesis 1:10 (KJV), "And God called the dry land Earth; and the gathering together of the waters called the Seas: and God saw that it was good."

What these American heroes did was give credit to the living God first. Now, you know why America is always at the cutting edge of the high-tech, and no one will catch up as long as America puts the living God, Jehovah, first and not any other god or manmade figurines before Him.

> Takeaway: Deuteronomy 5:6–8 (KJV),
>
> I am the LORD thy God, which brought thee out of the land of Egypt, from the house of bondage. Thou shalt have none other gods before me. Thou shalt not make thee any graven image, or any likeness of any thing that is in heaven above, or that is in the earth beneath, or that is in the waters beneath the earth.

(8/23/2023, Wednesday)

109. LAND ON THE MOON, BUT CAN'T LEND A HELPING HAND ON THE EARTH? IS IT MISSION ACCOMPLISHED?

India, Wednesday, August 23, 2023. India has landed a spacecraft near the moon's south pole, an unchartered territory that scientists believe could hold vital reserves of frozen water and precious elements, as the country cements its growing prowess in space and technology. This is an incredible achievement.

Congrats India, a small step for the moon lander, a giant step for India. You have earned your membership in the world's Space Race Club by landing on the moon. Now, can you land on the hearts and minds of the victims of socioeconomic exploitations, religious persecution, and the old shackle of casteism?

While I am penning this, the news flashes on the TV screen in California:

A steep rise has been observed in the illegal migration of Indians to the United States. Nearly 42,000 Indians reportedly crossed into the US through its southern border with Mexico. The numbers have almost doubled when compared to periods between 2021 to 2022 and 2022 to 2023.

On December 21, 2023, a donkey flight carrying some 300 Indian passengers was grounded in France on suspicion of illegal immigration.

Shah Rukh Khan's movie *Dunki* is said to be based on the "donkey route" or "donkey flight" that millions of Indians take to reach countries like the US, the UK, or some other European country. "Dunki," a regional pronunciation of donkey, is said to have originated from a Punjabi idiom that means "hopping from one place to another."

Let me be very clear: in no way can you ignore India's triumphant victory in mastering space technology, but at the same time, let us

not forget that India has to do more to bring the living standard of millions still left behind in small villages and towns.

In the twenty-first century, Disneyland's very popular attraction, "It's a small, small world," is now a reality. The world is watching India. India needs to address the burning issue of socioeconomic injustice, national shame of casteism, and violation of the international laws of religious freedom for millions and millions of her victimized minority citizens.

According to recent statistics published in 2024, the top one percent of India's 92 million adults own an average of 54 million rupees ($873,000) in wealth. Within this group, the 10,000 wealthiest individuals possess an average of 22.6 billion rupees in wealth, which is 16,763 times the country's average.

The remaining 99 percent are still struggling to achieve a decent living standard as in other technologically advanced nations. No wonder the largest number of illegal immigrants coming to America this year are from India, followed by China.

Takeaway: India may advance in space, science, and technology, but if the living standard and civility of the Indians are not raised at the same level as other civilized, advanced nations, India's progress is tarnished by the black cloud of shame and socioeconomic, religious injustice. It's our earnest prayer that India will now land on human hearts and minds so that millions of Indians do not have to immigrate legally or illegally to other nations. Demolish casteism, and let Christian missionaries share their love, compassion, peace, joy, and the good news of Jesus Christ to those you left behind. India, you will be blessed.

(8/24/2023, Thursday)

110. WHO CAN BE THE NEXT MOSES TO LEAD AMERICA IN 2025?

On August 23, 2023, the presidential election of 2024 first debate was paled out in Milwaukee, Wisconsin.

This year is heating up in the political arena due to the upcoming presidential election year. What is unique about this time is, first time in the history of America two opposite voices are emerging on the platform. Two hopefuls with Indian roots will compete first time in American history, one devoted Hindu from an immigrant family and the other who left Hinduism behind and followed Christ, also from an immigrant family. When our constitution was drafted 236 years ago, all founding fathers and people of the newly emerged nation, the United States of America, were Christians. When the nation became the wealthiest technical innovation hub in the world and invited the guests called immigrants to join the Christmas party, America never thought that after two hundred years of labor and the sweat of Americans, the new guests would pollute the Judeo-Christian faith.

But the wealthy, generous Americans invited them anyway with the hope that they would test our tradition, culture, and biblical values with apple pie, but it didn't happen for the majority of guests that entered from the gates of Asia and South Asia. Americans slowly got used to the test of chicken tikka masala and kung pao chicken instead of apple pie. But the irony is that the bitter melon is added to the melting pot of America by guests other than Judeo-Christian faith. You have arrived in the world's most advanced country where God is the living God and real God, not the man-made images. Can a king, warrior, political leader, great teacher, pandit or guru, mango tree, saint, disciple, Oscar winner actor, Grammy winner singer, or Nobel prize winner scientist be worshipped as a God? God is a Spirit;

it does not have a human body. But He is real and talks to you if you surrender to Him and acquire knowledge and wisdom that does not come from the university textbooks. You can't buy it with your wealth, but only by becoming humble and by His grace, not by your might. You can't please God by offering gold or flowers or sweets or coins. He wants a change of heart.

The president of the United States is not the CEO of the nation like any other country in the world, but he is the father of the nation who believes in the living God and the ten commandments. He is ordained Moses by the living God. Are you? Either you are or not. You can't mix hot mango chutney with Wisconsin cheddar cheese. By the way, don't misunderstand; we still love Wisconsin cheese at lunchtime, but mango chutney at dinnertime. Welcome to America!

If anything great came out of this debate, it was the wisdom of the highly educated Americans from a nation of Christian majority. Even though they disagreed with him, they peacefully and cordially listened to him, an unknown candidate from a slim Hindu minority in America. If a Christian from the slim minority in India stands on the election debate stage for the prime minister of India, the Hindu extremists will throw stones and shout racial slurs and bigotries.

This quality of education and wisdom separates lambs (and cows) from goats (and water buffalos in the Transatlantic); that's what is called a real democracy that sets an example for the rest of the world. I hope immigrants will learn a lesson from this year's American presidential election debates. God bless America. Believe in the living God if you believe God is real.

Takeaway: "Come now therefore, and I will send thee unto Pharaoh, that thou mayest bring forth my people the children of Israel out of Egypt" (Exodus 3:10, KJV).

Exodus 4:10 (KJV), "And Moses said unto the LORD, O my Lord, I am not eloquent, neither heretofore, nor since thou hast spoken unto thy servant: but I am slow of speech, and of a slow tongue."

You will be surprised by whom God will select to be the next president of America in 2025, but relax. He is in control; He knows what is good for America. The man who carries the rod (Bible)—the same rod that Moses carried.

(8/26/2023, Saturday)

111. INDIA, DID YOU KNOW?

India's high-tech victory/ energy independence has a root in America
On August 23, 2023, India landed near the south pole of the moon
with its Chandrayaan-3 lander. Congratulations, India, you have made
history, but don't forget who helped technologically, for food supply, and
in high education when you were still an infant baby after independence
in 1947.

**Did you know when India was still a newborn baby nation in
1947, it didn't have enough electricity to light up Bombay state towns
and villages? Here is the history your grandparents did not know or
did not tell you, or just ignored because of racial tone and national
pride. If you ever visit the Bhabha Atomic Research Centre (BARC)
in Trombay, near Bombay, read the inauguration plaque of India's
first Atomic Reactor placed by Jawaharlal Nehru, India's first prime
minister.**

In 1954, the first reactors at BARC and its affiliated power generation equipment were given by America with an understanding that the
technology would be used for peaceful purposes only. India's first power
reactors, installed at the Tarapur Atomic Power Station, were from the
United States.

CIRUS (Canada India Reactor Utility Services) was a research reactor at the Bhabha Atomic Research Center (BARC) in Trombay near
Mumbai, India. CIRUS was supplied by Canada in 1954 but used heavy
water (deuterium oxide) supplied by the United States. It was the second
nuclear reactor to be built in India.

(8/29/2023, Tuesday)

**Did you know the first satellite tracking station in Ahmedabad,
Gujarat State, India, was established, and the Indian engineers were**

trained by the American space agency NASA? How do I know? In 1974, I was teaching physics to the senior class at V. P. Science College, Vidyanagar, Gujarat State, India. I introduced two requirements for the students to achieve a BS with a major in physics.

1. Every student will build a medium wave/short wave radio. I built one with the vacuum tubes on a large piece of plywood and displayed it in the physics lab for the students to understand the circuit. The transistors were just coming into the market and were very expensive in India at that time.

2. I initiated the industrial tour for the Physics major students to expose them to the real world of industry experience for future job expectations. One of the stops was ISRA, a satellite tracking station in Ahmedabad. The plaque on the tracking station says, "NASA, USA." My students left a note in the visitor's diary,

"Thank you, America, the nation of fifty stars, thanks for teaching us how to aim the satellite star above the sky of Gujarat, the star of India, so one day India will launch its own satellite above the Pacific Ocean." That really happened in 1980.

Did you know an American designed India's first satellite called GRANY?

As a matter of fact, I documented the initial preliminary specifications and design of a few transformers for this program at the world's largest Boeing Satellite facility in El Segundo, California. A team of India's top-notch scientists and engineers came to the El Segundo plant. Indian Engineers Association of Boeing, El Segundo, California, invited them as chief guests for the annual association celebration. I was there. America aims bigger picture of tomorrow. These Indian engineers walked the assembly floor, from gate to gate, and saw how their GRANY was in baby state. Something went wrong, and in the middle of the program, India canceled the contract. Today, India builds satellites of its own, but the basics it follows are from America and American textbooks.

If you are a physics major and studied electromagnetic wave theory, you can easily build a radio. Almost fifty years ago, in 1974, I did while I was teaching physics at V. P. Science College, Vidyanagar (city of education), Gujarat State, India, and helped students to build one before they graduated with a physics major.

If you are a physics major or EEE, you can build a radio, and if you can build a radio, you can build a transmitter. I did a simple one. If you can build a transmitter, you can build a transponder, although oversimplified. If you can operate a nuclear reactor and if you are an expert in nuclear physics, it is entirely possible you can build a nuclear missile. If you can build a skyrocket firework, you can convert skyrocket into an advanced high-tech rocket if you hire a rocket scientist.

Connect dots together—now you know how to build a satellite, track the satellite, and build the nuclear missile; all you need is a launcher. If you can fly and track the satellite, you can guide the spacecraft. If you can guide the spacecraft, you can land on the Moon. If you can land on the moon, you can land on Mars, but wait until America will do it first.

I know I have oversimplified these new technology marvels, not to take lightly India's achievements, but to point out the fact that America always stood behind India.

Does the new Indian generation and major population of Indians living in small villages and towns know it? I hope so; if not, let them know India owes a gratitude-filled heart to America. Namaste, America. God bless America, and God bless India.

Takeaway: On July 18, 2005, Indian Prime Minister Manmohan Singh and US President George W. Bush signed America's Section 123 of the Atomic Energy Act 1954 Agreement for the peaceful use of atomic materials and technology in exchange for uranium from America.

On May 11 and 13, 1998, at the Pokhran range in the Rajasthan Desert, India conducted five nuclear tests of advanced weapons.

On June 23, 2023, Indian Prime Minister Mr. Modi attended a state dinner at the White House upon the invitation of US President Joe Biden.

America and India have been performing the rumba dance since 1947; we are still in romantic love but not married, and keep saying, "I will wait, I will wait until…"

---

112. FROM UNCLE SAM TO UNCLE GANDHI AND UNCLE MODI

Seventy-six years after its independence from the Brits, India is now a member of an exclusive club of world-limited nations that are capable of launching nuclear missiles and landing spacecraft on the moon, but if you trace back, the technology roots were planted in America. Kudos to America for technology nurturing while India was a new independent baby nation. I hope the new Indian generation will study the history and understand where their technological roots were planted before they were born.

Apple generation will never forget what America, including Five Eyes nations, has done for India. If you still don't believe it, get up at 2 a.m. and go to a town called Anand, the milk capital of India, in Gujarat State, India. There is a milk product giant company called Amul Dairy. Go to the back of the factory. You will see four stainless steel, refrigerated, and thousands of gallons capacity tankers donated by New Zealand around 1957. The large writing on the tankers says, **"Donated by the people of New Zealand to the people of India."**

These tankers every day loaded with milk at 2 a.m. to transport to Bombay every day. I was a chemist at Amul from 1960 to 1966 and certified the milk fat content of 8 percent before the milk could be loaded in the tanker, so I know it.

Although the cow is considered a holy mother, 90 percent of the milk in India is from black water buffalo, which contains about 10 to 12 percent fat and is very delicious and profitable. If you visit Gujarat State, India, you will see at least two black water buffalos parked in front of each farmer's house, just like you see at least two cars parked in the driveway of each house in the USA.

My job as a chemist was to monitor added skim milk to bring down the fat to 8 percent. There was not enough milk for hungry Bombay in those days. Thanks to two individuals larger-than-life, Mr. Tribhuvandas Kishibhai Patel, Amul President (Hindu), and Dr. Verghese Kurien, Amul CEO (Christian), who created the milk revolution in India, today India is the largest milk producer in the world. Kudos to Amul.

What has India done for New Zealand? Can India send a Bengal tiger, Girnar lion, and four tankers filled with pasteurized and homogenized Kesar Mango Lassi and Alphonso Mango Chutney from Gujarat state to New Zealand in appreciation for their Christ-like love, compassion, and generosity for India when India didn't know how to feed milk to Bombay?

Takeaway: New Zealand demonstrated the love of Christ from Christ Church to Anand, Gujarat State, India, by gifting four stainless steel tankers to carry milk from Anand to Bombay every day.

Today, under the deceiving name of forced conversion, India is not allowed to share the love of Christ with those who are neglected by their own countryman and living in poverty, without education and no opportunity for a bright future. What a contrast!

113. WHAT NEW ZEALAND DID IS WHAT CHRIST SAID ON THE CROSS AT HIS LAST BREATH

He saith to him again the second time, Simon, son of Jonas, lovest thou me? He saith unto him, Yea, Lord; thou knowest that I love thee. He saith unto him, Feed my sheep. He saith unto him the third time, Simon, son of Jonas, lovest thou me? Peter was grieved because he said unto him the third time, Lovest thou me? And he said unto him, Lord, thou knowest all things; thou knowest that I love thee. Jesus saith unto him, Feed my sheep.

John 21:16–17 (KJV)

God bless New Zealand; the city of Christ Church in New Zealand exactly did for India what Christ expects from the church of Christ.

On 23 January, 1999, an Australian missionary, Graham Stuart Staines, along with his two sons, Philip (aged ten) and Timothy (aged six), was burnt to death in India by members of a Hindu Nationalist group named Bajrang Dal in Keonjhar, Orissa, India.

Every day, thousands of Indians, 99 percent Hindus, arrive in New Zealand, Australia, Fiji, England, Germany, France, Italy, Spain, Switzerland, Denmark, Scotland, Holand, Belgium, Russia, Ukraine, Canada, USA, Mexico, Argentina, Brazil, and many other Christian nations where ever they can, legally or illegally. Have you ever heard any guru, pandit, sadhu, or baba was burnt alive in any of these countries? No. Why?

It is because they have heard the voice of Christ on the cross at His last breath, "Then said Jesus, Father, forgive them; for they know not what they do. And they parted his raiment, and cast lots" (Luke 23:34, KJV).

Gladys Staines, Mr. Graham's wife, used the same words and continued to serve the poor and needy, neglected by their own countrymen in Orissa, India.

(11/2/2023, in Staten Island)

It has been revealed that a record-breaking number of Indian immigrants are entering the United States through its southern border, according to the Daily Mail. Over the past year, approximately 42,000 Indian immigrants were intercepted, more than double the previous year's figure.

Ninety-nine point nine percent of these Indian migrants are Hindus. Will they create a Hindu majority in America to enter and win political positions and paint America with saffron color? Look what happened in England, Kenya, Uganda, Tanzania, South Africa, Australia, New Zealand, and Fiji. Can it happen in America?

America, be prepared to witness our Hindu friends; now, the mission field is here. Open your hearts, minds, and churches to these new immigrant arrivals. We have to win their hearts and minds for Christ because it is our mandate, "And he said unto them, Go ye into all the world, and preach the gospel to every creature" (Mark 16:15, KJV).

114. LET THEM EAT CAKE

I visited the Taj Mahal and took a back road tour. There, on the other side of the river, the naked kids were roaming around and begging for money on the filthy water of the Yamuna River bank. There is the rich history of the Taj Mahal on one side of the river and poverty on the other side of the river. What a contrasting world we are living in!

Then I went to the YMCA in Byculla, a suburb of Bombay (now Mumbai), and what I saw you wouldn't believe but it is a true story. There were two stories of makeshift slums made from tree branches collected from the trash of Bombay, and almost-naked kids were sitting there with no hope for any future. Bombay, India's financial capital on one side of the town and lost humanity on the other side of the town. What a contrasting world we are living in!

I came back and shared the story with the Indian Engineers Association at Boeing Company, Huntington Beach, California. All engineers were astonished, except one hardliner Hindu supremacist friend said, "Let them eat cake." It is an example of obliviousness to racist treatment of religious minorities, intimidation, and harassment of victims of socioeconomic injustice across India.

A man got an engineering degree from an American university, but the only thing he remembers is the *French phrase "Qu'ils mangent de la brioche" (let them eat cake)* **uttered by the eighteenth-century princess Marie Antoinette upon being told that her people are starving while she was feasting on a cake.**

This French phrase, as old as a caste system in the Stone Age, practiced by this man's ancestors 3000 years ago, is still alive in India, and it still prevails in the hearts and minds of some ignorant Hitlers.

Lately, credible reports reflect troubling signs in India towards the shrinking of political space, the rise of religious intolerance, the targeting of civil society organizations and journalists, and growing restrictions on press freedoms and internet access.

India was placed 161 out of 180 nations in the 2023 World Press Freedom Index. It slid down the Academic Freedom Index into the category of electoral autocracies, while the Democracy Index from the Economist Intelligence Unit ranked India among "flawed democracies." Where are the human rights, principles of democracy, freedom, equal opportunities, and the rule of law?

The Indian government dismissed these rankings as "perception-based" charges in a 2022 working paper. Unsurprisingly, human rights advocates rallied to protest Modi's state visit to the White House. On June 21, 2023, Hindus for Human Rights (HfHR) organized a rally outside the White House alongside the Indian American Muslim Council (IAMC), Dalit Solidarity Forum, North American Manipur Tribal Associations, and Friends of India Democracy.

The difference between casteism/racism and fascism is casteism/racism kills innocent people morally, socially, economically, and politically slowly, silently, and secretly, while fascism does all these instantly and openly, like a Holocaust.

If Hitler were still alive anywhere in the world, ask him to straighten out the four ends of the cross and follow the star of Bethlehem, a symbol of love and sympathy towards the poor, neglected, forgotten, marginalized, thrown to the bottom of the community, sick, neglected, victims of moguls of majority, as Magis did.

Do immigrants bend backward to get visas, but once in this country that advocates peace and equality for all, forget their obligations and bring their dirty laundry into this nation? Yes, a small fraction drunk in the old whisky of casteism and Stone Age culture has brought that inhuman ideology to this country.

You can't self-declare yourself as high class; you have to earn the status. It's not the freebie you are used to in your homeland. It's not your birthright. No man can put down any other man.

India is the only country in the world that classifies its own countrymen and women, brothers and sisters of the same skin color, same origin, same culture, and divides into upper/lower classes even before the babies are born and have a chance to reflect their God's

given talents, skills, scholastic potentials, and beauty of human being. What a shame!

Takeaway: Mother Teresa from Albania established the Missionaries of Charity to serve the poor of the poorest of Calcutta. She hugged them, opened the door for them, and fed them the same food she had. But their own countrymen said, *"Qu'ils mangent de la brioche"* (let them eat cake).

He raises the poor from the dust, And lifts the beggar from the ash heap, To set them among princes, And make them inherit the throne of glory For the pillars of the earth [India] are the LORD's And He has set the world [left behind] upon them.

1 Samuel 2:8 (NKJV)

115. GOLD SIDE AND TOXIC OXIDES OF AMERICA

(1/23/2024)

Golden Gate Bridge in Golden State, San Francisco, on the West Coast, is a symbol of the 3Ps: prosperity, power, and prestige.

On the East Coast, a shining torch in the hand of Lady Liberty at the New York harbor is a symbol of 3Hs:

- Hope for freedom, justice, and equal opportunities for all—it's in America's blood.
- Heritage to be generous and share the wealth—it's in America's DNA.
- "Huddled masses, give to me." Read the plaque under the pedestal of the Lady of Liberty—America is calling, can you hear it?

Lady of Liberty,

Cries she, With silent lips. "Give me your tired, your poor, your huddled masses yearning to breathe free, The wretched refuse of your teeming shore. Send these, the homeless, tempest-tost to me, I lift my lamp beside the golden door!"

Uncle Sam sent out an invitation on green cards to the world, "Come to the land of countless opportunities, turn your dream into marvelous reality and breathe the free air filled with the freedom and justice for all no other nation can offer."

It was true on October 28, 1886, is still true in 2024, and will remain true as long as America remains the Judeo-Christian nation, a lighthouse for the world. Show me any other nation that can claim this proclamation. There is none. This is the golden side of America.

Why is this nation blessed so much? It is because this nation has sent more missionaries than any other nation in the world to the

darkest corners of Africa, India, and China. The people who could not read or write their own language now log in on the Internet.

America exchanged its gold with the ashes of the poor, neglected, needy, tortured, and victims of religious persecution. Why? It is because that's the only thing they had to exchange for a new life and because America kept the promise when the living God led the people to the new promised land.

Today, this promised land is called Silicon Valley in the west, where the micro sand of the desert turns into the golden microchips, Wall Street in the east, where Dow soars the world record, keeping GDP higher than the Everest, and all forty-eight stars in the middle, called heartland of America, the diamonds on the neckless of Queen Liberty, the bread basket for the world table.

It is because the Bible says, "I will make you a great nation; I will bless you, And make your name great; And you shall be a blessing" (Genesis 12:2, NKJV).

> And He said: "Behold, I make a covenant. Before all your people I will do marvels such as have not been done in all the earth, nor in any nation; and all the people among whom you are shall see the work of the LORD. For it is an awesome thing that I will do with you."
>
> Exodus 34:10 (NKJV)

What is true for Israel, it's true for America because America is a new Canaan.

Let us be honest: there are toxic oxide spots also in America, although, slowly fading away. An all-time high, larger-than-life, powerful, spirit-filled, true Christian missionary at home said, "I have a dream" on August 28, 1963.

One of my heroes, Baptist minister Martin Luther King Jr., the black Billy Graham, is still alive in spirit and challenges the world powers at UNO. "Dismantle casteism, racism, persecution for practicing the religion of their choice."

Another toxic tent covers my heroes, the veterans of the ugly wars. They gave everything they had so that the world could live in peace and be prosperous again. What did we give them? Torn-apart tents on the sidewalks from Los Angeles to New York and from Seattle to San Deigo.

They deserve better from Uncle Sam and the US. Let every house of worship, church, and synagogue in America, one nation under the living God, invite every veteran's family on Veteran's Sunday Potluck and hug them and say, "Thank you, my brother and sister. Job well done. God bless you."

Another toxic bottle is the bottle itself. Alcohol, divorce, and drugs have ruined millions of beautiful, precious lives in America. I saw myself when I lived with them at the alcoholic rehabilitation center (ARC) at Salvation Army in Santa Ana, California, because I didn't have a home to go to when I immigrated to America. America, wake up; the Salvation Army alone cannot do such a monumental task.

One more toxic blanket is the blanket thrown on the homeless and victims of mental sickness living on the sidewalk on winter nights across America.

There is no country in the world where every house has a garage with a minimum of two cars parked on the driveway and driven bumper to bumper on the park ways. How in the world can America have a homeless or victim of mental sickness person living on the sidewalk? America, before we build a base on the moon and Mars, let us build a shelter on the earth for every homeless American.

Takeaway: "Wealth maketh many friends; but the poor is separated from his neighbor" (Proverbs 19:4, KJV).

How true! America has many friends, but the homeless are separated on the sidewalks. America will be seven times richer when every homeless person will have a place called a home.

According to Habitat for Humanity,

More than 4,300 homes could be considered a "Carter House" because the President Jimmy Carter have helped build that many homes with more than 100,000 volunteers in 14 countries over nearly 40 years.

Wow! American president! Can any other president of any other nation have done this? Why can't we have a house for every homeless person in America?

116. BRIGHT SIDE AND DARK SIDE OF INDIA

(7/17/2023, Monday)

The bright side of India:

The world's largest democracy is not only bubbling with a population like a soda bottle but also filled with the saffron of unsurpassed love, friendship, and hospitality.

You have to experience it to believe it. Intimacy is another name of India. Everybody knows everybody in the town, like a big family. There is no such thing as a private life, including how much you make and whom you date.

If you are a teacher, the whole school faculty shows up and brings gifts on your wedding day. I can't even think of it happening in the Western world. It happened on my wedding day. An American takes a cab in Bombay, and the taxi driver invites him to dinner at his home to meet his family. Don't expect it in Los Angeles or New York.

Why is the majority of hotels in America owned by Patels?

It's because a milk bottle of entrepreneurship is given to every Gujarati child at birth, and a mantra of brotherhood and adventure is bestowed on people when they leave their homeland for the land of opportunities, America.

There are twenty-two main languages and twenty-eight states with totally different lifestyles, food, garments, and cultures, and still, they are one nation under Red Fort, like a honeycomb. Unbelievable! India is the most diverse country in the world, with hundreds of gods and goddesses, but there is no freedom of religion; go figure that out.

So, today's India is 20 percent Russia (borrows technology from Russia), 30 percent China (one-party rule, intolerance for religion),

40 percent America (H1 visas, student visas, large immigration quota, business), and 10 percent original spices to complete hot sweet curry.

The dark side of India:

Ninety-five percent of immigrants agree that in spite of improvement in health care, achievement in high tech, progress in education by using American textbooks and increasing economic index, the living standard of a common person is still well below the average American standard.

It will take another hundred years for India to match the Western living standards if they can eliminate casteism/racism/religious intolerance and establish the American education system and industrial revolution.

The aromatic grape wine of the democracy winery has not filled the old broken barrels of villages and towns where 90 percent of the population resides.

Millions and millions of indigenous and neglected people living at the bottom of the pyramid, called the caste system, still live in darkness, poverty, illiteracy, and humiliating sanitary conditions.

Under the doctored name of forced conversion, the so-called upper class wants to neither embrace them, invite them into their homes, allow them in their temples, marry their sons and daughters, nor let anybody else do it.

The victims do not know that they are the victims of socioeconomic-religious persecution. They never had a chance to see the sunrise that would bring them to the same level as their persecutors. New India, offer a new life to these victims that will bring out the skill, talents, and beauty granted free by their living God. Their health, wealth, and strength were snatched away by their own egotistic countrymen and women and buried inside their caves for three thousand years. Now is the time —let them go free.

India, it's about time. If you really believe in a real democracy, let God's people go, release them from your invisible slavery, and let the bell of freedom of religion, equal opportunities, and justice for all ring from the Red Fort every 15th of August. Then, the world will recognize you as the New United States of India.

Takeaway:

Open India's eyes, Lord; they want to see You,
Reach out and touch them, say we love you.

Open India's ears, Lord; they want to hear You,
Reach out and call them; they want to tell You.

Open India's hearts, Lord; they want to hug You,
Reach out and tell them, "It is finished." India will follow You.

117. THANK YOU ALL MY READERS AND SUPPORTERS

This is my real story, woven with the true stories of millions like me in India, and a memoir of how the living God, not the man-made figurines, raised me from a humble adobe in India to lead and manage a nuclear missile-loaded submarine navigation system Navy Program Office in Huntington Beach, California.

Amazing truth for a Christian pastor's ordinary son! The story you read was about growing up in poverty and fighting against discrimination, violence, and racism posed by a few Hindu extremists among the majority group in India. It is a story of trials and triumphs.

The Gatha also tells you: A fight between Goliath and David. Failure is the first step to leading the spiral staircase of success; it will take you round and round, but don't give up until you see the open door to the galaxy. You will see the spectacular panoramic galaxy studded with a million stars of opportunities just waiting for you.

The dream of America, the land of milk and honey, is still alive for millions like me. I hope this book will ignite a spark to flame their Olympic lamp to run a chariot of fire on a legal racecourse to reach America, as I did and then love her, leave rugged luggage behind, be American, pay back your due to America, accept Judeo-Christian values and tell the truth back to your homeland. Read on; you will be glad you did. You will be blessed, guarantee.

If you don't believe in God, you will see Him face-to-face. In America, if you don't believe in tomorrow, tomorrow will believe in you and will hackle you, "Hey, my friend, I am here. Get up. The Son has risen on Easter Sunday, so you will also be. Follow me, and I will lead you to a new Canaan, a land of milk (prosperity) and honey (the powerhouse of science and technology)."

If you don't have a friend, you will have one now. This book is your friend, and that will teach you to find a friend whom you can trust and the one who will take you to the next level. His name is Immanuel (God is with us), Son of God, Jesus Christ.

Isaiah 7:14 (KJV), "Therefore, the Lord himself shall give you a sign; Behold, a virgin shall conceive, and bear a son, and shall call his name Immanuel."

Matthew 1:23 (KJV), "Behold, a virgin shall be with child, and shall bring forth a son, and they shall call his name Emmanuel, which being interpreted is, God with us."

Takeaway: I want to thank you, all my friends, who read this book and are partners in lending a hand to millions in India and around the world through Glass Cross, my nonprofit, to uplift underprivileged students.

Remember, we all are given Joshua's horn; whenever you face Jericho, blow it seven times, and the wall will come down crumbling.

It shall be that when they make a long blast with the ram's horn, and when you hear the sound of the trumpet, all the people shall shout with a great shout; and the wall of the city will fall down flat, and the people shall go up, everyone straight ahead.

Joshua 6:5 (NKJV)

118. FINAL SALUTE

I salute all my readers worldwide, fans and veterans of American wars, and those who are in active service in the Army, Navy, Airforce, Marine, Space Force, and Coast Guard. I owe you a lot; all I can give is my sincere love, heartful thanks, and humble prayer for you and your families.

I end this book with a prayer from the heart, unconditional love, and a deep, genuine request to remember and support those victims of social-political-religious persecution and casteism in India through the Glass Cross nonprofit I will launch.

Now go in peace, stand up, speak up, reach out, and touch these children their own countrymen have exploited, put down, and neglected in India and in many other dark corners of the world.

God bless you for your encouragement, God bless America for giving me a new life, and God bless India for nurturing me in my childhood. There are no words for how thankful I am to my living God, who brought me and millions and millions of others like me to this land of milk and honey. Amen, amen, and Amen.

"The grace of the Lord Jesus Christ, and love of God, and the communion of the Holy Spirit be with you all. Amen" (2 Corinthians 13:14, NKJV).

9 798893 334104